PEACE
IN THE
HEART & HOME

A Down-to-Earth Guide to Creating a Better Life
for You and Your Loved Ones

WHAT PEOPLE ARE SAYING ABOUT CHARLETTE MIKULKA'S
PEACE IN THE HEART AND HOME

"A highly readable, accessible and very practical guide to living a more emotionally fulfilling life, both with oneself and in relationships."
—ALAN S. GURMAN, PhD, Emeritus Professor of
Psychiatry, University of Wisconsin School of Medicine

"Charlette Mikulka has written a deeply insightful and compassionate book that weaves her many years of experience as a psychotherapist with the most up-to-date research on the value of affiliative relationships and relating—including relating kindly to ourselves. Textured with heartfelt stories and ways in which we can address our own pain and suffering, this is a book of wisdom and immense helpfulness. An uplifting and empowering book."
—PAUL GILBERT, PhD, FBPsS, Mental Health Research
Unit, Kingsway Hospital, Derby, United Kingdom and
author of *The Compassionate Mind*

"This meaty book describes the variegated sources of contemporary stress and provides practical tips on how their adverse emotional and somatic effects can be avoided or significantly alleviated. These simple techniques are much more cost effective and safer than drugs, and in many instances, can satisfactorily reduce or eliminate them."
—PAUL J. ROSCH, MD, President of The American Institute
of Stress, Clinical Professor of Medicine and Psychiatry,
New York Medical College, Honorary Vice-President,
International Stress Management Association

"Charlette Mikulka offers us a one-stop shopping handbook for life. In a folksy, straight-talking manner, along with references for authenticity, she lends a wise and comforting hand to her readers as they tackle the nuts and bolts of life's many journeys."
—ELANA KATZ, LCSW, LMFT
Ackerman Institute for the Family

"Charlette Mikulka's book conveys the 'Peace in the Heart' she is writing about, allowing the reader to feel her sincerity, care, and understanding about how to handle emotions and cultivate spiritual awareness, so important in these changing times. She provides a wealth of information and resources along with her own experiences in using them, so that readers can look more deeply into what resonates most for them. This is a beautiful book."

—DEBORAH ROZMAN, PhD, author of *Transforming Stress: The HeartMath Solution for Relieving Worry, Fatigue and Tension*

"This book is just what it says it is: a down-to-earth guide to creating a better life. We all can use reparenting, coaching and discipline on our journey through life in order to understand and overcome our mistakes and heal our wounds. So read on."

—BERNIE SIEGEL, MD author of *365 Prescriptions For The Soul* and *101 Exercises For The Soul*

"*Peace in the Heart and Home* is a user-friendly book for the general public. It not only presents 'self-help' materials, it helps the reader understand how past experiences (family of origin) influence current perceptions. While self-help interventions are clearly outlined, professional interventions (EMDR and other interventions) are also explained in layman's terms, with case presentations to validate psychotherapy interventions. In summation, a nicely written book that addresses reader's need for information, self-help interventions and understanding of when and what potential professional interventions may help."

—ROY KIESSLING, LISW
EMDRIA Approved Training Provider and Consultant

"Charlette's profoundly important book seamlessly integrates complex theory with down-to-earth clinical wisdom. The true life stories of people courageously confronting their fears to claim their universal right for love and connection are an inspiration to all readers. *Peace in the Heart and Home* delivers much-needed healing and will likely change the lives of many who invest in perusing its pages."

—GEORGE FALLER, LMFT
Director, New York Center for Emotionally Focused Therapy

PEACE
IN THE
HEART&HOME

A Down-to-Earth Guide to Creating a Better Life
for You and Your Loved Ones

CHARLETTE MIKULKA

KITTACANOE PRESS
NEWTON, NEW JERSEY

Published by Kittacanoe Press

Cover art by Lisa Torrieri

Publisher's Cataloging-in-Publication
(Provided by Quality Books, Inc.)

    Mikulka, Charlette.
      Peace in the heart and home : a down-to-earth guide
    to creating a better life for you and your loved ones /
    Charlette Mikulka.
      p. cm.
      Includes bibliographical references and index.
      LCCN 2010904206
      ISBN-13: 978-0-9844903-0-1
      ISBN-10: 0-9844903-0-2
      ISBN-13: 978-0-9844903-1-8 (audiobook)
      ISBN-10: 0-9844903-1-0 (audiobook)
      [etc.]

      1. Families—Psychological aspects. 2. Peace—
    Psychological aspects. 3. Self-actualization
    (Psychology) I. Title.

    HQ519.M55 2011   306.85
                    QBI10-600068

Peace in the Heart and Home

is dedicated to:

Francine Shapiro, the developer of EMDR, whose genius and integrity have brought peace and rebirth to countless tormented souls;

The courageous people, who have sought my professional help, taught me so much and enriched my life with their humanity. Each one has been as unique as a snowflake and an absolute pleasure to know;

My dear life-long friends, Melissa, Paula and Lisa, with whom I have shared walks, talks, laughter, delectable meals and precious companionship;

My sons, Michael and Christopher, who have known me at my loving best and unconscious worst and, like all sweet beings, deserved only the former

And,
My husband and life partner, Joe, for his loving devotion, open mind, responsiveness and the ample grist he provides for my spiritual mill.

Table of Contents

Acknowledgments

The creation that you have before you has one name under the title and yet the nutrients that nourished its growth come from the minds and experiences of dozens, if not hundreds, of other individuals. I have been influenced by personal relationships throughout my lifetime, by the courageous people who have engaged in therapy with me, by professionals I have heard speak throughout my career as a social worker, by colleagues in various settings and by people I've never personally met but whose written or spoken words I found compelling.

I am also indebted to all the clinicians, researchers, scientists, philosophers, authors and spiritual explorers whose inquisitiveness, enthusiasm and dedication bring us increasing success in understanding, managing and transcending the problems with which human beings have grappled for ages. I am especially thankful for all that I have learned through training, workshops or consultation with Sue Johnson, Jon Kabat-Zinn, Daniel Siegel and April Steele. Though I have not had direct experience with Thich Nhat Hanh, Francine Shapiro or Alan Watts, the fertility of their minds and work have enriched my life immeasurably.

Much of what I am presenting in this book is a simplified overview of very complex and evolving research, theories and treatments. There are other authors who are capable of going into much greater scientific elaboration and academic rigor on each of the subjects I address. Those of you who are interested in further exploration of what I have covered can find authoritative works in the Bibliography. Just like my book, each of those works rests on the shoulders of many others.

I would like at this time to express my gratitude to those who invested time and energy into reviewing my manuscript and giving me helpful feedback: George Faller, Paul Gilbert, Alan Gurman, Elana Katz, Roy Kiessling, Barry Litt, Joe Mikulka, Melissa Montimurro, Lori Petry, Paul Rosch, Deborah Rozman, Bernie Siegel, Paula Slomsky and Lisa Torrieri. The valuable counsel of my editor, Marian Sandmaier, spurred me on to greater clarity and improved structure. (www.mariansandmaier.com) Thank you also to my friend, since fifth grade (!) and graphic artist Lisa Torrieri for her cover art that captures the peaceful, warm glow that comes from putting *all* the pieces together. (www.lisatorrieri.com)

After 92 years of life, my mother has passed on. The book you hold in your hands would not exist had it not been for her. Here is the poem that I wrote to describe the essence of my mother, as I knew her.

The Varied Dances of a Soul Known as "Ginny"

A stunned child at the top of the basement stairs

A mute swan frozen in fear and clinging to her adored brother and sister

A compliant caretaker of a woman in grief, whose refrigerator is bare

A budding artist named Ginger strolling through Prospect Park with a friend who brought her back to life and taking art classes at the Museum

A woman with a flashing smile, warming with her glow a community of singers and dancers

A tender mother who calls her child "bunny" and "little one"

A woman with an open heart of gold—wherever she feels safe

A flitting butterfly, never landing on earth for more than a minute at a time

A collector of everything—best left stored away and forgotten

A lost gypsy who hands me a comb and says, "Cha, would you fill in the gaps?"

A magical, benign presence, full of eccentric surprises and buoyant joy

A fading visitor, who awakens with bright eyes and beaming smile, takes a few sips and sighs: "That was wonderful!"

In writing this poem, I discovered that I have been responding to my mother's request my whole life: I've been filling in the gaps, in more ways than one. I hope this book helps you to fill in your own gaps.

Introduction

PEACE IN THE HEART AND HOME is a collection of lessons learned and wisdom gleaned by an imperfect, evolving human being, wife, mother and psychotherapist. My adult life has been fueled by a passion to understand what causes people and their relationships to fail, thrive or merely survive. The well-being I want to foster in myself and others encompasses the full spectrum of human experience: body, mind, heart, spirit and relationships, which, as you'll see, are all intertwined and inseparable. My knowledge started to unfold with my formal education as a social worker but became far deeper and more meaningful through my experiences assisting my clients on their healing journeys. I've always been eager to learn and have taken advantage of professional reading and training to provide more competent service to my clients. Equally beneficial in developing understanding has been the examination of my own inner world, behavior and relationships over the past twenty years.

Much of what I've discovered I've attempted to weave into my personal life and professional work. Like everyone else, I've learned many things the hard way, through failure as much as through success. Over time, I've come to distinguish which efforts result in spinning my wheels, which make matters worse, and which ones pay off. The more I learn and the more effective I feel, the more hopeful and confident I am that others, too, can reliably find peace in their heart and home. As I develop personally and professionally, I always feel that where I am now is even better than where I was before. I'd like to help you, too, experience the satisfaction of creating a better life for yourself and your loved ones.

I have found that many books on psychology, relationships, well-being and spirituality are written in abstract language and readers are left to wonder, "How do I actually put this into practice?" You will find that *Peace in the Heart and Home* is full of explicit advice, skills, resources and methods for achieving greater peace and happiness. Also, rather than limiting the focus to one aspect of human difficulty, this book covers the gamut, providing a full understanding of the factors playing into physical and emotional distress, behavioral problems and relationship drama. No matter what your unique circumstances are, if you are alive and struggling, this book will have a lot to say about what you can do to rise above and prosper.

While we human beings and the social organizations we create can be dysfunctional in so many ways, we are very fortunate to be living in these times. We are in the midst of an explosion of science, research and clinical experience that is generating an increasingly solid understanding of what conditions lead to suffering in individuals, couples and families and ultimately nations. More and more, we are recognizing how to reduce suffering, heal the wounds and alter the patterns that interfere with optimal health and effectiveness. I don't believe that it is humanly possible, or even desirable, to eliminate pain, but I do believe that dramatically reducing suffering and increasing peace and joy are realistic goals. The new approaches we're acquiring to help people heal and thrive inspire me and make me enthusiastic.

This book is jam-packed with information and images that I believe will resonate with your most meaningful life experiences. On the one hand, I expect that you will feel validated, reassured, encouraged and inspired. On the other hand, much of what I present and recommend may be quite eye-opening and not a "walk in the park." Inhaling my words may be hazardous to your delusions. But that is the very reason why this book's path has the power to dramatically alter your life, unlike other's you may have followed. The bottom line is this: I am foremost an optimist and would never walk someone through a disturbing scenario unless I was certain that there were clear and achievable ways to move beyond it and flourish.

Some of you might have a pattern of absorbing emotionally-charged information like a sponge and becoming overwhelmed or alarmed. As you read this book, you may be quick to judge yourself harshly as having too much wrong with you, having too much to overcome or having caused too much harm. *But this book is not about increasing shame and blame. It is about increasing awareness, understanding, compassion and wise action.*

Or you might feel a sense of urgency and panic to fix things quickly and pressure your partner to "get with the program." I suggest that you instead slow down the process of exploring this material, take smaller bites and keep your focus on your own self-nourishment. It will also help you to remember that what I am describing is the human condition, which means that *we are all in the same boat.* We're all striving to feel more effective and fulfilled in our relationships and to be at peace. Trust me; it's not coming easy for any of us.

You may also be comforted to know that human beings are resilient. We possess inherent healing processes that can be tapped to bring us back to qualities of being that are our birthright. These qualities include courage, curiosity, calm, clarity, confidence and compassion. Consider how well the human body recovers from cases of chicken pox or poison ivy. It seems as though our bodies are going to be scarred forever, and yet, there is barely a trace when the condition passes. Likewise, the human psyche has a built-in capacity to return to wellness. We may need assistance with this healing process when harm is traumatic, extensive and deep-rooted, but now, more than ever before, effective help is available. Hang in long enough with me and you'll find out about a wide range of healing approaches. In the kind of therapies I will be telling you about, clients develop abilities and engage in unique experiences they had no clue existed, but which they discover to be highly effective. Many people have only experienced talk therapy and taking medication, which can be beneficial, but often are insufficient.

We will be taking a look at some newer, less-known approaches that are surprisingly powerful.

As you begin to read the material in this book, some of you might be inclined to dismiss it as relevant to only a small portion of the population and not applying to you. You might think, "I know all that already" or "people have to stop being so fragile and whiny and grow up." You may not reflect deeply on how this information relates to the drama of your own life. I hope instead you will dare to open your mind and heart a little because, day after day, people suffer needlessly due to being in the dark. Knowledge truly is power. Understanding the forces that shape our personalities, relationships and even physical well-being increases our ability to work with them and even to transform them. Many conditions and problems that people consider hopeless are not at all beyond hope to a psychotherapist. We make it our business to help people not only learn and accept what is outside their control, but to recognize what absolutely *is* within their control. We also know which solutions people are inclined to pursue that are actually dead-ends or illusions.

I expect that *Peace in the Heart and Home* will benefit a wide range of people, including:

- those who feel baffled, overwhelmed, trapped, stuck, frustrated, disgusted and tired of spinning their wheels;
- those who suffer various psychological symptoms such as anxiety, depression, rage, panic, phobias, obsessions, compulsions, addictions or problems with attention, memory and decision-making;
- those who endure chronic or recurrent physical health problems, whether mild or severe, or have a family history of significant health problems;
- those who have experienced childhood trauma and deprivation;
- those who learned long ago to be satisfied with crumbs;
- those who don't believe they have any psychological needs and don't see any point in dwelling on problems, emotions, relationships or the past;
- those who are frustrated by their inability to make their spouse happy;

- those who have suffered a series of relationship failures;
- those who care deeply about the relationships they are in and are aware of their unmet needs, dissatisfaction and pain;
- those who are noticing that their marriage and parenting aren't going as well as they had hoped;
- those who haven't yet married nor had children and want to learn how to prevent the problems they see so many other people experiencing;
- those who want to be better at marriage and parenting than their parents were;
- those who can't imagine doing things better than their parents did.

Whoever you are, I hope that you and your loved ones will benefit from my experience and heartfelt words. Like the Olympic Torch, I transfer my flame of knowledge to you. May it guide your journey and lighten your life.

Charlette Mikulka
Newton, New Jersey

CHAPTER ONE

What it's Going to Take

D EEP INSIDE, MOST PEOPLE WHO are suffering or struggling don't want to limp along through life. They want to thrive. But thriving requires that we get to the root of our problems. If we simply clip off the leaves and stems of a poison ivy plant and don't remove the roots, the toxic plant will just grow back. In our society, we have a pattern of looking for the quick fix and putting band-aids over gaping wounds. If there is a pill for whatever ails us, we don't have to stretch ourselves or face anything that makes us feel uncomfortable. It is human nature to move toward what feels good and avoid anything that makes us feel anxious.

The reality, though, is that most emotional, mental, physical and relationship problems simply persevere, reemerge, escalate or morph into new symptoms when we don't dedicate ourselves to addressing the underlying causes. When we begin to dig deeper than we usually dare, it can be somewhat destabilizing and therefore frightening. But that is the nature of all creativity and growth; it starts with some degree of confusion and disorientation but evolves into a new and better order.

Substantial and lasting personal change requires venturing into the unknown and making significant investments of courage, energy, time and effort. Those who have taken such journeys with proper guidance know firsthand the benefits of extending themselves beyond their comfort zone. M. Scott Peck, author of *The Road Less Traveled,* defined love as "the will to extend one's self for the purpose of nurturing one's own or another's spiritual growth." *Peace in the Heart and Home* is all about cultivating this kind of love.

Previous generations did not have the benefit of the extensive knowledge and modalities of sharing information that we now possess. Our parents really did the best they could within their level of psychological sophistication. Nowadays, we have little excuse for not bettering ourselves for our sake and the sake of our children. I must say though, that because of the information explosion and the profusion of therapies, alternative interventions, pop psychology books, exploitative and reality television shows, self-help products, pharmaceutical commercials and Internet websites, people can be confused, overwhelmed or misdirected. This often leads to wasting energy, making matters worse or becoming discouraged.

My most important message is this: the missing crucial elements in our efforts to improve our relationships and lives are emotional intelligence, self-awareness and the courage to face our personal fears. Rational understanding alone won't cut it. Good intentions are never enough. Personal vows to not make the same mistakes as our parents have limited holding power. Flying by the seat of our pants gets us exactly what we should expect. Putting all our eggs into a New Age basket of organic food, supplements, aromatherapy, crystals and the like won't protect us. A meditation retreat in India won't set things straight. Living in our dream house or a bucolic setting makes no difference. Attending the best schools is not the key. Watching Dr. Phil and reading books and articles won't suffice either. In my own life, extensive cognitive knowledge, fresh air, exercise, a healthy diet and a powerful urge to be loving and conscientious were all sensible factors that were inconsequential, as long as my emotional blind-spots and hijacks prevailed and self-knowledge was sorely lacking.

Some people may not be able to conceive of another way of being, perceiving, relating or feeling in their own skin. They may believe that the state of mind and body and quality of relationship they have experienced so much of their life is just the way it is, "as good as it gets." They may think that whatever damage done to them is permanent. Not so. I have repeatedly experienced the deep satisfaction of witnessing people who, through great courage, open-mindedness and perseverance, rediscovered their unscathed spirit. I have seen clients become able to connect more effectively with loved ones. I have watched them recover their physical vitality as a number of chronic physical ailments faded away.

I'm here to show you the way to peace in the heart and home, to shed light on what may seem to be a mystery and to reveal the method in the madness. There is a rapidly evolving science of the mind, relationships and well-being and I intend to make it as clear and relevant to your lives as possible. *Peace in the Heart and Home* points a finger directly at where and how you need to travel, but unless you get on the path and pursue it diligently, you will not have the depth of experience required to evolve to a new state of being and functioning. You will need to provide an open mind, courage, determination and self-discipline. This is a hero's journey. I'm offering you a Course in Mindful Caring, not a course in miracles.

Though when you care mindfully, miracles in fact happen!

CHAPTER TWO

Attachment: The Foundation for Our Quality of Life

OUR CHILDHOOD RELATIONSHIPS and their corresponding emotions have everything to do with the quality of our physical health, psychological well-being, intimate relationships and our own children's functioning. They are the soil that nourish—or poison—our development and functioning. The impact is pervasive, insidious and long-lasting. Of course, other factors contribute to our level of health and functioning, such as prenatal care, diet, exercise, sleep, education and access to community resources. However, both research and clinical experience indicate that the most prominent factors causing emotional, mental, physical and social suffering are the unresolved emotions, deprivation and self-defeating lessons stemming from significant childhood relationships.

Day in, day out experiences with parents, siblings, relatives, peers and teachers leave their mark on our personalities, for better or for worse. Our early relationships create the lens through which we perceive ourself, others, the world and our future. The effect on our personalities is not one-dimensional or always evident. Parts of our personality may function absolutely fine, reveal strengths and resourcefulness and show no evidence of having been wounded. This state of mind and body is often called the Public Self. For most of us, the emotionally traumatized parts of our personality emerge only in certain times and contexts, usually with people who remind us of those who had previously hurt us. The magnitude of the impact of the past on our daily lives is absolutely astonishing—and for most of us, it remains invisible. It is analogous to a fish being oblivious to the water it lives in because it is so pervasive, persistent and taken for granted.

In this chapter I will be providing an overview of early human development, particularly the "attachment bond" between mother and child. While it may be a bit challenging to grasp, it is crucial as it lays the foundation for understanding relationship dynamics. The rest of the book won't make as much sense without this basic knowledge. As you continue reading the book, this chapter's material will help you to better understand the physical, emotional, mental and relationship experiences you've had throughout your life. All of the other chapters will be much more accessible, personal and colorful. One last thing: I will be referring to the child in this chapter as "he" to avoid confusion whenever referring to the mother as "she." So, let's begin.

The Developing Brain

Great strides in neuroscience and attachment research are helping us to understand the earliest and most powerful events and dynamics that shape our brain, mind, self-image, identity, emotional core, perceptions, defenses and relationships. Louis Cozolino, PhD is one of a number of contemporary mental health clinicians who is translating the wealth of new knowledge for the benefit of therapists and their clients. In his book *The Neuroscience of Psychotherapy: Building and Rebuilding the Human Brain*, Cozolino explains what happens in the first years of our lives. He states that the newborn emerges from the womb with a large portion of the brain unformed. This allows the brain to be shaped according to the needs and values of the particular culture and environment the child is born into.

The down side of the unformed brain is that a great deal of the brain's development is dependent upon the psychological state and social-emotional environment of the child's primary caretaker. As Cozolino writes, "The infant and mother gaze into each other's eyes, linking their hearts and brains." Through this intense bond and continual flow of subtle interactions, the mother unknowingly transfers her store of conscious and unconscious emotional memories and lessons from her emotional brain to the child's emotional brain.

The first 18 to 36 months of human life are a highly sensitive and expansive period of brain development. The child's daily interactions with caretakers and other close family members literally shape the architecture of the child's brain. The cognitive brain plays a very minor role during this period. Instead, the majority of development takes place in the young child's social-emotional brain. This is the more primitive part of the brain and is concerned with survival, emotions, human connection and the felt sense of the body. All of a child's experience during this period is wired in and stored away without any language to consciously remember or verbalize it. So when people say of a very young child, "Thank goodness he is too young to know what's going on," the child is in fact having intense emotional and sensory experiences that are being stored for posterity.

According to Cozolino, "The fact that early interpersonal experiences are visceral and preverbal, make them even more resistant to change. Because our networks are sculpted during early interactions, we all emerge into self-awareness preprogrammed by unconsciously organized neural networks." Because the child is entirely dependent upon the parent for survival, he is very vulnerable to anxiety and fear. For a helpless creature whose life is utterly in the hands of another, isolation and abandonment mean death. If the parent doesn't respond to the child frequently, quickly or empathically enough, the child *feels as though* he is dangling from a cliff. Along with fear comes a sense of helplessness. And along with helplessness come feelings of shame when the instinctively longed for and expected responses don't occur. One way we know that shame is experienced by children is that their body language reveals shame. A child's posture may be slumped, with head lowered and averting of eye contact. They may turn or run away whenever they cry. Another way we know is that adult clients often speak to their therapists of the shame they felt when their parents did not respond to their psychological and social needs.

The mother and child participate in an ongoing dance of "harmony, rupture and repair." Harmony occurs when the parent is attuned to the child's emotional and physical needs and responds appropriately. Rupture of harmony, or disharmony, takes place when the caretaker, *being human,* misses, ignores or misunderstands the child's cues. *Ruptures are absolutely inevitable.* Children need to be able to tolerate some degree of inconsistency, because that's the reality of human interaction and because it is through repair that the child learns that pain is temporary.

Repair takes place when the parent provides sufficient comfort and soothing to realign with the child's rhythms and needs and return the child to emotional balance. The more the child experiences the mother's return to "attunement" with him, the more the child's brain stores memories of safety and contented connection, and therefore, confidence that others will be there for him in the future. When human beings feel secure that others will be there when needed, then their mental energies are freed up to explore the world and express their unique selves.

The more the parent reestablishes attunement, the more the child learns to expect reconnection. Cozolino writes: "The learned expectation of relief in the future enhances the ability to tolerate more intense affect in the midst of the stressful moment." This is trust, the cornerstone of relationships and the core of a solid sense of security. The ability to repair a rupture and return to harmony and attunement is also a core dynamic found in secure adult intimate relationships.

Returning to the young child, the mother's primary job is to help soothe and regulate her child's strong emotions and body sensations. The aim is to keep the child in an "optimal arousal zone" so the child isn't either over- or under-stimulated. Being overwhelmed and emotionally flooded can lead to the child shutting down, disconnecting in self-protection. At the other extreme, being neglected and under-stimulated interferes with psychological safety, feelings of self-worth and the development of the brain. In extreme situations, children who have been severely deprived of close contact, comfort and a bond with a personal caregiver have failed to thrive, to the point of death. Neuroscientists and therapists call the management of emotions "affect management" or "affect regulation." There is probably no more critical parenting behavior that a child needs to experience than affect regulation. The parent's level of ability will become the child's level of ability to self-soothe and manage his own emotions throughout his life.

The mother's ability to be emotionally present, attuned, responsive and soothing to her child is directly related to her own experiences of being parented. As Alice Miller wrote in *The Drama Of The Gifted Child; The Search For The True Self*: "The empathy and care (a child) has received and the assistance she has gained in articulating and understanding her own inner world will influence her future parenting abilities. A mother's childhood can determine whether she is prepared to emotionally provide for her newborn or if she will require her child to give to her the love and attention she herself failed to receive as a child." If her own mother didn't provide adequate, reliable soothing, a parent would be expected to have great difficulty tolerating, processing or appropriately responding to emotions in herself or others.

Miller's work focuses on the adaptations and sacrifices of their authentic self that children feel compelled to make in order to respond to their parents' expectations. In some families these family rules are explicit, while in others they are unspoken. Examples include: I must never disagree with my parents or complain. I must never express anger. I must never look unhappy. I must be number one at whatever I do. I must show sympathy for Mom and make sure she feels loved.

These early messages and patterns of dealing with emotions get wired into the emotional brain, becoming the process through which all future relationships are experienced and managed. Thus, no matter the parent's convictions, intentions or cognitive knowledge, the emotional brain—also known as the unconscious—is going to run the show. We can resolve this predicament, however, via new life experiences that bring the unconscious to consciousness and alter the wiring. In later chapters of this book, we will explore these growth and healing processes in more depth.

When a parent does provide "good enough mothering," she is creating a secure "holding environment" enough of the time to give her child a bodily sense of security, which translates into a psychological sense of security. The child develops confidence that the parent won't leave or become overwhelmed in response to his needs and strong emotions. The mother is secure enough, calm enough and strong enough to be with him and his emotions. She is neither shut down nor over-reactive. She can tolerate his emotions and patiently, lovingly respond in a way that brings relief.

When the child learns from his mother's behavior that his feelings and emotions are okay, he can allow himself to experience, identify, express and work them through. The child is neither detached from his emotions nor flooded by them. Any child whose experiences have permitted these emotional management skills to be wired into the emotional brain is the most fortunate of children. It is the basic condition for physical, emotional, mental and social health. It is not a well-appointed bedroom or a plethora of toys and early educational opportunities that determine a child's ability to thrive, learn and function well throughout life. The single most important factor is an accessible, responsive and engaged caregiver.

The Family Dance

The other major contribution to a child's functioning is the ability of family members to adequately regulate *their own* emotions. Children are highly sensitive to family members' emotional states and body language. In fact, non-verbal emotional communication within the family has a far more powerful impact on *all* members than the actual words that are spoken. This kind of communication includes facial expressions, eye contact, tone of voice, timing and intensity of response, body gestures and a multitude of other non-verbal signals that are picked up unconsciously and instantaneously. Emotions, positive and negative, are highly contagious. If either parent is numb, distant, detached or, at the other extreme, fearful, agitated or angry, the child can't feel the secure, calm connection he needs to soothe his body and, therefore, his mind.

"Developmental trauma" and "attachment trauma" are the names for the day-in, day-out experience of a social-emotional climate that is toxic and devoid of adequate protection, connection, empathy and reassurance. Cozolino refers to it as, "Experiences of pain and isolation in the absence of support, and the struggle to make sense of life without adequate help." *Many adults, who can't recall any distinct memories of childhood abuse, assume that there's no explanation or justification for their emotional distress. They don't realize the insidious harm done by attachment trauma.*

Cozolino writes, "The strength of learning during these sensitive periods, results in early experiences having a disproportionately powerful role in sculpting the networks of attachment and affect regulation. Because this experience is essentially unconscious, it has the additional power of organizing our background affect, our views of the world and relationships, prior to the development of conscious awareness." *How we perceive, feel about and respond to people and situations is far more guided by the lessons of early childhood than we would like to believe. We may be adults, chronologically and physically, but too often the youngest parts of our personality are invisibly, yet actively, living our lives.*

Cozolino writes further, "Many of the most important aspects of our lives are controlled by reflexes, behaviors and emotions learned and organized outside of our awareness . . . it is obvious that despite the massive development of the cortex, our primitive emotional brains continue to exert great influence over us." This is why I often say to my clients, "Emotions rule." *So, if you do not become an expert on your own childhood relationship history and emotional landscape, sensitivities and vulnerabilities, you'll continue to be at the mercy of them.* Later chapters of this book will introduce you to the mindfulness and affect management skills and trauma treatment that can help you cope with and heal this emotional history.

The Architecture of the Emotional Brain

One of the most significant parts of the emotional brain is the "amygdala," which has the role of appraising the environment for cues of danger. It serves as a warning system, like a smoke alarm. Whether threats are real, imagined or experienced vicariously through witnessing another being threatened, these frightening experiences are stored in the amygdala. Since so many of our threatening experiences in childhood involve not being able to connect with or derive comfort from our caregivers, much of what is stored involves what we can expect from those we depend on. Because these memories were formed at a time when threat felt like risk of death, these memories are stored as threats to physical survival.

So throughout our lives, whenever we face an experience that has the slightest resemblance to a previous threat, the amygdala whips through its emotional history vault and makes a quick-and-dirty assessment. Whenever there is any chance of risk, the amygdala will err on the side of caution and sound the alarm, triggering a cascade of bodily changes that can rock one's whole physical and psychological being. In most cases, we're overreacting. But in nature, it is better to be safe than sorry, for the top priority is survival. Responding quickly to perceived threats increases longevity, even if those lives are prone to chronic anxiety and fear.

The amygdala, our built-in alarm system, is on-line at birth. Not on-line until years later are the parts of the brain that use logic, reason, discrimination and perspective, which help us to reduce our sense of danger. Because all of us have stored early memories of threat, without the softening effect of reason or perspective, all of us are prone to anxiety. To try to cope, human beings have created a wide range of defenses to minimize close contact with difficult emotions. Sometimes, these defenses are helpful. The amygdala's capacity to trigger the stress response, which includes the *fight-flight-freeze* reaction, is adaptive when the anxiety that ensues causes us to take action or use caution in situations in which we may be truly in danger.

Unfortunately, like a dysfunctional smoke alarm, the amygdala can also cause us to misread situations and act inappropriately. We may become aggressive and alienate others. Or we may avoid situations that actually are important and beneficial to our lives. We may become passive and submit to situations that are harmful or unfair to us. As we will discuss later, the amygdala plays a vital role in marriage and family relationships.

The Social Brain

The brain, of course, does much more than warn us of danger. It also helps us to develop as social beings. Psychiatrist Daniel Siegel, author of several books, including *The Developing Mind, Parenting From The Inside Out, The Mindful Brain* and *Mindsight,* is the leader of a new field of study called "Interpersonal Neurobiology." According to Siegel, the basic unit of human life is not one but two, because the brain is a social organ, shaped through a relationship with another human being. We are hard-wired to be connected to other brains. Not only does the brain get shaped through relationships with others, but the mind itself evolves from more than one brain.

Siegel says that the ongoing interaction between caregiver and child develops critical brain circuits that profoundly affect our relationship with ourselves and with others. These include—are you ready?—our ability to:

- tolerate and manage emotions
- engage in self-reflection
- develop self-awareness
- control our impulses
- respond flexibly (as opposed to knee-jerk reactions)
- experience empathy
- perceive objectively
- engage in problem-focused (as opposed to emotion-focused) coping
- feel safe
- feel loved
- trust closeness

For a human being to thrive in life, there are no more crucial abilities than these. If we are really honest with ourselves, we will admit that many of these capacities are underdeveloped in ourselves, particularly in our relationships with our partners or those who mean the most to us.

Siegel has written, "Human connections create neuronal connections from which the mind emerges." He frequently quotes Hebb's axiom: "Neurons that fire together, wire together." In simple terms, the word "wire" means chemical substances and electrical charges connect and activate different neurons when different events occur together. This is called a "conditioned learning response." Neural networks create patterns of information throughout the nervous system linking perception, biochemical reactions, sensations, emotion, thoughts and behavior. Too often what are paired together are fear and shame and an event involving other people.

Siegel states that mindfulness is at the heart of nurturing relationships. When parents relate with "intention" they consciously and purposely choose their behavior with their children's well-being in mind. (The concept and practice of mindfulness are so important that I will discuss them in great detail in Chapter Nine.) Consciously choosing our behavior requires "response flexibility," the capacity to delay gratification and inhibit impulsive behavior.

Delaying gratification basically means tolerating the difficult feelings involved in doing the right thing. Impulsivity, by contrast, means following an urge to do something that will provide quick emotional relief in the short-run, even though it causes pain for oneself or another in the long run. While impulsivity can involve becoming angry, aggressive, critical and judgmental, it also includes doing things such as coping with relational distress by overeating, over-drinking or having an affair. Another kind of impulsivity that is equally damaging is giving in to the urge to emotionally shut-down and "disappear" when emotional challenges emerge. The ability to delay gratification is a cornerstone of emotional maturity and compassionate relationships.

When a child's psychological as well as physical needs are inadequately met, ongoing stress hormones destroy neurons in the hippocampus, a part of the brain needed for processing and storing experiences productively. When the hippocampus functions properly, an event is stored away as an "explicit memory," something we can recall and that no longer has any emotional charge to it. Inadequately processed and stored experiences leave the child with "emotional baggage." This sets the child up for more trauma, because the more stress he or she experienced early in life, the less developed the hippocampus, and therefore the more he or she relies on the primitive, unconscious emotional brain to deal with ongoing life challenges.

When experiences are overwhelming to a child, the memory stored is "implicit" rather than "explicit." "Implicit memories" are those that haunt people throughout their lives without their recognizing that the emotions, physical sensations, impulses and core beliefs are coming from the past, not the present. As I'll demonstrate later in this book, *the average adult's personal and family lives are permeated with implicit memories.*

One of Dan Siegel's favorite take-home messages is that the nervous system has "plasticity," which means it is not set in stone. Throughout life, the nervous system can change through new responses to emotionally-charged experiences. New experiences that are repeated and replace self-defeating patterns can create new connections between neurons, new firing and new wiring, leading to new brain architecture. Emotionally secure attachment relationships in adulthood can restructure the brain and therefore the mind. This can occur when people experience an ongoing relationship that provides sensitivity, reflection and attunement. Additionally, traumatic memories can be reprocessed, leading to new, adaptive, "gut level" beliefs about oneself and others. We'll further explore this lifelong potential for growth in upcoming chapters.

The Power of Attachment

Most of us are very familiar with the landmarks of physical development in the young: rolling over, sitting up, crawling, cruising, walking and running. Likewise, we are aware of other achievements such as grasping objects, self-feeding, potty-training, speaking and learning the alphabet. Yet, the social-emotional development that is simultaneously occurring and getting established in the brain is too often misunderstood, overlooked or mishandled. How we attend to our children's social and emotional needs will show up in their ability to handle relationship and life challenges with competency and grace or ineptness and pain.

The brain's unique development is the fruit of our first love relationship, our attachment bond with our mother. Infants have an instinctual drive to connect, attach and interact with their mother. This "instinctual attachment drive" is abundantly clear in all young children, but is also what drives adult intimate relationships. Research on child and adult attachment has burgeoned in the last several decades. It has finally caught up with and is validating the powerful interest that generations of adults have expressed in music and poetry. A vast proportion of twentieth century popular song has rested on lyrics that reflect attachment longing, fulfillment and loss. Back in 1932 Noel Coward wrote: "Will it ever cloy, this odd diversity of misery and joy? I'm feeling quite insane and young again and all because I'm mad about the boy." In *A Hard Day's Night* the Beatles sang: "When I get home to you, I find the things that you do will make me feel alright." In *She's Got A Way* Billy Joel sang: "She comes to me when I'm feeling down, inspires me without a sound, she touches me and I get turned around." And then there is Gilbert O'Sullivan's *Alone Again (Naturally):* "It seems to me that there are more hearts broken in the world that can't be mended, left unattended. What do we do? What do we do?"

The key dynamics involved in attachment are as follows:

- Seeking physical and emotional closeness and connection with another person.
- Using the other person as a "safe haven" to provide soothing when under stress.
- Internalizing the other person as a mental image that provides a sense of a "secure base."
- Experiencing predictable, sensitive, perceptive and effective communication.
- The capacity to reflect upon the mental state of another person resulting in a sense of "feeling felt" by the other.
- Sharing a non-verbal focus on each other's emotional states, that is, attunement through the senses.
- At later stages of development, there is also a shared verbal focus on mental states, which includes stating perceptions, memories, thoughts, feelings, intentions and beliefs.

Attachment scholar Mary Main has been successful in predicting the kind of attachment pattern a child will have by asking the pregnant mother to discuss her childhood in a specialized "Adult Attachment Interview." In her research, Main discovered something surprising: The child's level of secure attachment could be determined, *not by the degree of harm his or her parent experienced in childhood, but by how coherent a story the parent can tell of her early life.* If an adult has been able to integrate the *emotional* reality of her past into her conscious mind, even if it was traumatic, then that emotional integrity, that ability to talk about and put those experiences into perspective, will be a major advantage for the parent and her children.

If a parent is still emotionally triggered by her past, she will find it hard to focus on the past because the emotions and beliefs will have so infiltrated her present relationships. On the other hand, if a parent has *buried* emotion-laden memories and detached from anything disturbing, her description of her childhood will be sparse. Her overall conclusions and remarks will be significantly incongruent with the facts. For example, one of my clients told me that her father was an alcoholic, her mother had bipolar disorder and there was domestic violence throughout her extended family. Yet, several minutes later, she concluded that "I had a wonderful childhood. I can't imagine anything I'd want to change."

Four types of relationship attachment patterns have been identified through extensive research by Mary Ainsworth with infants and their mothers. Her "Strange Situation" research studies show that by eight months of age, children have already developed a clear attachment pattern that will serve as a template for future significant relationships. The study begins with an eight month old child playing with toys in a room accompanied by his mother and a stranger, the researcher. According to a pre-arranged plan, the mother leaves the room briefly while her child remains with the stranger. Of course, this is a frightening situation for a child, especially at this age. When the mother returns, the response of the child indicates the type of attachment he has with his mother.

A child with a "secure" attachment will seek and experience comfort and soothing from the mother and then soon return to playing contentedly. All three of the other forms of attachment are known as "insecure" attachments, each marked by its own particular pattern of approach and avoidance. A child with an "avoidant" attachment will ignore the mother's return and continue playing with the toys as if he had no disturbed feelings or emotional needs. Interestingly though, the monitor that tracks the child's physiology indicates that the child actually is in distress but is making an effort to dismiss his feelings.

Meanwhile, a child with an "anxious-ambivalent" attachment pattern will cling to the mother and express prolonged distress but, despite the mother's attempts to comfort, will not feel relief. This child will be too preoccupied with the relationship to return to exploring the play environment. The most insecure attachment pattern of all is called "disorganized" or "fearful-avoidant." This child experiences and expresses emotional distress, but is confused about what to do. He rapidly flips back and forth between approaching and avoiding the mother, seeing her both as a source of comfort and a source of threat. His instincts say he should go to Mommy for comfort, but his experience tells him she's not safe.

Perhaps not surprisingly, children with secure attachments are at lower risk for being traumatized or developing mental health problems than those with insecure attachments. In adulthood, those who have maintained a secure attachment status will be able to self-soothe, enjoy their own company, understand and accept their emotional past and present and create trusting relationships with others, *including* their partner and children. They are comfortable with both interdependence and autonomy and with intimate connection as well as solitude. I must admit that in all my years of life, I'm hard-pressed to recall a person who came into adulthood with a solidly secure attachment.

Some children may have enjoyed a secure attachment for a number of years until a traumatic experience ruptured the trust and damaged the secure attachment. Fairly common is the scenario in which the parents' childhood wounds gradually emerge and the marriage bond weakens, with the spouses ineffectively coping with pain through conflict, emotional withdrawal, drinking, Internet or porn addiction, avoiding home, affairs and/or separation and divorce. Inevitably, the ongoing tension and turmoil damage the child's sense of security.

Anxious-Preoccupied Adult Attachment Style

Children with an anxious-ambivalent attachment style become adults with an "anxious-preoccupied" attachment style. (Throughout this book, I will use the term "anxious" to describe these individuals.) They are extremely emotionally aware, expressive and reactive and have an excessively strong drive to seek connection, approval and support from others. When they want to express something, they do; there is very little editing. Their speech may be long-winded and rapid. Their propensity for emotional flooding fuels their drive to take action—verbal or otherwise.

Adults who are "anxious-preoccupied" have so little capacity for self-soothing and such a strong need to connect that other personal goals are often relegated to the shadows or ineffectively managed. They have an insatiable appetite for attention, approval and control so as to avoid relentless feelings of invisibility, insignificance, shame, vulnerability and helplessness. This can lead them to become critical, demanding and aggressive as they *desperately protest their experience of disconnection and aloneness.*

Sometimes, those with an anxious-preoccupied status exhibit the opposite pattern, ignoring their own needs and feeling compelled instead to meet the emotional needs of others who appear wounded or deprived. They can be highly preoccupied with, and sensitive to, others' pain and problems and have a compulsive need to fix, protect or take care of others. Anxious individuals have an undying hope that they should and can make those who suffer happy or that others should and can stop the anxious person's pain. By focusing on goals that others have not "signed up for" or are incapable of achieving, anxiously-attached people may feel like they are constantly trying to move a dead weight.

Another common pattern of anxious individuals involves channeling their abundant intensity, passion, energy and motivation into achieving goals. Anxiously-attached individuals may become high achievers in the realms of education, career, social status, talents and/or travel. They often are "family heroes" who bring much pride and satisfaction to the family. While they are able to meet many of their goals, because they aren't scratching the true "itch," their itching, like all compulsions, can escalate out of control.

Those with anxious-preoccupied attachment sometimes burn out like a comet from their intense and desperate efforts to fix or control others in the hope of experiencing connection, security and peace. Their pattern then changes to dismissive-avoidant attachment. For many people, a long period of preoccupied anxiety is followed by a long period of avoidant withdrawal and depression. For others, the swing back and forth between being revved up and shut down occurs within a week or even a day. Sometimes these individuals are diagnosed with bipolar disorder. In any case, they are experiencing extreme physiological and emotional dysregulation. I will speak about these swings within the autonomic nervous system in the next chapter.

Dismissive-Avoidant Adult Attachment Style

Children with an avoidant attachment status become adults with a "dismissive-avoidant" attachment style. (Throughout this book, I will use the term "avoidant" to describe these individuals.) Avoidant individuals have been disconnected from their attachment feelings and needs, probably since infancy, and so they focus whatever energy they have on activities and tasks rather than people and emotions. Because they are disconnected from their emotions, they tend to be shut down in relationships. They are highly self-sufficient and guarded, having learned that it is safer to not get close to or rely on others. They don't expect to be understood, accepted or supported, so their major defense is "sour grapes," "who needs it anyway" and "I couldn't care less." The dismissive-avoidant adult is the flip side of the anxious-preoccupied adult, and people with these contrasting attachment styles tend to attract each other like magnets.

Even when they are highly accomplished in the work world, avoidantly-attached individuals often are haunted by a sense of inadequacy, especially in their relationships with important others. Many feel helpless to make their partner happy. This is a painful belief to hold about one's self. The avoidant individual's primary strategies for dealing with these circumstances are restricting awareness and withdrawal. In order to turn off their emotional needs and urges, they have to shut down their emotions across the board. That means dramatically reducing attention to the body, feelings, relationships and the past. As a result, many become all "left brain," dominated by logic, reason, intellect, coldness and detachment. These "Spock-like" individuals may be silent or give mono-syllabic answers, or their speech may be sluggish and run on in a dull monotone.

Often, family members are disturbed by the avoider's forgetfulness, distractibility and seeming inability to "be all there." They may attribute these behaviors to Attention Deficit Disorder, but the behaviors are more likely a survival-motivated self-defense against circumstances that trigger emotional distress. Those who rely on this strategy long enough are likely to suffer major depression or dysthymia, a milder form of depression. Psychotherapist Terrence Real wrote an excellent book devoted to the pervasive problem of male depression: *I Don't Want to Talk About It: Overcoming the Secret Legacy of Male Depression.*

Because they have disowned their emotional history and are so allergic to emotions, avoidant individuals have very little awareness of what makes them, their partners and their relationships tick. They lack empathy and compassion either for themselves or others. Avoidant individuals will edit out anything that is painful or discouraging, insisting that "everything is fine" and becoming disturbed by their partner's focus on problems and the past. *While avoidant status is a common attachment status for men, women are not exempt. Likewise, plenty of men as well as women have an anxious attachment status.*

Some children have an avoidant attachment with one parent and an anxious attachment with the other parent. As a result, they may grow up to be avoidant in some relationships and anxious in others. Sometimes adult partners switch attachment styles during the course of their marriage. At first the man is avoidant and the woman is anxious. Later in the marriage the woman may become avoidant and the man will become anxious. Usually, all of this occurs out of consciousness. Sometimes those with avoidant attachment may be detached with their partner but anxiously attached to others who aren't perceived as rejecting or threatening. While they may be highly esteemed in those relationships, the fact that they feel so ineffective and unappreciated in their key attachment relationship, takes a heavy toll on their emotional and physical well-being.

The Fearful Adult Attachment Style

Children with a fearful-avoidant or disorganized attachment status become adults with a "fearful attachment status." They are fearful of intimacy and socially avoidant, due to distrust and fear of rejection. They both want and fear intimacy. These individuals will alternate between intense awareness of their need for connection and love and an equally intense rejection of closeness. They have low self-confidence and high self-consciousness. They inhabit the worst of both worlds: I'm not okay *and* you're not okay.

People with a fearful attachment status can alternate between episodes of highly-agitated, volatile, demanding and threatening behavior and benign, good natured stretches. Despite their pleas for attention and support, they will push away anyone who tries to respond. This behavior may be fueled by a deep distrust of others' motives, feeling unworthy of care and becoming anxious due to the unfamiliarity of the situation. During periods of their lives, those with a fearful attachment status may suffer great pain inwardly with no outward sign of their chronic insecurity, anxiety, distrust, loneliness and longing.

While these distinctive attachment styles have been identified, it is important to remember that people's attachment bonds are anxious or avoidant to different degrees; it's not a black and white situation. Also, it is not uncommon for an individual to simultaneously have an avoidant attachment in one relationship, an anxious attachment in another relationship and a secure attachment in a third relationship. In later chapters, I will be exploring adult attachment relationships in great depth.

Earned Secure Adult Attachment Style

A final category of attachment in adulthood is "earned secure attachment." The great news is that, no matter the severity of our childhood deprivation and trauma, we can heal the wounds of our emotional past and acquire the same emotional intelligence, confidence and trust in self and others as those who have always been blessed with a secure attachment. In later chapters, we will explore how to develop a strong, secure attachment at any time in our lives.

CHAPTER THREE

Personality in Day to Day Life

I FIND MYSELF ON SURGING, *wild waters that are emanating from my childhood living room and propelling me out the front door onto a vast raging river. As I watch the shoreline rushing by I am aware of my vulnerability and that there is no place I can go . . . and then I see a stone fortress up ahead. I know that only children and animals live there, so I will be safe. I find myself inside the fortress, hiding within massive, heavy, dark wooden furniture. I can barely breathe. I'm astonished that my life could have dwindled to such a tiny flickering flame that still refused to go out. Suddenly a child approaches me, points to me and says, "I see you there!" While he is laughing, I'm alarmed and tell him, "This is not a laughing matter! No one must know I exist." Then out of the corner of my eye I see, through an open doorway, a harbor with a ship. I see my chance to escape. When I become aware again, I am in an apartment of my own. I'm very pleased to discover that I have successfully escaped and survived. I am on my own and intact. Then, I look out the window and realize that, while the world outside is full of color, my world is black and white. My heart sinks.*

This is the most significant dream I ever recall having. I experienced it in adulthood during the period when I was in therapy and actively reconnecting with my childhood memories. I've held onto it for almost twenty-five years because it captured so poignantly and vividly what my life had felt like prior to my decision to face my emotional history. Most of us do not find the safety and guidance we need to face and heal our pain until we are adults. Many of us go to our graves never having been freed from our past.

As we go through our daily lives there are patterns to how we typically feel, perceive, think and behave, especially in relation to other people. Many of us don't allow enough time to reflect on these patterns; we take the way we are for granted. We may assume that we are set in stone and there's nothing we can do about it, so why think about it? Plus, it would only make us feel miserable. Indeed, many people *are* tormented, drowning in awareness of their feelings, emotions, thoughts and experiences, and feeling absolutely confused, stuck and overwhelmed. As we move along in *Peace in the Heart and Home*, I will provide a framework that enables us to imagine a way of being that is neither a "done deal" nor utter chaos. That framework will involve effective ways of being in touch with difficult emotion-laden reality.

The World of Emotions

Human beings are capable of experiencing a wonderful palette of emotions. Without emotion, there is lifelessness, a lack of color and vitality. It is not possible to suppress only the painful emotions and hold onto the pleasurable ones. A rich life is one in which we know what it is to feel hurt, disappointment, loneliness, sorrow, helplessness, remorse, envy, betrayal, disgust, shock, fear, desperation, humiliation, outrage and horror as well as compassion, confidence, enthusiasm, dignity, hope, delight, wonder, ecstasy, peace and love. Our knowledge of these emotions makes it possible to connect and share a depth of understanding with others who also know these emotions on an intimate level. The wider and deeper our emotional experience, the richer our lives, provided we have the language and skills to articulate and manage them.

Emotions are the substances that animate the world. Without feelings, there would be no motivation to do anything. I once read of a case in which a man had suffered damage to his emotional brain. The man retained his high cognitive intelligence, but without access to his emotions, he totally lacked motivation or direction to initiate any action. He couldn't make decisions because all actions were equally devoid of meaning. Some avoidantly attached people may experience this state of mind. Without exposure to their emotions, they have no rudder to guide their life. I know of a few avoidant individuals whose speech is riddled with the phrase, "I don't know."

Speaking of avoidant attachment, I believe that many men who are emotionally shut down and detached from their wives turn to spectator sports to safely invest their big hearts and to restart their emotional engines. They care deeply about their teams, are ecstatic when they win and express deep disappointment when they lose. The same men who play it emotionally close-to-the-vest at home openly express huge amounts of enthusiasm and hope over groups of men chasing a puck, swinging a bat, outmaneuvering a tackle or shooting a basket. They can openly express expectations and complaints, something they may not do with their spouses. In the domain of sports they experience a deep sense of belonging, connection and pride (and sometimes disgust). What I'm suggesting here is that men and their families have a lot to gain when men bring their hearts, courage, enthusiasm and hope to their personal relationships as well. Picture Cuba Gooding Jr. with his wife in *Jerry Maguire*—and then take it down a few notches.

On the other hand, many people with anxious attachment and racing physiologies may feel compelled to spend an inordinate amount of time engaging in physical activities in order to release all the energy that their nervous systems keep generating. They might become involved in team sports or individual activities such as running, bike racing or working out at the gym. Each excursion is a fix that provides relief until the next wave of adrenaline, anxiety or tension rolls in. Some people with anxious attachment thrive on crisis and are drawn to working in high-pressure settings like emergency rooms or on rescue squads. Then there are those who handle their excessive emotion-generated energy by plunging into business, the media or politics, thereby providing a reason to always be on the go. This process may entail working long hours, winning people over and feeling a sense of urgency that can't be stilled, that can only be temporarily appeased like a hungry lion.

Some people's tremendous creativity is fueled by a relentless rush of emotional energy and drive. The pressure to always be on, to perform, entertain and get a reaction may benefit those of us who are their audience, but at quite a cost to the drama or comedy king. The inability to be one's authentic self, to be accepted for who you are, not what you achieve and the inability to tolerate or enjoy stillness is a tragedy.

Those with anxious attachment, being highly aware of their emotions and physical sensations, are prone to taking excessive action since their intense e-*motions* demand that they *move*. They have a powerful sense that what is happening right now isn't right, must be changed and that it's up to them to make things different than they are. This powerful drive to control people, events and the future prevents them from recognizing and enjoying what is here, right now in the present moment. It also results in a never-ending battle because nothing ever becomes or stays perfect. And so, like Sisyphus, the man of Greek myth who was condemned to rolling a rock up a steep mountain, only for it to roll back down, the anxiously-attached person struggles fruitlessly for self-efficacy, fulfillment and peace.

While emotions can provide us with vitality, meaning, direction and fuel to act, they can mislead us when we have been seriously hurt in the past. Often, they are basically flashbacks of implicit traumatic memories, without the content—time, place and person—to explain their origin. In those cases, emotions arise and the rational mind looks for justification for the feeling. Our perception is colored by emotions without our even being aware of it.

Perhaps you can imagine how these misperceptions can cause big trouble in relationships. It is a common phenomenon that we see what our wired-in emotions tell us to believe, rather than believe what we actually see. But, if you understand that your amygdala is being triggered unnecessarily due to its overcautious nature, you may be able to respond differently to your emotions. Just because you feel afraid doesn't mean you face a genuine threat. Just because you feel guilty doesn't mean you actually did something wrong. Just because you feel enraged doesn't mean you actually were mistreated. Just because you feel shame doesn't mean you actually are unworthy or are going to be judged. Just because you feel helpless doesn't mean you actually are helpless.

The reservoir of painful emotions that we re-circulate within our being and relationships also create behavior patterns that keep us stuck in the same shame-reinforcing experiences. When we carry a lot of shame, then we expect others to perceive our defectiveness and unworthiness, which leads to us becoming defensive. We tend to defend ourselves in a fight, flight or freeze mode. Fighting might involve speaking loudly and passionately about our worth and entitlement. This conceit, pushiness and self-centeredness may provoke others to dislike and avoid us. The only ones who are likely to stay with us are those who feel inadequate, lack better judgment or are guilt-driven and desperate, and at some level we know that. Picture the arrogant villain Lex Luther, the clueless Otis and the gullible Miss Tessmocker in *Superman*.

If we choose flight, we might shy away from people in order to avoid putting ourselves in a position of being judged and found wanting. Then our isolation, loneliness and feelings of being unlovable reinforce our shame. If we react by freezing, we might submit to mistreatment from others because we don't feel we deserve better or we don't feel competent to walk away from someone who is abusive or neglectful. Then the continued mistreatment reinforces our shame. Freezing can also involve waiting for someone to choose us and staying as long as they want us, whether or not they meet *our* needs.

Whether we recognize them as emotions or mistake them for physical ailments, the longer intense emotions stay stuck in our being, the more those feelings distort our sense of identity. Shame and guilt tell us we are horrible, undeserving people and responsible for others' suffering. Fear and anxiety tell us we are helpless victims. Rejection and inadequacy tell us we are defective outcasts. Sadness and despair tell us we are tiny and insignificant. However, when emotions are properly and fully processed and released, we discover our true identity. I imagine our true nature as a brilliant copper pipe and stuck traumatic emotions as corrosive deposits that mask the pipe. When the emotions are helped to finally run their course, the deposits dissolve, revealing our hidden brilliance. Accessing our true Self will be discussed at length later in the book.

Our Worried Minds

Another source of emotional misdirection is the excessive use of our thinking process to worry about problems, past and future. Obsessive thinking about things that have already occurred can fan the flames of guilt, anger or hatred. Obsessing about things that might happen can trigger fear, hopelessness and helplessness. These extreme feelings can cause extreme behaviors. Slipping into imaginative fantasy can produce uplifting or disturbing emotions, depending on the scenario. The brain does not distinguish imaginary images and emotional experiences from real-life ones. So if you imagine yourself being rejected by others, your brain registers that as an actual event and alters your body's chemistry to meet the situation. People often cause themselves so much unintended injury by the practice of imagining disturbing events. Generalized anxiety disorder is fed by such catastrophic scenarios.

When our minds are filled with the white noise and congestion of disturbing thoughts and images, it creates a confusion that makes us more susceptible to entering a time warp. The past and present get jumbled up and we can feel more like a child than an adult. The younger we experience ourselves, the more we feel helplessness, self doubt, shame and fear. In such a state of body and mind we are more likely to handle our problems in a "finger in the dike" manner. For example, we might tolerate abusive treatment hundreds of times rather than reflecting on how the experience is hurting us, gathering the strength to let the other person know how their behavior is damaging the relationship and identifying courses of action should the person's behavior not change. Or, we might express anger, hostility and disappointment hundreds of times at our annoying child rather than reflect on how our behavior is impacting him emotionally and provoking his behavior in a "chicken and egg" negative cycle.

Many people are under the false assumption that worrying, hyper-vigilance and tension prepare them to take action should something threatening occur. *Purr*haps they should reflect on the nature of cats, which are among the laziest, most relaxed creatures on the planet. They also have some of the quickest reflexes in the animal world, being able to come to attention and burst into action the second they recognize an intriguing opportunity or a potential threat. These two states might be linked. The fact that the feline nervous system is so serene and its energy so well conserved might give a cat the flexibility and energy it needs to swing into action at the drop of a hat.

Humans are capable of this, too. I'm reminded of the one time in my professional life that a client acted inappropriately in my presence. As we sat and talked for the first time, this confused and nervous 13-year-old boy suddenly lunged his hand under my dress, and just as rapidly I yelled, "What the f__ are you doing?!" He immediately pulled back and expressed remorse. Up until that moment I had been calm, alert and friendly—my common state of being with clients—which allowed me the flexibility to take instant defensive action when the situation required it.

Unfortunately, our calm state of mind and body is too often polluted, such as through catastrophic thinking and imagination. An example of how the imagination can actually trigger a sense of threat is depicted in the following story. One morning, after I had dropped my son off at a friend's house, I began to have a fantasy that some violent intruder was entering the house. Instantaneously I felt my hands grip the steering wheel tightly, my heart rate increase, my eyes widen, and a feeling of panic spread through my body. Fortunately, I was mindful enough to catch what I was doing to myself. I reminded myself that this was just a fantasy, not based on any evidence, and that the likelihood of it actually happening was extremely low. In this way I was able to snap myself out of the scenario and bring myself back to reality. Instead of causing us needless distress, our imagination can be intentionally used to nourish and heal ourselves. This capacity will be addressed later in the chapter on Self-Care.

The emotions that typically torment those who have unresolved traumatic memories and attachment trauma include fear, panic, anxiety, overwhelm, vulnerability, helplessness, shame, inadequacy, guilt, anger, sadness, loneliness and despair. Fear is probably the most common disturbing emotion that drives behavior between human beings, especially fear of being abandoned, alone and isolated, seen as inadequate, rejected, humiliated, betrayed or annihilated. Like everything else in life, emotions are waves; they rise and fall, come and go. But in the case of unresolved traumatic experiences, they rise, peak and get stored in the brain in that heightened state. Emotions are problematic when they get stuck in either an "on" or "off" position. In life, elasticity and fluidity are signs of health, while rigidity is limiting. The Dalai Lama is said to feel his emotions very powerfully, but they recede quickly and he regains his composure and equanimity.

I often explain to my clients the relationship of emotions to reason using my hands. I call it the "Island of Reason and Ocean of Emotion." Make a fist with your left hand; that is an island and represents your left hemisphere, cognitive faculties, reason and composed adult perspective. Now, flatten and stretch out your right hand; that is the ocean and represents your right hemisphere, emotions and physical sensations. When the emotional ocean rises too high, there is the risk of flooding the island of reason. The island can disappear under intense anger, fear, shame and despair. At the other extreme, if emotion recedes too far, the resulting aridness can stunt life and growth. Optimally, the ocean washes across the island's shores, continuing to provide its riches and vitality, without jeopardizing the island's presence.

Extreme Stress and Defenses

As long as we have the ability to self-soothe, maintain perspective and reach out to others we trust for comfort and connection, we can manage to stay within what is called an "optimal arousal zone." *To be truly healthy, we need to be able to do both: care for ourselves and ask for help when needed.* We maintain optimal arousal through the process of homeostasis, which allows us to gently fluctuate between being energized and relaxed. If a disturbing event occurs, that causes intense fear, and we are unable to manage that fear, then we will experience "hyperarousal." We are hyperaroused when our amygdala registers threat and triggers the stress response. The resulting biochemical arousal enables us to fight or flee. If we are unable to take action or get the support we need, the hyperarousal will escalate. This can lead to panic, disorganization and plummeting to the other extreme of numbness and "hypoarousal." If we have nowhere or no one to run to for safety and comfort, if we are vulnerable and unequipped to take action on our own, then that leaves only one option—to freeze. All of this is the case with children.

Children who are exposed to experiences that frighten them and whose parents are unavailable or unable to provide protection and soothing, often reflexively shut down emotionally and physically as a way of coping with threat. *In all humans, the freeze response is not a conscious choice; the nervous system automatically takes action on behalf of the organism's survival.* This phenomenon, which involves the defense mechanism "dissociation," spares children full awareness of the wild and raw feelings that are surging through their body and consciousness. Sometimes their minds become foggy, blank and still, while their bodies are still raging. At other times they are so shut down that they are completely numb. In some individuals, their consciousness will disconnect from their bodies and they will observe the frightening events from a safe distance as if it were happening to someone else.

When we are hyperaroused, it means that the "sympathetic branch of the autonomic nervous system" has been activated. It's equivalent to a car's accelerator pedal being pushed to the floor. In this state, anxiety compels us to take action and our physiology is radically altered so that we have the capacity to do so. Think of an adrenaline-fueled person lifting a car to rescue a child.

By contrast, when we are hypoaroused, the "parasympathetic branch of the autonomic nervous system" has become activated to keep us from completely burning out. It's equivalent to hitting the brakes. When we are hypoaroused to the extreme, we go virtually into hibernation, with just a pilot light keeping us alive. This is the state I experienced in the dream that opens this chapter. But as mentioned above, some individuals experience the worst of both worlds: intense internal activation *and* complete immobility. They may experience them simultaneously or alternating over time. These opposing physiological states and accompanying behavioral extremes may be experienced by those with bipolar disorder, previously called manic-depression. These swings are also found in people with Post-Traumatic Stress Disorder. People who have experienced chronic, pervasive stress in their lives can go through this exhausting process daily. The chemical bathing of stress hormones their whole system experiences takes a dramatic toll on their bodies as well as their minds. We will explore this in more depth in the chapter on Physical Health.

I'd like to mention at this time that many people have been told by psychiatrists that they have a chemical imbalance and the cause of the imbalance is never really spelled out. If anything, it might be explained as a genetic issue or a neurological fluke. *My basic premise is that the majority of cases of chemistry thrown out of whack are the result of insecure attachment relationships, psychological trauma, emotional flooding and chronic or severe stress.* It is also my belief that being told that taking medication to correct the imbalance is *all that is necessary* is a huge disservice to a suffering human being, especially in times when there is so much more that can be done.

Getting back to our main subject, in the earliest years of life, a very young child has only a few defenses to rely on: crying to seek attention, enraged screams to protest the lack of response, and, when that fails, a resigned, defeated numbness that shuts the body and awareness down to a faint flicker. As children reach ages five, six, or seven, their unconscious minds begin to create other defenses to help them cope with their lack of parental nurture. Many, if not most, of the defenses that cause major problems in adulthood are lifesavers for the child. Without these defenses, children would feel absolutely devastated, stay frozen in helplessness, be unable to function in daily life, fail to meet basic developmental challenges—or die of a broken heart.

Deprived of dependable parental care, children will seek comfort wherever they can find it. Turning to fantasy and imagination can be a great relief. Savoring a relationship with a warm and affectionate pet can be soothing. For a teenager, having a friend with whom to share problems is helpful and reassuring. While all of these resources play a role in organizing a child's emotional life, they are no substitute for a relationship with a dependable, empathic and responsive adult. In studies of resilience, children who have at least one adult they can turn to for understanding and support are more likely to thrive in the future, despite having endured challenging circumstances.

Because too many children don't have the relationship resources to help them cope with their hurts, fears and losses, they become very dependent upon their defenses. When they grow up and leave the source of the traumatic memories, they take their defenses with them. They have become integral to their personality. Added to this is the societal pressure, especially for males, to be a self-sufficient, achievement-oriented individualist who is too strong and self-respecting to whine or have needs. We're encouraged to suck it up, tough it out, get over it. Some people, out of compassion for another's suffering, may encourage us to avoid focusing on our pain, thinking that's the best way to experience relief.

But when we don't face our pain, we simply create a bigger and deeper reservoir of unresolved emotions that must stay buried; a psychological toxic waste site. The longer we rely on our defenses, the more we fear the emotional truth that lies behind them and the more power the disowned emotions possess. By the time many people arrive at a therapist's office, their defenses have multiplied, backfired, become ineffective, or escalated to the point of compulsion. They often feel out of control and depleted from the relentless battle with physical, mental and emotional symptoms that arise from ignoring painful realities. There is no peace when we are haunted and on the run. As Thomas Merton observed: "The truth that many people never understand, until it is too late, is that the more that you try to avoid suffering, the more you suffer, because smaller and more insignificant things begin to torture you in proportion to your fear of being hurt."

A story is told of a stress management lecturer who raised a glass of water to the audience and asked, "How heavy is this glass of water?" A range of answers were called out. Then the lecturer said, "The absolute weight doesn't matter. It depends on how long you try to hold it. If you hold it for a minute, that's not a problem. If you hold it for an hour, you'll have an ache in your arm. If you hold it for a day, they'll have to call an ambulance. In each case, it's the same weight, but the longer you hold it, the heavier it becomes." When we dam up our wounds and losses, we create a tremendous back log that is a heavy weight to hold. People can carry these weights for decades. The energy it takes to suppress this inner world can deplete a person's resources. As I work with clients to gradually heal this huge reservoir of pain, I am absolutely astonished at the volumes of human drama that live within the shelves of their being, without others who have known them having read a single page.

Some of my clients, in the early weeks of therapy, have wondered why they still feel so terrible after years, if not decades, of struggling. The fact that they still feel so helpless, afraid and ashamed reinforces their belief that they are damaged goods. The actual reason they can't get free of their pain is that, like a jack-in-the-box, each time the toxic memories emerge, they keep pushing them back down. Traumatic emotions are the equivalent of hot volcanic materials that are hell-bent on coming out and staying out. A lesson can be taken from these powerful eruptions. The longer the lava is released, the cooler it becomes. Volcanic materials ultimately break down and form some of the most fertile soil on Earth. This same soil has been cultivated, produced abundant food and fostered civilizations. My experience with guided releases of traumatic material has proven to me and my clients that new growth and thriving are the fruits of their labor.

Defensive strategies vary in the degree to which they distort reality in order to achieve the goal of reducing anxiety. This means that, while delusional and severe dissociative states are the exception, all of us are prone to misperceiving people and situations. In fact, for all of us, daily life is comprised of hundreds of live "Rorschach tests," in which we project our emotionally-based beliefs and judgments onto the world. While defenses can drastically stunt a person's development and make life difficult for other people in their life, I feel compelled to say that, along with emotions, defenses add much richness to the world. So much of human drama, theater and literature are filled with characters whose defensive behaviors are colorful, fascinating, alarming, offensive or tragic.

Some common defenses that the human psyche packs in its arsenal include: arrogance, defiance, blame, sarcasm, perfectionism, approval-seeking, placating, minimizing and denial. There are dozens more that can be found in Appendix A at the end of this book and you might find it helpful to take a look at this list in order to identify the defenses you typically employ. Add to this list the many types of compulsive behaviors that help us avoid silence, stillness, reflection and the anxiety-provoking material lurking there. Any activity can be done excessively and be motivated by avoidance, for example: exercise, sex, gambling, caretaking, shopping and Internet surfing. I had a client who spent six hours a day losing herself in novels and catalogs. All of these compulsions are short-lived quick-fixes and substitutes for the soothing that comes from a nurturing relationship with oneself and emotionally authentic and secure relationships with other adults.

Trying to overcome any of the above compulsive behaviors without exploring and addressing the underlying emotions, gut-level self-beliefs and traumatic memories is doomed for failure. It's removing those poison ivy leaves and leaving the roots intact. Carl Jung once said "Neurosis is always a substitute for legitimate suffering." Later chapters in *Peace in the Heart and Home* will thoroughly explain how adults can develop self-soothing skills, resolve traumatic memories, cultivate secure intimate relationships and develop a connection with the fullness of the present moment.

I'd like to mention here that some people who have been angry, aggressive, paranoid or highly agitated for years and years may eventually become subdued. While it may seem on the surface that they are healthier, that most likely isn't the case. They may be calmer because they are drinking heavily, are depressed or are relying on dissociation. They may be less troublesome and less confrontational, but people in this state are half alive. Their decades of sympathetic nervous system overdrive and futile protesting of disconnection and pain have come to an end. Their nervous system has shut down; they are basically in parasympathetic collapse.

We need to recognize that tuning out and distraction are defenses. When I provided psychotherapy to adolescents in a school setting, I noticed a pattern with students diagnosed by others as having ADD or ADHD. Most of them came from families where there was severe marital distress, parent-child conflict, parental addiction, child abuse and/or domestic violence. When your family members are in pain and the way they behave is excruciating to witness and experience, it makes sense that you'd not want to pay attention. It makes sense that you might experience or cultivate a distractedness that provides a smokescreen against reality. It's also the magical thinking of a child to believe, if I don't notice it, maybe it will disappear or not hurt me.

While avoidant children become detached, forgetful and sluggish, anxious children cope by using the opposite strategy—hyperactivity. Constant activity can provide the flurry necessary to keep suspected or actual painful truths from ever clearly registering. It can also help regulate the excessive physiological arousal that keeps getting generated at home. Cozolino states what I've often suspected, "Sadly, many children with manic defenses are mistakenly diagnosed with ADD."

A common practice of males (and the occasional female) in our society is "busting chops." It probably serves a number of purposes, one being, "the best defense is a good offense." Males learn early in life, as a survival tool, to be merciless with each other. Most of the time, it's commonly understood to be all in good fun. "Busting chops" is one of the few acceptable ways for a male to show delight and joy. At times, and for some people, it could be used as a form of passive-aggression, a way to let off emotional steam. But it could also shift into full-blown bullying. "Busting chops" seems to be the psychological equivalent of two rams butting heads, each not wanting to be the pathetic loser, each needing to be the "king of the hill." There is no middle ground; you are either the Lion King or a "pussy." Fathers want their sons to be "a man" and can't trust that they will be without a lot of toughening up. They would be horrified if their son were to show vulnerability. The feelings of unworthiness and shame would be too much to bear. Men may also be reenacting the kind of relationship they had with their father (or male relatives and peers), *but this time, the son has the power.*

Additionally, in order to prepare each other for the expected threats of a harsh world, it's advantageous for males to practice attacking and withstanding attack. It's analogous to pulling the rug out from under someone to help them gain experience getting back up on their feet. Unfortunately, the more males become insensitive to aggression, the more they participate in creating the cruel world they expect. It may also be their way of flexing their fearlessness and apathy muscles and toughening the wall around their heart: "I'm never treated with empathy or sensitivity and that's fine with me. I'm not feeling deprived or hurt at all. In fact, this is great! Bring it on!"

This pattern certainly is the antithesis of the kind of relating that creates emotionally secure relationships, whether out in the work world or at home. When people who rely on this defense are in relationship with people who are in touch with their emotions, they honestly don't get what the other person's upset is all about. Such a relationship represents two contrasting response patterns to the childhood experience of emotional deprivation and lack of safety. One person builds excessive tolerance of lack of love and safety, while the other person is hypersensitive, never having forgotten how painful it is to be deprived of basic needs. The counterpoint to this avoidant pattern is the following defense strategy often associated with, but not limited to females.

Those who have experienced childhood deprivation, abandonment and helplessness may devote themselves to rescuing and taking care of others. Such people are often called "co-dependent." The deep empathy they possess from experiencing and witnessing so much pain in themselves, parents and siblings, can make them highly sensitive to the pain and vulnerability of others. They may have an oversized sense of loyalty and responsibility. This can be played out through becoming a medical professional, social worker, therapist, firefighter, police officer, rescue squad member or animal shelter volunteer. I've also known a number of people whose urge to connect with, care for and protect animals and pets (speechless, defenseless creatures) was so powerful, that their primary preoccupation and attachment was with the animals in their lives, not humans. Sometimes those who have lost all faith and trust in people are sustained by their relationship with their pets.

When we feel compelled to advocate for the underdog, whether it is an animal, a child, a person in crisis, the homeless or third world peoples, we are overlooking the victim closest to our heart—the child within who has no one to turn to. No matter how much effort we put out, it never seems to be enough because there is always someone else who is vulnerable and deprived of what they deserve. Everywhere we look we see someone else in need and we can't tolerate others' distress. While our dedicated efforts on behalf of others are valuable, admirable and sorely needed, they are not a substitute for self-care. After we heal our inner wounds, these passions and commitments can still be pursued, but with a healthy enthusiasm, dedication and satisfaction that is very different from the previous state of being tormented and driven.

Why Our Defenses Don't Work

Relying on our defenses to bring us peace is like throwing thousands of darts at one wall when the dart board and bull's eye are on the opposite wall. Here are some examples of how we can expend huge amounts of energy investing in pursuits that have us absolutely missing the mark.

Sandra has enjoyed a highly successful career in the field of child development. She is considered an expert on children's needs and feels very confident professionally. But in her private life Sandra has been haunted for decades by the memory of multiple losses of parents and substitute parents in childhood. While in her work life she cognitively understands the psychological needs of young children, in her personal life she runs from the internal cries of the lonely, forgotten child who longs for comfort from a compassionate, responsive adult. No matter how many children Sandra positively impacts through her career, the child inside her remains fearful, neglected and in pain. What we resist persists.

Throughout childhood, Kevin was at the mercy of his father's insensitivity. Whenever Kevin was upset, his father called him a "kidder." When he was eleven, his father managed to bring him to tears at the dinner table every single night. Making it worse was the fact that his mother made no effort to provide comfort or protection. In adulthood Kevin has delighted in teasing and fooling others. There is a mischievous and undermining adolescent inside the grown man. Over the years, he has done things to members of his family and extended family that provoke feelings of confusion, helplessness, fear, disappointment, embarrassment or anger. Each time he watches unperturbed with a veneer of innocence and benign good humor. He has created quite a trail of memories of people with egg on their faces, people who've tripped over his outstretched foot. While each incident by itself is minor, it adds up to a legacy of disharmony, untrustworthiness and disrespect. Kevin has become a carrier of the disease that was acquired by him in another time and place. It infiltrates his adult family and spreads the feelings of insecurity and shame. And with sad irony, it does not in any way bring confidence, security or love to Kevin's inner child who was the victim of far more tragic and heartbreaking events.

As a child Linda was constantly bullied, blamed and rejected by her older sister Kathy, who often threatened Linda's life if she didn't jump to Kathy's demands. Linda's feelings of fear and of being loathed, inadequate, rejected and helpless followed her throughout her childhood into adulthood, coloring her every experience. As an adult, Linda pursued karate and became a black belt. Small and slight of frame, she nonetheless entered tournament after tournament going up against competitors who were often physically intimidating. Each time, Linda struggled to overcome her fear. The sense of power and confidence she felt with each win couldn't be sustained. It was like scooping up water with a strainer or casting again and again into a dead pond. Despite her competency and high achievement in karate, Linda still felt like a little girl—inadequate, helpless and frozen in fear—in all other realms of her life.

Linda's strategy is quite common among men. They are highly competitive and set before themselves one risky physical challenge after another such as aggressive racing, snowboarding, biking, weight-lifting, rock climbing or high contact sports. No matter how many dangerous or intimidating experiences they tackle, to me they are not as courageous as the men I have worked with who faced their traumatic memories and relationship fears. Now those are brave men.

Physical challenges can also be a way of activating the sympathetic nervous system for avoidant individuals who are depressed and lacking a sense of identity, purpose and drive. Such individuals might be considered adrenaline junkies. For others, the intense focus demanded by risk-taking activities may provide a barrier from feelings of emptiness, sadness, helplessness and loneliness. One last possible dynamic is that when people persistently seek physical and mental ordeals, they may be reenacting the childhood experience of facing one difficult challenge after another—on their own.

The emotions and beliefs about self and others, stemming from our family of origin relationships, enter a pipeline that goes underground and reemerges in peer relationships, romantic relationships or relationships with authority figures. Anytime we are triggered by another person, we can assume that it is reminiscent of a past wound or deprivation. Over time, the pipeline can wear out in a slow manner or break in a brittle way. Our emotions can leak out in small doses giving us brief exposure to disturbing material that we can dismiss as a fluke, a momentary being out of character. We may experience an intense rupture that repairs fairly quickly, postponing further our motivation to face the music and heal. Sometimes psychiatric medications help patch up those ruptures, resulting in another decade going by without those wounds being addressed.

There are people who manage to maneuver around potential growth-provoking crises for decades and then a major event turns their lives upside down. For some people, the past can burst through the defenses with such strong emotions and extreme behaviors that there are alarming repercussions that can't be overlooked or suppressed. Then there are some people with an anxious or fearful-avoidant attachment status who barely have any respite from relentless awareness of anxiety, fear, shame, helplessness and anger.

Adults with a dismissive-avoidant attachment status may look on the surface as if they are devoid of any emotional distress. They rarely, if ever, reveal any hurt feelings or show interest in others' hurt feelings. They may look as cool as a cucumber, but remember the avoidant eight month olds who looked unaffected while their physiology was markedly distressed. It's like a duck that is tranquilly gliding on the surface, yet all the while is working overtime underneath. Avoidant individuals may be engaged in constant worrying, analyzing, judging, procrastinating, catastrophizing and second-guessing everything—while never letting on.

The suppression of difficult emotions and aversion to sharing feelings and needs with another human being are a recipe for eventual suffering. It could be in the form of serious medical conditions like heart disease or cancer. It could be chronic minor physical complaints that migrate from one part of the body to another. It could mean a series of relationship failures and rejections due to being distant, uncaring and unresponsive. It could be burrowing into one's work or hobbies, alcohol or Internet relationships, thus putting salt on our spouse's open wounds and intensifying his or her messy emotions. One way or another, life insists that we deal with pain. It won't be denied.

States of Mind or "Ego States"

"But he seemed so timid and polite—the last person to do such a thing." Following a murder-suicide in the community, this kind of shocked remark is typically made by neighbors and co-workers. A similar kind of disbelief and confusion may follow the news that the compassionate clergyman molests children. Then there is the pillar of the community who ignores his wife and drinks himself to sleep; the feisty "tough cookie" who at home appeases her domineering husband; the man with the perfect life and family who is having an affair with his sister-in-law, the jovial guy at work whose presence provokes dread in the hearts of his wife and children; the superstar athlete whose amazing feats are sandwiched between battles with cancer, the vegetarian parent whose children are obese and the organized perfectionist whose procrastination puts him in bankruptcy. How could these contradictions exist in the same person?

Every one of us has multiple sides to our personality. Different sides become activated in different situations. Some people who were angry, impatient and critical as parents turn out to be benign and loving grand-parents. In some situations, we consciously make changes in how we behave, such as when we attend a funeral or meet with our boss. Other sides can be triggered unconsciously by strong emotions or potent cues in the environment. Each aspect of our personality has a corresponding "neural network" in our brain which is the wired in pattern and memory of this particular way of being, perceiving, thinking, feeling and behaving.

Generally, when we are in public, we tend to be more conscious of the impression we are making and less likely to let down our guard. But at home behind closed doors, with the people who mean the most to us and who we depend upon the most, we are far more likely to experience "emotional hijacks," courtesy of our ever-vigilant amygdala. As soon as an old wound is triggered and we feel vulnerable, one of our protective parts is bound to jump in to try to come to our rescue. The response will be fight, flight or freeze, one of the ways we once discovered would give us relief, a method that we have used hundreds of times and has become a well-worn neural pathway. At these times, we are basically possessed; our mature state of mind is nowhere to be found. Perhaps this is why so many of us are fascinated with stories and movies like *Dr. Jekyll and Mr.Hyde*, *The Wolfman*, *Alien*, *The Incredible Hulk*, *Sybil* and *The Exorcist*. Instinctively we recognize that we, too, harbor a deeply irrational side.

The more mindful we are, the more we can recognize when a "hurt part" or "protective part" of our personality is kicking in and, kindly but firmly, take back the reins of our decision-making and behavior. These hurt and protective parts were predominantly created during childhood and adolescence and therefore lack adult judgment and perspective. They are in a time warp and have no clue that times have changed, that they are safe now and have resources and choices that they didn't have before. Most of us are not aware enough of our "inner child states of mind," their fears and unmet needs.

As a result, when one of these states emerges, the child who belongs in the car seat ends up in the driver's seat, taking over the steering wheel. The adult part of our personality gets locked in the trunk and when we finally escape, we wonder, "What just happened?" If we don't invest in exploring and processing highly emotional events like these, we can go through our whole lives feeling ineffective and limping away from car wrecks. But if we choose to become more mindful of our emotional states, our adult self can stay in the driver's seat most of the time. A later chapter of the book will be devoted to this extremely important subject of mindfulness.

Sometimes parts of ourselves become polarized, wrestling with each other for control over our lives. "Polarized parts" are two parts of our psyche, each trusting only itself to protect us. For example, I have a client who alternates between caving in to her husband's demands and utterly dismissing his concerns and following her own impulses. The more one part escalates its particular strategy, the more the other escalates to gain back control. Eventually the person's life becomes out of control because of their extreme and contradictory beliefs, emotions and behaviors. When we are under stress and don't take the time to be mindful of our inner landscape, we are more susceptible to being over-taken by these wrestling protective parts.

We might evidence excellent judgment and give sage advice when we are helping a friend, loved one, coworker or client. But when it comes to our own personal lives, our sound judgment may be nowhere to be found. A certain person in our life may resemble in a deep yet subtle way some significant person from our formative years, provoking powerful emotions that drive us to behave in self-defeating ways. For example, we may feel undying longing and hope with someone who anyone else could clearly see as incapable of responding. As a result, we may be stuck for years in futile states of mind and behavior. One of my clients put it this way when she finally saw the light: "I've been a wind-up robot facing a wall and trying to move forward."

Another variation on polarized parts is when a vulnerable, hurt child ego state is offset by a protective ego state. "Busting Chops," intense competition and extreme risk-taking are examples of "reaction formations." This is a type of defense in which we exaggerate one type of behavior and attitude to mask emotions or impulses that are unacceptable. In so doing, we fool ourselves and possibly others. Additional examples of reaction formation are the following:

- People-pleasing and approval-seeking to hide feelings of hostility and aggression
- Sermonizing against sexuality to counteract shame about one's own sexual impulses
- Over-compliance to rigid rules to offset the shame-tainted need to spontaneously express one's true self and desires (picture the rigid and suppressed Dwight and Angela in *The Office*)
- Power-seeking to substitute for helplessness and emotional deprivation (think *Citizen Kane*)
- Intellectualizing and indifference to avoid awareness of vulnerable emotions
- Domination and contempt to hide vulnerability and shame
- Perfectionism to avoid feelings of inadequacy

I like to use the example of singer Judy Garland to demonstrate the importance of distinguishing which part of our personality is requiring attention. When we don't know where the unmet need is, it's like drowning a well-watered plant while neglecting the plant that is dry and wilted. Whenever Judy sang her heart out, audiences adored her. What made her stand out as one of the major musical talents of the twentieth century was her ability to express deep emotions such as vulnerability, longing, hope, sadness, love, joy and dignity. In her live performances, Judy was showered with love, recognition and admiration. When she sang special songs to her young children on stage, she seemed the epitome of a devoted, attentive mother.

Yet, off stage, Judy was irresponsible, unpredictable, demanding, ill-tempered, self-centered and volatile. She went through five marriages and four divorces. She had an eating disorder as evidenced by dramatic swings between weight gain and loss. Unable to understand the source of her relentless emotional pain or how to resolve it, Judy self-medicated with food, alcohol and prescription drugs. At age 47, she died from an overdose of barbiturates, a medication used for treating anxiety. Despite her outstanding career success and all the energy she expended seeking and successfully obtaining an emotional response from her audience, not one ounce of the love and attention she received from her fans was felt by her wounded inner children. Therein rests the tragedy of Judy Garland's failure to ever feel secure or loved—to ever experience life "Over the Rainbow."

When we don't recognize that the parts of our personality that feel deprived are intrusions from the past, we can misunderstand their signals. A client of mine, who chronically felt the urge to eat, be lazy, sleep, not think and avoid responsibility, regularly acted on those urges. As a result, she was undisciplined, obese, and unable to be emotionally present or provide guidance for her children. In coming to understand that these infantile needs were appropriate to another time and stage of her life, she was able to exchange living out these urges with imaginally providing the infant part of her personality with the experience of being held, fed, cared for, and allowed to sleep and just be. This enabled her to meet the infant's needs while retaining an adult state of mind and appropriate adult behavior. This strategy of "imaginal nurturing" will be discussed in the chapter on Self-Care.

Sometimes the misdirected energy and efforts to manage our emotions and unmet needs are played out with other family members. For example, an adult who feels empty and worthless may feel an urge to take care of others, which was probably her fundamental childhood emotional experience and role. Since she has social anxiety and only feels safe in her home with her family members, instead of investing her energy into causes or relationships that actually are in need of attention and support, especially her own healing, she indulges a family member. The family member can end up feeling smothered, losing his own identity, doubting his competency and becoming the under-functioning, needy person he is believed to be. He may even become physically or mentally ill.

A useful exercise I do with clients is to have them draw an "Egogram," a bar graph that depicts common ego states: hurt child, carefree child, adult, nurturing parent and critical parent. (The Egogram was created by John Dusay, author of *How I See You and You See Me*.) I first show my client a diagram of an adult who was raised with good-enough parenting and a diagram of a person who was deprived of adequate nurturing and protection. Those who had good-enough parenting have a hurt child ego state that is minimal, on a scale of 0-100%, maybe 20%. This gives them a significant capacity to feel carefree, spontaneous, playful and joyful. The carefree bar may be about 75%. They have had the expected emotional bruises that come with being alive in an imperfect world, but whatever trauma they experienced was minor or there were responsive adults present to process the experience and provide comfort and safety.

This means that in adulthood these individuals aren't haunted by huge amounts of residual pain and fear. They are able, therefore, to make sound, rational, adult decisions. Their adult ego state may be about 80%. When they do experience losses and challenges in adulthood, they have a healthy-sized, nurturing parent ego state with the ability to be self-compassionate, comforting, patient and supportive. The size of that ego state may be about 80%. Correspondingly, the critical adult part of their personality is small, perhaps representing about 20%. When they evaluate their behavior and attitude, they can do so with honesty, yet kindness. Because they are not highly judgmental of others, they generally feel safe and trusting that the world is a good place to be.

Contrast this way of being in one's mind and the world with the adult who was deprived of sufficient adult support, understanding, protection and guidance in childhood. The bar graph of these people would be the reverse of those with adequate nurturing. These anxiously-attached adults have significant traumatized parts of their personality that leak or gush disturbing emotions, which distort or flood their adult state of mind. As a result, they often are unable to maintain an adult composure and perspective. Their decision-making and actions are highly compromised. These adults are highly judgmental and critical of themselves and have an extremely limited capacity to nurture, comfort and support themselves. They perceive others as totally "together" and able to rescue them, while they see themselves as fundamentally flawed, helpless and unlovable.

Or, if they have an avoidant attachment style, they will perceive themselves as helpless victims of others who are irrational and impossible to please. Those who are avoidant generally are not spontaneous, joyful or carefree and do not have a nurturing relationship with the parts of them that are suffering. Those who have a fearful attachment style also perceive others as untrustworthy. Their constant belief is: I'm miserable, unlovable and helpless *and* others will hurt me if I turn to them. Their ability to take in the beauty and wonder of the world is crushed under the weight of just trying to survive and keep despair at bay.

Some people who have been deprived of sufficient nurturance develop a defensive part that edits out any flaw or source of shame in themselves and projects these "bad" qualities onto others. This sense of superiority and contempt or paranoia toward others is certainly not a desirable state of mind or conducive to the welfare of others. When your goodness or composure depends upon others being bad or out of control, you're doomed to live in an alien world, populated by those you neither trust nor respect. In the extreme, it leads to a kind of fundamentalism that puts one's own group on a pedestal and involves an urgency to eradicate or convert the bad that is "out there." The sooner we can recognize the dark side within us and process it until we regain our sense of self-worth, the sooner we can feel safe with others and "live and let live."

Getting back to the egogram, I explain to my new clients that our first priority will be fostering the growth of the nurturing parent part of their personality through the use of the self-care and self-soothing skills and resources found in Chapter Five. Also, they are taught mindfulness skills, found in Chapter Nine, to strengthen their Adult ego state. The more they invest in developing these new habits, the more their carefree and adult parts will emerge. The hurt child part will become less insecure and energy will be transferred to the secure, carefree child. At the same time, their critical parent ego state will begin to shrink from replacing harsh judgment with compassion and support. Later on in therapy, I have the client redraw their egogram so that they can graphically see the progress they've made.

Symptoms

Feeling anxious is part of being human. Between the fact that we are born with an amygdala that views every new experience through fearful eyes, the fact that so much of our neural wiring for perceiving the world is developed while we lack reason or self-reliance and the fact that the world we live in is rife with legitimate threats, we have a lot of anxiety to manage. To have all that anxiety unbridled would be chaotic and overwhelming, so our psyche and body find ways to package and contain it. It's analogous to the difference between having a basement that looks like mayhem hit and having all the mess put in stacked, orderly boxes. It's still all there, but it's more tolerable—at least for awhile.

Besides the earlier-mentioned defenses and compulsions, there are other means of providing a kind of containment, while at the same time alerting us that we're not functioning optimally. And so we have physical, psychological, emotional, social and behavioral symptoms. Emotional symptoms and defensive strategies have already been described. Additional behavioral symptoms that impact our relationships with others include:

- angry outbursts
- argumentativeness
- passive-aggression
- harassment
- bullying
- impulsivity
- self-harm
- theft
- vandalism
- violence
- recklessness
- underachieving at school or work

When such behaviors are heavily related to emotions and our relationship with ourself and significant others, to think we can solve these problems with moralizing, lecturing, preaching, rules, laws, punishment, consequences and rewards, is totally missing the gate. But even if we manage to control or stop those behaviors, the larger and deeper problems remain unaddressed. *So much of family, community, societal and international conflict, dysfunction and drama are the tragic blooms of unresolved trauma and/or insecure attachment.*

Psychological symptoms may include:

- difficulty concentrating
- mind going blank
- poor memory
- distractibility
- confusion
- difficulty making decisions
- intrusive and disturbing thoughts or feelings
- flashbacks
- feeling like you are outside your body
- feeling like you are in a dream or a fog
- loss of pleasure and interest
- racing thoughts
- pressured speech
- obsessive thoughts
- hallucinations
- being easily startled
- delusions
- hyper-vigilance
- paranoia
- suicidal thoughts
- fantasies of harming others
- phobias about particular settings and circumstances, such as enclosed spaces, open spaces, heights, crowds, bridges, driving, swimming, public speaking and socializing

When we are in a physiological state of hyperarousal and heightened sense of threat, neutral faces appear to be angry. Hypervigilance causes us to overlook or dismiss evidence that we are safe and seek out justification for our feeling of danger. We are prone to misperception and give even benign situations a negative connotation because, when it comes to survival, we have to play it safe. In contrast, the calmer we are, the more we can see the whole picture without distortion and the more accurate and trustworthy our perceptions and judgments.

While moderate stress, complexity and challenge actually stimulate learning, severe stress can impede it. Many children as well as adults have difficulty performing cognitive tasks due to severe stress which interferes with learning. They find that their memory, concentration and ability to make decisions are impaired. Many children who do poorly in school have home lives that are painful or chaotic. Some adults find that their high level of anxiety interferes with their ability to be organized and efficient while other adults channel their anxiety into compulsive organization. Sometimes, when children have sufficient defenses to manage their difficult emotions, they are able to excel in school. They may feel safer and that things are more predictable at school than at home. They may be able to experience a sense of competency and self-esteem that is not possible at home.

Psychological symptoms and issues can sometimes have a behavioral counterpart that reflects the person's deepest predicament. I once worked with a truck driver who, despite driving over sixty hours a week, repeatedly told me in our first sessions that he felt stuck and couldn't move on. He believed that what kept him stuck was his inability to cry over a devastating loss. Interestingly enough, this man, a recovered alcoholic, drank well over a gallon of beverages each day. It would take his bladder being on the verge of bursting to get this man to stop so he could "relieve himself." Despite all this releasing of fluid throughout the day, the man could not release one drop from his eyes…and so could not experience relief.

Another example of a behavioral habit reflecting a psychological condition is the following story of a woman who relied heavily on repression and dissociation to manage emotionally-laden material. When she passed away, her grown children were astonished to discover that her bedroom furniture was packed with thousands and thousands of pieces of useless, out-dated, broken or torn paraphernalia, the accumulation of a lifetime. The woman never disposed of anything. Her drawers were a metaphor for her mind. Literally everything was stuffed away. Nothing was ever processed, edited or organized. Any objects of value were lost in a mass of nonsense and chaos. Let me close this anecdote by adding that one of her daughters is now a quilter and therapist, both of which involve putting a multitude of pieces together, recognizing what is no longer relevant or needed and discovering the beauty of what remains. We are blessed to live in these times when we can understand more fully the price we pay for avoiding pain. We are blessed again to have increasingly more respectful and effective means of alleviating our pain.

As will be seen in the chapter on Physical Health, many of us also suffer from a wide range of medical ailments and disabilities that can be related to chronic anxiety and stress and unresolved emotions from relationship distress. Physical symptoms may include:

- lowered immunity or resistance
- accident proneness
- difficulty falling asleep or staying asleep
- restless sleep
- nightmares
- muscle tension
- loss of appetite
- excessive appetite
- digestive system problems
- fatigue
- excessive energy
- restlessness and agitation
- nervous tics and gestures
- muscle spasms and twitches (e.g. eyelid)
- preoccupation with the body and health
- rashes
- allergies
- hypersensitivities to everything under the sun
- compulsive skin or scab-picking or hair pulling
- stomach aches
- headaches
- pervasive aches and pains
- migraines
- jaw tension and pain
- all or some of the symptoms found in panic attacks: racing heart, shortness of breath, dry mouth, sweating, dizziness and trouble swallowing

When one family member suffers psychologically or physically, he or she rarely suffers alone. Instead, the individual's self-absorption, helplessness, anguish, fear, desperation and irritability are felt by family members, adding to their reservoir of emotional burden. It often leads to a family imbalance in which all attention and resources are funneled to the member identified as "the one who *really* is in need," while other hurting members are ignored or dismissed.

The Paradox of a Perfectly Imperfect Self and World

A major premise of *Peace in the Heart and Home* is that we need to recognize that most of what people bring to medical, mental health and marriage and family practitioners are symptoms, the tip of an emotional iceberg that requires our looking under the surface and dealing with the reality of what's there. If we just scrape off the tip, we are going down like the Titanic. Fortunately, human "sinkings" don't have to be the end of the story, for we have the capacity to discover our vulnerabilities and become stronger in what had been the fragile places. Human beings are resilient and can resurrect, like the phoenix from the ashes, with the help of loving compassion, courage and awareness.

M. Scott Peck wrote in *The Road Less Traveled:* "Mental health is an ongoing process of dedication to reality at all costs." That means employing a minimum of defenses and cultivating the courage to face our fears and blind spots, to overcome our fear of the dark. Anais Nin knew this well when she wrote, "Life shrinks or expands in proportion to one's courage." We all have a dark side and that's alright. It's pretending it's not there that is not alright.

"Welcome to the human race" can be a comforting insight. It helps to put our shame to rest. Apparent imperfection is what makes a universe possible and worth existing. Without our wounds, conflicts, personal and interpersonal challenges, trials and tribulations, without the struggle, humility, dignity and glory of joining with others to face and overcome our difficulties, what use would there be for a world? A heavenly existence with non-stop beauty, peace and contentment would become meaningless and boring eventually. The basic dynamic of existence is what the ancient Chinese philosophers called the yin and yang. Contemporary Quantum Physics confirms it. Life is about co-existing opposites, each having inherent value because it is essential to the whole. You can't have one without the other: particles and waves, light and dark, inhale and exhale, joy and pain, dreams realized and crushed, vitality and deterioration. It's about the ride, not just the destination. It's touching the earth and the divine.

CHAPTER FOUR

Psychological Trauma, Healing and EMDR

Psychological Trauma

Psychological trauma is pervasive. I used to think that only a minority of people were wounded and struggling. Now I realize that it is the human condition. Much of adulthood is spent grappling with the aftermath of childhood as we purposely or blindly try to free our bodies and souls from the ropes that bind us. While we clearly recognize when people are desperately in need because of being in the path of a hurricane, tsunami, earthquake or war, the masses of us invisibly struggle day after day for decades, trapped under the weight of our personal and family dramas. My intention in writing *Peace in the Heart and Home* is to shine a light on what I believe to be a difficult but dependable road to freedom and our reclaimed spirit.

In addition to developmental or attachment trauma, there are also a wide range of other stressors that impact the developing psyches of children and haunt their future lives as adults. Stressors are situations that are perceived and experienced as threats and that exceed a person's perceived available resources. Get ready for a long list.

- Death of a significant person or pet
- Parental depression, anxiety, Post-Traumatic Stress Disorder, rage, paranoia, personality disorders, unresolved trauma or grief
- Parental overwhelm due to financial problems, discrimination, unsafe neighborhood or bullying at the workplace
- Domestic violence or marital alienation, strife or infidelity
- Abandonment by a parent
- Parental separation and divorce
- Conflict between divorced parents
- Dating and remarriage of a parent
- Parent's unavailability due to work, travel, military assignment, addiction or compulsive behaviors
- Chronic physical illness of a parent or child
- Serious accidents, hospitalizations or surgeries involving self or family member
- Physical deformities or shortcomings
- Physical child abuse
- Being forced to experience something frightening or repulsive
- Mental and verbal abuse by an adult or another child as well as bullying or teasing at home, school or neighborhood
- Witnessing a sibling be mentally or physically abused
- Sexual abuse of self and/or another sibling
- Rape or other sexual assault
- Physical assault
- Harassment due to sexual orientation
- Parental or sibling substance abuse
- Chronic school failure or poor grades
- Cut-offs from extended family members
- Family isolation
- Criminal behavior of a family member
- Aggressive, controlling, acting out behavior of a sibling

- Witnessing crime or violence
- Being a victim of crime or violence
- Natural disasters

All of the above stressors are common. In my professional experience, the majority of those seeking psychotherapy have histories of pervasive, chronic childhood trauma and/or attachment relationship injury that fully explain the multitude of symptoms with which they have struggled. Most of my clients have each experienced between 10 and 20 traumatic events or chronic conditions. Each individual's personality, brain and body reflect their emotional and relationship history. Like the Grand Canyon with visual evidence of millions of years of geological influences, our brain and mind are carved with layer upon layer of experience. But unless we come close enough to look into the gorge or get to know ourselves in depth, we have no idea just how much is there, how much it or the person has been through.

Some people who suffer multiple psychological, physical and behavioral symptoms have been spared the most severe childhood stressors such as parental addiction, domestic violence, physical abuse, sexual abuse, divorce or poverty. But enduring just a few chronic, pervasive stressors, like having parents with anxiety, depression, uncontrolled anger or heavy reliance on defenses, can take a huge toll on a child's sense of self-worth, safety and competence. I recall one client whose mother alternated between idealizing her and giving what my client called "zingers" and what I call "verbal sucker-punches." Woven into daily life were guilt trip messages like, "If you refuse to get me that can of soup from the basement this minute and I die trying to get it myself, you'll have to live with that." Yet early in the therapy process, this client had cheerfully described her family home as being like *The Donna Reed Show*. Mom wore pearls and a smile as she delivered her blows; so the little girl told herself she was happy and smiled back.

Making Contact with Your Vulnerable Inner Child
If you are one to minimize the difficult experiences you went through as a young person, it may be helpful to find some photographs of yourself

at the ages these experiences occurred. Look deep into the eyes of that child and notice what body sensations come up inside. Some of those photographs may present you and the family dressed in your Sunday finery or in a smiling group picture. Only you know, deep inside, what percentage of the time your family was that calm and contented.

Also, think about the children you know and love now who are those ages—your own children or your nephews and nieces. Ask yourself whether you would wish those events or circumstances on any of these children. If you don't have children in your life, just notice the children present when you are in a public place and allow yourself to experience how innocent, impressionable and vulnerable they are. You were once that age. You were once that vulnerable. For those of you who may feel tough now, *you weren't then*. And that hurt child still lives inside you.

I want to reassure you that, while owning the painful aspects of your childhood may significantly alter the image of your childhood and parents, it doesn't remove any of the uplifting memories. It is not uncommon for people to feel compassion for their parents, as well as themselves, when they see more clearly and from the heart what was happening in their family. It would be cruel of me to encourage people to dig up the graves of the childhood experiences that wounded them, if it weren't so that the memories aren't at rest at all, are in fact haunting them and their current families and if there weren't other, more genuine and secure ways of feeling loved, whole and connected. The honesty, bravery and integrity that take place in a therapist's office make it a concentrated pocket of human dignity at its highest. I imagine that, as seen from above, each office is a star that is shining with a vibrant light from the authenticity occurring within.

I should also make clear that recognizing that you were hurt by your family members does not mean you have to confront them or seek apologies. You can heal without your parents ever having to know the many ways they didn't come through for you. If they now are more emotionally mature, know you are attending therapy and express genuine curiosity and eagerness to know what you're discovering, then you might want to share some of your experience. Unfortunately, that's rarely the case. If the person who traumatized you is no longer alive, that in no way prevents you from healing. If your parents are now elderly and frail or if they remain toxic, it would serve no good to reveal how much and long you suffered. If you are now on very good terms with the sibling who tormented you in childhood, you don't need to change your current relationship, but you will need to own how those early experiences impacted your life.

The most important goal is to come to peace within yourself—by putting the memories *genuinely* to rest. The one valuable way you can use your self-knowledge with those who have hurt you in the past is to better tend to the relationships that you have with them today. As you become more aware of your emotions and needs and better able to articulate them, you will be able to assert yourself as necessary to make sure that your needs are met today. And by the way, asserting isn't limited to voicing what you expect others to do. You can protect yourself by the actions *you* choose to take or refrain from taking.

While some traumatic experiences result from particular events, like 9/11, most are ongoing patterns, so insidious that they are just "normal life" to the child. Specific traumatic events have been called "Big T traumas" while ongoing, attachment traumas are called "Small t traumas." A few clients of mine have wondered whether their current difficulties were due to trauma in a previous lifetime, because they so minimized the attachment injuries throughout their formative years. They learned to dismiss their painful experiences because their parents dismissed them.

For a number of reasons, children will always trust their parents' experience and perception before their own. First, a young child is highly aware of his parent's far superior knowledge, competence, autonomy and strength. The child is in the learner role and the parent in the teacher and authority role. Second, a child's self-image and interpretations of events are acquired from the parent. Third, because children are so dependent upon their parents, it is imperative that they not give up hope that their parents are good, right and trustworthy. Without adults who know what they are doing, a child is totally lost in chaos. It is the lesser of evils for children to absorb their parents' perspective and give up on themselves. Fourth, the loyalty and attachment bond may create a powerful conviction that viewing the parent as imperfect or responsible for harm is denying the parent love and gratitude. This emotional conviction is often the last and most powerful tether holding an adult in a child state of mind.

It is important to mention that some children have received most of their care from siblings who, out of tremendous compassion, guilt or fear, have felt compelled to respond. This often happens when parents are emotionally unavailable due to dissociation, depression, addiction, self-absorption, narcissism, marital strife, domestic violence or chaotic family life. As adults, these child-parented individuals, not knowing any other way, may consider their emotional needs to have been met. However, a child's emotional needs can only be adequately met by an adult, not a fellow sufferer. Often, "parentified children," those who have had the inappropriate burden of caring for their parent and/or siblings, in adulthood become anxiously-attached, overly-responsible caretakers whose functioning deteriorates as their underlying unmet needs and wounds increasingly break through. This family dynamic will be discussed later in greater detail as it is a very common occurrence in family life.

Sometimes we can get clues about our deepest emotional truths from dreams or favorite songs, stories or plays. Even objects can reveal and express our emotional life story. One woman I know, who had felt helpless her whole life, displayed in her living room a statue of Venus de Milo, the armless woman. Just like Venus, this woman wasn't whole, because her emotional truth was lost and forgotten. And without arms, she was vulnerable and unable to embrace and connect with others.

The client mentioned before, who dismissed and minimized her pervasive childhood trauma, was so taken by the play, *Les Miserables,* that she saw it well over a dozen times. She also had dreams in which she was an impoverished, starving child imprisoned while watching another child outside the bars eating to her heart's content. Her unconscious was preoccupied with what she consciously discounted. Another client, who was horrified by having to visit a creepy grandfather every Sunday, grew up to be obsessed with watching horror movies. This same woman had suicidal feelings starting in elementary school, and throughout her life her favorite book has been one in which a child longed to join the ghost of a dead child in a lake.

In my daily interactions with the world, the young Charlette was often among the most bubbly, upbeat people present in a room. Yet, whenever I took long walks by myself in childhood and adolescence, I loved to sing the spirituals, "Nobody Knows the Trouble I've Seen" and "Sometimes I Feel Like a Motherless Child . . . a long way from home, a long way from home." Most of the time, the deep emotion and meaning these songs, stories and dreams hold for us are never consciously examined or understood, as we are caught in their familiar trance and may have no one with whom we feel safe enough to share them.

While human beings are resilient, traumatic experiences become more damaging and harder to heal spontaneously when:

- they start early in childhood
- when the event is personal, involving another human being
- when the perpetrator is someone the child depended upon or trusted
- when the threat is severe
- when it lasts a long time
- when it reoccurs
- when there is no adult to turn to for protection or comfort
- when there is a prior history of insecure attachment, victimization or trauma.

The earlier in development trauma occurs, the greater the sensitivity and risk of having a traumatic reaction to even mild or moderate stressors. Just as kindling can restart a wood fire, additional smaller traumas thrown on top of the hot embers of previous trauma, can flare up old wounds. Neuroscientists actually use this word, "kindling," to describe the lowering of the threshold for a traumatic response as a result of repeated triggering.

Whether or not a person is traumatized by an event depends on the individual's unique history, perceptions and interpretations. What is inconsequential or a minor disturbance to one person may be traumatic for another. Sometimes other people's reaction to someone who has been traumatized is more damaging than the trauma itself and adds on a secondary layer of trauma. An example might be a parent who refuses to believe her child's claim of abuse, which only deepens the child's sense of utter helplessness and lack of protection.

Another factor in trauma development is whether or not people are able to take action to protect themselves through fighting or fleeing. Those who freeze and dissociate, because there is no way to fight or flee, may be vulnerable to developing Post-Traumatic Stress Disorder (PTSD) because of the intense state of helplessness. PTSD is a severe anxiety disorder with symptoms related to hyper-arousal, numbness, avoidance and reexperiencing of the trauma. During traumatic events, people who dissociate may appear on the surface to be unaffected, but in fact, their nervous systems have been deeply damaged. They have become hypersensitive to the slightest cue resembling the original incident and self-defeating beliefs about themselves and others have been wired into their brains.

Sometimes children, lacking judgment, perspective and help in understanding events, emotions and life, can misinterpret another's motives and feelings and make the worst possible interpretation of an event. As a result, even when circumstances are benign, children may take away harmful messages and lessons about themselves and relationships. Conscientious parents can sometimes prevent this negative impact by being attuned to changes in their children's demeanor or habits that may hint at something troubling them. Then they can sensitively initiate a discussion.

An example of a misinterpretation is the following. A client of mine slammed a door in anger when she was four years old and part of the ceiling collapsed. Her mother ran into the room expressing upset, swept the child up and deposited her in another room out of harm's way. The door to the child's room was closed to make sure she was safe while the other room was examined and cleaned. Because her parent failed to provide an explanation, reassurance or comfort, the child assumed that she was bad and her anger was dangerous. This is why being in touch with our own emotions and being sensitive to the states of mind of others is so critical. Without deep knowledge of our self and human nature, we don't make the empathic connection that enables us to provide soothing responses to others. This incident was just one of countless "small t" relational traumas my client experienced. It was reflective of pervasive family interactional patterns, leading to a lifetime of distrust, cynicism, self-doubt, passivity and depression.

Trauma does not occur only in childhood. Adults, too, can be traumatized by such events as prolonged illness or sudden death of a significant other, a hostile divorce, harassment, discrimination, job loss, financial collapse, accidents, surgery and hospitalization, natural disaster and war. Being treated insensitively during a time of vulnerability, such as a husband making an accusatory remark following a wife's miscarriage, can also cause trauma in adults. Although some people are able to work through a trauma or loss and come out unscarred or stronger, others develop highly distressing and persistent symptoms. An unresolved trauma is like an emotional splinter; there is a highly sensitive area that hurts whenever touched. When we've been traumatized, we can't do things we want to do and we do things we don't want to do. We feel stuck and experience a discrepancy between what we know, what we feel and how we behave.

When clients come to my therapy office, some are very aware of the sources of their emotional pain. They know they are tormented by the past but don't know how to stop it. Others have no idea of the impact of their formative years on their current difficulties and attribute their pain entirely to current relationships and circumstances. The reality is that emotional pain and symptoms are caused by a mixture of past and present distress. Most of the time, we don't consciously connect the emotional dots. While current circumstances may be legitimately challenging, they are often magnified by their resemblance to past wounds. The old traumatic pain piggy-backs on top of the current hurt. The emotional reaction the person is having may be totally out of proportion to the actual triggering event, but in another time and context, the emotions make absolute sense and are normal.

Many difficult experiences in our lives may have been deeply disturbing but, between talking about them, receiving empathy and hugs from those who care, reflecting on them and dreaming about them, these matters get resolved and stored in our memory bank in a benign way. However, when an experience is too overwhelming to process, it stays stored in a form that keeps the event as "hot" as the day it occurred. Some people have discussed their painful memories for years with friends, family and therapists and yet the emotional charge of these memories and its impact on daily functioning barely budge. Some traumatic memories are always present to some degree, lurking in the background of our lives, tainting our present moment. Other traumas go completely underground and, like a volcano, lie dormant for months, years, or even decades. The way we react all depends on the strength of our defenses and the presence of powerful environmental cues.

I would like to mention here, for those who have read Eckhart Tolle's *A New Earth,* that what he calls the "pain body" I would call a trauma-tized child part or a demanding, desperate protector part. I absolutely love Tolle's books but I don't agree with his depiction of the pain body as an entity deriving pleasure out of being miserable. As mentioned earlier, protector ego states don't know any better way to help defend the child from emotional pain because they never had anyone to turn to for support and they had no models of how to appropriately ask for needs to be met. To others, these behaviors are dramatic, manipula-tive, threatening, controlling, smothering and obnoxious. Such an ego state is self-defeating because, while it initially may garner sympathy, it eventually burns people out and causes them to withdraw or express contempt. This confirms the worst fears of those who are ruled by this ego state, that they are unlovable and will be rejected and abandoned.

Also, the reemergence of painful emotions and the perceiving of threat are not because a pain body needs more pain to survive. The inner child is protesting the experience of painful isolation and making desperate and ill-fated attempts to gain soothing. At other times, these eruptions might be traumatic emotions being triggered by an over-reactive amygdala. Later chapters on Self-Care, Intimate Relationships and Mindfulness will address cultivating more appropriate and effective ways of getting emotional needs met.

Healing

As I said in an earlier chapter, the brain is plastic; it has the capacity to change its shape and form. The synapses between neurons that were cre-ated in childhood may be like dead end streets where we get mugged, but new synapses can be formed that lead us to feelings of self-worth, safety and self-efficacy. As you'll soon see, this is not pie-in-the-sky thinking. This is scientifically-based, clinically-proven reality. And if you'll pardon my far-from-scientific analogy, this path to safety is forged by heading directly into our disturbing emotions, like Dorothy, the Tin Man, the Lion and the Scarecrow heading straight for the Wicked Witch's castle. When we have a safe enough holding environment, we can dare to face emotional experiences that show us what we are made of. Dorothy and her fellow travelers had each other and the Good Witch to provide a sense of community and safety. Contemporary travelers have psychotherapists. Dorothy and her friends were rewarded for exercising their courage, intellect and heart. So can we.

In fact, these are the very requirements for overcoming trauma: the cognitive, rational intellect of the brain's left hemisphere; the emotions, body sensations and imagery of the right hemisphere; and the courage and wisdom of our heart and gut. Neuroscientists have recently discovered that the heart and intestines are surrounded by thousands of neurons, making them significant sources of intelligence along with our brain. Talk therapy does not elicit all these sources of experience and intelligence, which is why it merely processes the tip of the iceberg. It is good at creating insight, but insight without peace is the booby prize.

Over the last few decades, the field of psychology has become increasingly aware of the importance of integrating mindfulness of thoughts, imagery, emotions and body sensations into any treatment. This is especially so when the condition has trauma and insecure attachment at its root, which as I've said, is the case for most people. The approaches that rely primarily on teaching new behaviors to solve problems and changing thoughts to reframe perspective, alter emotion and manage impulses are called "top down." The approaches that go directly to the body and process what is felt there are called "bottom up." I see top down approaches as equivalent to a salmon relentlessly fighting a powerful current. I see bottom up approaches as turning off the current. Phew, can't you just feel the difference? It's the difference between struggling to stay on top of an issue and there being no issue.

The process of healing and change is spiral, not linear. That means you're likely to take two steps forward and one step back, and then three steps forward and another step back. As you begin to move forward, healing one trauma at a time, it's as if you're coming into a clearing within a deep, dark jungle. You begin to feel less suffocated; you begin to feel the sunlight of hope. Then, you reenter another part of the jungle, become disheartened and wonder, "will I really ever get out?" Then, as you labor on, you eventually come to a bigger clearing and experience relief and peace. To keep moving forward requires courage, because you need to keep reentering the jungle and facing another threat. But after you have healed all your past traumas, you have truly come out of the jungle once and for all.

The new neuronal pathways that are created through repeated, mindful, courageous walks will become your brain's new default position. The old paths will now become overgrown from lack of use. This is what it is to "grow oneself up" again; rewiring the brain, removing harmful software and rediscovering the program that is our birthright. Our True and Higher Self exudes calmness, confidence, courage, clarity, and loving compassion for self and other. There is a genius and wisdom within us that gets tapped through the healing process. It far surpasses what our cognitive brain alone can offer. When we integrate our adult reason and perspective, our unconscious healing processes and the traumatic memory lodged in the emotional brain, what we end up with is beyond the combined conscious intellect of the client and therapist.

"Integration" is the key word in healing and thriving; bringing together and valuing both the yin and yang, top down and bottom up, reason and emotion, uplifting information and disturbing information, body and brain, strengths and weaknesses, awareness and what has been hidden, courage and fear, adult state and child state, self and other. Crossing from the painful side of the river to the peaceful shore requires going into the swift current. As we wade deeper into the difficult waters, and hold onto our hats, we gradually expand our comfort zone. The less left that frightens us, the more we feel safe in the world. The more the world is our oyster.

EMDR

It is hard for me to imagine how most people would be able to access their Higher Self and function from a place of heightened spiritual awareness while they still have psychological and physiological anxiety being broadcast every day, creating white noise in their consciousness. I have found that once people's traumas have been healed, spiritual insights may arise naturally and easily. In the past several weeks, I have seen evidence of this with a man who was referred to me by his therapist specifically to do EMDR, the trauma treatment I am going to tell you about. From an early age, Peter had been emotionally, verbally and physically abused by his father. As a result, when Peter began attending school, he behaved oddly, cringing when other children approached. He was the limping gazelle to the hungry hyenas in his classroom. Every school year from that point forward, he was the victim of bullies, especially at the special school he attended for troubled adolescents.

By the time I met Peter, he had made some valuable gains in his two years of talk therapy. He was far better able to function in the world and with others. He still however, had a fearful attachment status, Post Traumatic Stress Disorder and major depression. On his second EMDR session devoted to his first memory of classroom victimization, in which all the children joined in with the bully in telling him how weird he was, Peter came to some gut-level insights. He felt a strong connection with the other children, realizing that they would have felt just as badly as he did, had they been the object of cruelty. He realized for the first time that he was no different than them.

Peter, who had felt his whole life that he was defective and an outcast, finally felt normal, worthy and strengthened from his new sense of being connected to others in the class and the world. It was clear by what he was expressing, verbally and non-verbally, that he had experienced a powerful spiritual insight and he had accessed his Higher Self. He left the session feeling calm, relieved, encouraged and actually eager for the next opportunity to work on a traumatic memory.

During the next EMDR session, Peter worked on the memory of being chased by peers in the playground during recess and being filled with terror as he ran for his life. The following week, when I assessed how disturbed he felt about that particular memory, his level of upset was minor. I thought that perhaps he had not much more to process. Instead, the session bloomed in a way that neither Peter nor I anticipated. During a 40-minute period of processing, Peter unveiled layer after layer of new perceptual clarity about the reality of the recess experiences. He came to realize that there were actually only a few children who bullied him, and that the majority of the children were just being kids, chasing each other in a playful way, without any malice. He remembered doing that himself, playfully running after other children. He remembered actually enjoying the company of some of the children and them liking him.

During EMDR, Peter recognized how much he'd always focused on disturbing details, and that, until now, he'd had no recall of good memories. He was surprised to discover how much about those recess periods had been benign and that his perception had been mistaken. His fear had generalized from the few who had mistreated him to the belief that all children would do the same. He compared it to burning your hand on a stove and never wanting to get burned again. He recognized all of this in a non-judgmental way. Again, Peter had accessed his Higher Self, his capacity to view reality from a meta level, the level above the ego. He was able to see the scene impartially yet compassionately, from the other children's perspective as well as his own. Now that he was able to see the larger picture, he found that he'd always possessed the necessary elements to create a peaceful understanding and resolution in his mind and body. He said that, just like I had promised him, he *did* have the inner wisdom to heal his own trauma. By the end of that EMDR session, Peter was astonished to find himself feeling fully calm, safe and happy as he recalled the once-excruciating memory. "We were just being kids, doing what kids do."

While there are other effective approaches to trauma treatment, EMDR is the method I know best and that I strongly recommend. I have been practicing EMDR for the past eight years and have used it successfully with more than a thousand traumas. It is, without a doubt, the most valuable training I have ever received. Before I learned it, I often felt that the tools I had were inadequate for the task, like chipping away at a stone statue with a dental tool. EMDR is a systematic, complex and comprehensive approach, not just a clever technique. *It is a very powerful method and therefore should only be implemented by licensed mental health professionals with proper training, clinical judgment and ongoing consultation to ensure mastery and safety.*

EMDR stands for Eye Movement Desensitization and Reprocessing and is an information processing therapy. The approach was first discovered and developed by psychologist Francine Shapiro in the late 1980s. Initially it was used to treat rape and combat victims who suffered from Post Traumatic Stress Disorder. Since then, about 50,000 therapists worldwide have been trained in EMDR and it has been used to treat a wide-range of conditions, including depression, low self-esteem, anxiety, obsessions, compulsions, addictions, eating disorders, chronic pain, panic attacks, phobias, anger and aggression, complicated grief and personality disorders. EMDR has also been used to develop inner resources and achieve peak performance.

The current treatment guidelines of the American Psychiatric Association and the International Society for Traumatic Stress Studies designate EMDR as an effective treatment for post traumatic stress. EMDR was also found effective by the U.S. Department of Defense, the United Kingdom Department of Health, the Israeli National Council for Mental Health and many other international health and governmental agencies. Extensive information about the effectiveness of EMDR can be found at the following websites: www.emdr.com and www.emdria.org. Mental Health Professionals can learn more about EMDR by reading Francine Shapiro's, *Eye Movement Desensitization and Reprocessing (EMDR): Basic Principles, Protocols and Procedures,* 2nd Edition. Trainings are available throughout the United States and internationally. The public can gain a better understanding of EMDR by reading the book by Francine Shapiro and Margo Silk Forrest, *EMDR: The Breakthrough "Eye Movement" Therapy for Overcoming Anxiety, Stress, and Trauma.*

Practitioners of EMDR believe that *any experience that results in damage to a person's sense of self-worth, safety or personal power is traumatic.* Self-defeating core beliefs about self and others are related to those three categories. The following are very common irrational beliefs or lessons people learn from traumatic experiences, especially those suffered in childhood:

- I'm responsible for others' suffering or happiness
- I have to be the strong one—I can't trust others to share the burden
- I have to put others first
- I have to be perfect
- I'm unlovable
- I don't matter and am unworthy
- I'm not good enough
- I'm stupid
- I can't trust myself or I'm untrustworthy
- I'm a disappointment
- I'm damaged and defective
- I can never forgive myself
- I'm powerless, weak and can't protect myself
- I'm in danger
- I can't trust others to not hurt me

The rational part of the personality may know that "I did the best I could, I deserve love and kindness and I can protect myself." But the traumatized part of the personality still believes, at a gut level, that "I am unworthy and helpless." People can expend a great deal of energy fighting an inner tug of war between their adult perspective and their traumatized child perspective. For some people, these painful self-beliefs pound loudly every waking moment and there is no respite, except perhaps through numbing substances, self-mutilation or awareness-obliterating rage. For others, there is a steady, background drip, drip, drip of insecurity and malaise. Perhaps these are the "lives of quiet desperation" of which Thoreau spoke.

An EMDR therapist has a number of ways to help clients identify memories in need of healing. A client will be asked to identify their worst memories. The therapist will also be able to recognize potential

EMDR targets from the history-taking session and the clients' ongoing anecdotes about members of their family of origin. Another way that a therapist can help a client identify sources of his or her difficulties is to do what is called a "floatback." By identifying the emotions, negative self-beliefs and body sensations that get triggered the most in their current disturbing relationships, clients can often "connect the emotional dots" to the earliest times in their lives when they felt that very same way. The emotions, self-beliefs and body sensations are implicit memory fragments that need to be integrated back into the scenarios from which they keep breaking loose.

Speaking of integration, EMDR integrates, in an elegant way, some of the most beneficial dynamics and interventions found in psychotherapy and healing. The approach is client-centered, which means that it is responsive to the particular needs of each individual. The client is provided a safe "holding environment" for exploring the trauma. The therapist's role is that of an attuned, emotionally available, compassionate and respectful facilitator. The therapist's interventions are kept to the bare minimum as the healing process arises spontaneously within the client, rather than being directed by the therapist. The EMDR procedures jumpstart the healing process, which involves the client simultaneously observing and experiencing the internal images, emotions, self-beliefs and physical sensations that percolate up. EMDR is a "somatic" or body-centered approach in which the memory is considered fully healed only when the person can stare the memory in the eye and feel their body free of any distress or tension.

Mindfulness, the subject of a later chapter, is the mental state that clients access during EMDR when they observe their inner experience which is comprised of emotions, body sensations, images and thoughts. The trauma is broken up into bite-size pieces, alternating between a minute of observing and experiencing the trauma and a very brief break to report what's coming up. This makes facing the trauma more manageable and allows the client to keep touching base with the therapist for safety and comfort.

The process is predominantly non-verbal, enabling rapid-fire processing of all the neural networks that are being activated. In the midst of experiencing the worst of the memory, words often can't keep up with, or adequately express, what the client is experiencing internally. But as the emotions are processed, the individual is more and more able to find words that capture the meaning of the experiences. As mentioned in the chapter on Attachment, the ability to create a coherent narrative that reflects the emotional reality of one's childhood relationship experiences is a marker of secure attachment. Putting emotional experience into words is also a valuable skill, particularly when it comes to relationships, as will be discussed in the chapters on Intimate Relationships and Family Life.

Considering my earlier discussion of the first few years of a child's life, you may be wondering how we can heal experiences for which we lack explicit memory. Anything that has deeply impacted us in our earliest years is going to bleed into and become a sensitivity in later situations and relationships. So in EMDR, when we process the emotions, beliefs and body sensations connected to a memory that the client does recall, the sensory and emotional material being processed will likely also emanate from earlier, pre-verbal childhood experiences. Also, in EMDR, it is not always necessary to have an image or words to connect with and process a memory. In some cases, particularly with pre-verbal memories, emotions and body sensations can be enough.

While the client is focusing on the inner experience, the therapist is simultaneously providing what is called "bi-lateral stimulation." The original form taught by Dr. Shapiro involved the therapist moving her hand side to side, guiding the clients' eyes back and forth in a horizontal direction. This produced eye movements similar to what occurs during dreaming in rapid eye movement (REM) sleep. Over time, other forms of bi-lateral stimulation were offered to clients, such as alternating tones through head phones and taps to the clients' knees or hands. With the use of one of these forms of stimulation, the client's attention is focused dually—on the present and the memory. The dual awareness grounds the client in the present, so that they don't get sucked into the memory. Also, many clients find the stimulation provides a relaxation response, which helps make facing the trauma more manageable.

One theory on why EMDR works is that the bi-lateral stimulation is activating both hemispheres of the brain. This process enables the right hemisphere's unconscious emotional, imaginal and somatic perspective to be integrated with and tempered by the left hemisphere's conscious, rational adult perspective. Cross communication between the left and right hemispheres stimulates, and may therefore strengthen, the part of the brain that joins the two, thus facilitating greater future processing and integration of experience.

The client's inner experience during EMDR is equivalent to having one foot in the right hemisphere, one foot in the left hemisphere, one foot in the past and one foot in the present. The therapist has prepared the client in earlier sessions to make sure the client has adequate skills and resources to maintain this balanced perspective. If clients are too guarded and fearful to allow the traumatized state to be accessed, nothing will happen. At the other extreme, if clients have no boundaries, little adult perspective or minimal affect management skills, they are at risk of being re-traumatized. *For this reason, EMDR must be practiced by trained mental health professionals who are capable of assessing and developing a client's capacity to manage strong emotions.*

Over the course of the EMDR session, the client processes a range of emotions. Each layer of emotion will start out at a tsunami level, but just by staying with and observing the experience, the client will feel the emotion gradually decrease until a different emotion becomes more compelling. A person may start out with strong feelings of shame and fear, followed by helplessness and inadequacy, then anger, then sadness and grief, then disappointment and regret. Some memories are resolved in one session while others need further work or fine-tuning in a second or third session. Some complex traumas may require several sessions.

The earlier metaphor of island and ocean may be used here to explain the EMDR process. As the prepared client intentionally observes the strong waves of emotion that dominate his or her awareness, they gradually get processed. As the emotions begin to recede, the island of reason reappears. With the return of reason, the client can begin to put the traumatic emotions and experiences in greater perspective. The more perspective the individual develops, the more the waves of emotion recede. By the end of the EMDR processing, the ocean has returned to its pre-tidal wave position.

The process the client goes through during EMDR trauma work has been called "sublime free-association." (Freud would have been very impressed.) I liken it to a kaleidoscope. With each step into the traumatic memory, the multitude of memory fragments get altered and rearranged into new patterns, as the client's adult perspective integrates with the childhood memory. Over the course of an EMDR session, the pattern continues to shift until finally, a new design has formed that is free of any negative charge. The individual can recall the memory and feel calm, both mentally and physically.

The client also emerges from the experience with new, appropriate and healthy beliefs about him or herself, which are wired into the brain and become the new default position. For example, instead of just intellectually believing, "I'm a good person," "I can take care of myself," or "I deserve to be happy," people treated with EMDR come to experience these statements at a gut level. The healing and shifts take place at the levels of physiology and emotion, as well as the level of reason. This makes all the difference in the world.

Another analogy to describe the EMDR process is a crystal ball, the type that was part of the 1970s Disco scene. Each time the client reenters the memory, his attention and awareness are like a light that shines on another facet of the crystal ball. Once a facet has been clearly seen and felt, the ball shifts, exposing another facet. The memory is healed when all the aspects of the trauma have been revealed and processed. My way of understanding it is that each emotion-charged piece of information is clamoring to be heard, recognized and appreciated. The message is critical and insists on being delivered. Once that happens, the job has been done.

When someone has a core self-belief like, "I'm not normal," it typically will be stemming from multiple traumatic experiences. I tell my clients that it's like being trapped alive in a coffin with about ten nails holding the lid closed. Each traumatic memory related to that core self-belief is a nail to be removed. As each trauma is healed and each nail is removed, the lid can be pushed out further and further, giving you bigger breaths of fresh air, fuller views and tastes of freedom. To be completely freed from the negative self-belief, you will need to remove most of the nails before you'll have enough momentum to push off the lid once and for all. Anytime people end their therapy treatment prematurely and work hasn't been completed, it is likely that they will be more prone to relapse. A person who has been in an accident wouldn't want a doctor to leave five of fifteen pieces of glass still inside and consider the treatment complete. Thoroughness is important for optimal health.

It seems counterintuitive to seek out pockets of fear, shame, helplessness and loneliness. All our mental energy throughout our lives has been invested in avoiding pain. Yet, in EMDR work, we actively look for these raw spots. In EMDR training there is a metaphor used of entering a dark tunnel. As we face our disturbing emotions, there may be the urge to freeze or retreat. Yet, when we find the courage to keep moving forward, further into the dark, eventually we begin to see the light at the end of the tunnel. As we finally exit the tunnel, having felt all there is to feel, the tunnel vanishes. It's like Dorothy having faced and stood up to the Wicked Witch. Once she did that, the witch melted away, never to be a threat again. It's a wonderful feeling to know that we've conquered our greatest fears.

I should mention here that EMDR is also used to heal memories in which the client has committed an act or acts of which they are deeply ashamed or are relentlessly stuck in guilt and regret. Through fully processing their emotions, such clients can be able to take responsibility for their behavior, recognize what they have learned from their experience and seek ways in which they can make amends.

Proper EMDR treatment provides desensitizing of not only past traumas but current triggers of the memories. For example, an obese client of mine named Peggy had been deeply humiliated about 20 years ago when she was refused cake at a party, being told sharply, in front of everyone, that "the last thing *you* need is cake." When Peggy entered therapy with me, she had totally forgotten that incident. Recently, she attended a family party that she was fully enjoying until it was announced that cake was being served. Suddenly flooded with anxiety and the urge to leave, she abruptly left the party.

In exploring this experience with me, Peggy recalled the earlier party humiliation. She realized, too, that for the past 20 years, whenever dessert was being served at social occasions, she left prematurely. This provided us with a past trauma and a current trigger for EMDR work. An earlier related memory was that her mother always baked sweets for herself each night after the children went to bed and never left any for the children to enjoy. As an adult, at home, Peggy indulged herself with desserts, which triggered old conflicting feelings of deservedness, longing and shame. These eating sprees occurred in the middle of the night, the unconscious trigger for the time her mother had made and gobbled treats. As a result of Peggy's EMDR work on these and many other childhood traumas, she has been able to experience far greater calm in her body, sense of self-worth, conscious decision-making and comfort in social situations.

One of the most awesome aspects of EMDR is that each individual's trauma and healing process will be experienced in a completely idio-syncratic way, one that neither the client nor the therapist could ever predict or consciously elicit. There have been a number of EMDR sessions when I have wondered to myself, "How is this person ever going to be freed from this emotional quicksand?" Over the years, witnessing and facilitating thousands of EMDR sessions, I've come to trust the process. At those exceptional times when a client's processing becomes blocked, the therapist can make a brief intervention that will provide the piece of information the client needs to get unstuck. For the majority of EMDR sessions, the therapist stays out of the way and the client's inner wisdom brings him or her out of the dark woods into safety. As long as the client can ride the strong waves of emotion and hold onto their adult state of mind, healing is inevitable.

Journeys of Healing

Marina's Story

Marina came to therapy because she was severely anxious and distraught over the relationship between her grown son, Tony, and his girlfriend Carol. Marina felt a huge responsibility for the relationship and the harm she anticipated Tony was going to suffer. She felt she had made a catastrophic mistake by being cordial when Tony introduced her to Carol, a single mother with a history of relationship problems. Marina cried to me: "I'm afraid I'm going to lose Tony because of this woman. I don't want to control him, I want to protect him. My child is in the fire and I need to get him out!"

Rather than focusing our attention on the current situation, I helped Marina identify the childhood and adult traumas that made her feel such powerful guilt, shame, helplessness and fear. These included being constantly judged, criticized and controlled by her father and uncles; having accidentally caused two fires when she was a child; and giving birth to and raising a child with a life-threatening condition.

Over time, as Marina healed each trauma through EMDR, she was able to discontinue medication for anxiety and depression. Her mood lightened and her inner youthful enthusiasm and spirit began to sparkle. At one point, she told me that her friends, also in their late fifties, assumed she was having an affair because, what else could possibly cause a married woman her age to be so happy? Marina and I got a great kick out of that. Once the past traumas were resolved, Marina did EMDR on her son's relationship with Carol. By the end of our work, Marina had hosted an engagement party at her home for Carol and was eagerly planning the wedding. Carol hadn't changed, but Marina could perceive Carol and her son's future in a more realistic and benign way. Most importantly, she was no longer taking on responsibility for others' lives and happiness.

Marina also did EMDR on the issue of her daughter whose death at an early age was inevitable. About a year or two after our work ended, Marina came for a few sessions following the death of her daughter. In our discussion, it was clear that Marina wasn't depressed but that her grief was being stifled by well-meaning friends and relatives. Once Marina regained permission to let her emotions flow, she quickly reclaimed her joy of being alive.

Louis' Story

Louis was conceived by two teenagers, who hastily married as a result of the unintended pregnancy. From the day he was born, Louis' father made it clear how much he resented, loathed and despised the boy for ruining his life. All the misery the father felt was blamed on Louis. Louis' mother was verbally abused as well and unable to protect Louis or herself. A number of years later, the young couple had another child who was put on a pedestal by the father. Louis, on the other hand, never knew parental kindness, support, love or protection.

Louis must have known deep inside what he had needed as a child, because he became a loving and devoted father. He also compensated for his deprivation by being overly generous to his children. Not surprisingly, Louis married someone who he could never please. She never showed any gratitude for all his efforts to meet her every desire, nor did she show empathy for any difficulty he experienced. When I met Louis, intense anxiety, terror, helplessness and shame radiated from the pores of his being. He suffered from chronic Post-Traumatic Stress Disorder and Major Depression. His relationship with his wife was driving him crazy and his rage was escalating in the direction of physical aggression.

Over the course of two years of EMDR treatment, Louis processed many painful memories involving both his childhood and adult families. He was able to achieve a sense of self-worth, dignity, self-confidence and safety he had never known before. He also was able to dissolve the sense of impending doom that had followed him every day of his life. When I spoke with him about a year after our last session, Louis was happy with himself and his life, even though there were certain unfortunate aspects that were out of his control. His tone of voice was lighthearted as he said, "What are you going to do? You just have to laugh." And he did.

Sarah's Story

Sarah grew up with a mother who had a parade of men entering the house. Many of these men sexually abused Sarah. She was able to recognize these men as self-centered exploiters, but her mother was clueless and childlike. Sarah was very protective of her younger sister, Lynn, and when these men began to show interest in Lynn, Sarah offered up herself so that her sister wouldn't have to experience the abuse she was enduring. Because of this horrifying childhood, Sarah never married nor had children.

When she arrived in therapy for the first time at age fifty, Sarah was filled with anger, fear and helplessness over her married best friend's relationship with another man, who was an irresponsible, flirtatious alcoholic. Sarah's friend lacked good judgment and resisted Sarah's increasingly desperate attempts to warn and protect her. Sarah told me, "I can read people and detect when they are conning, self-centered and exploitative. I'm extremely angry and untrusting. Then I feel guilty for being so mean. This isn't me. I'm not like that. When I'm angry, I'm a bad person and I push people away."

After Sarah did EMDR on her childhood traumas, she was able to let go of the burden of trying to protect her dear friend. She was able to continue the relationship and feel peace as she accepted the fact that her friend was an adult, responsible for her own life. She could live with the reality that her friend was not ready at this time to deal with her own issues. Instead of threat and anger, Sarah felt more secure in all her relationships and experienced joy every day.

To me, Sarah is an excellent example of the way that our childhood wounds and emotions inevitably infiltrate our adult lives. She may have avoided marriage and parenting in an attempt to protect herself, but because she had people in her life who mattered to her, she was still vulnerable to her old fears. Those perceptions, beliefs and emotions will get projected onto and attached to something in our present lives, regardless of how many defenses we've erected. They will not be denied.

Gordon's Story

Another client of mine was Gordon, whose father was an alcoholic. Throughout his childhood and youth Gordon was pushed into the role of the man of the family. His mother was too helpless and shut down to take charge of the situation and protect her son. Each night, Gordon would hear his father's depressed, drunken mumblings in the living room and later see his father passed out on the floor. At the end of every family function, Gordon helped his uncles carry his incapacitated father into the car. He was the one to contact professionals about getting his father help—help that his father would never accept.

Meanwhile, Gordon had no one to provide him love, guidance, encouragement and comfort. He went through life trying to figure everything out on his own and feeling totally overwhelmed and unequipped to meet the challenges. His father's shame became Gordon's shame and he feared being "found out" as defective and incompetent.

As an adult, Gordon had attended talk therapy on and off for years, but still suffered a nagging sense of anxiety, overwhelm, helplessness, dread and panic. Although Gordon didn't realize it at first, these were the same emotions that haunted him as a young person, but had never recognized or articulated because no one was there to help him talk about what he was experiencing. His greatest fear in daily life was that his business would fail, putting him and his family out on the street. He was so preoccupied with money and where it was going to come from that he had no energy to pursue pleasure or to simply enjoy the present moment.

During his initial EMDR sessions, Gordon had some difficulty accessing his emotions for a number of reasons. He felt, as a male, that he should not be such a wimp. He felt ashamed for still being so insecure and needing therapy after so many years. He assumed I must feel the same about him—that I thought his feelings were pathetic and not deserving of attention. I needed to respond to each of these concerns before we resumed the EMDR. Once Gordon began to fully engage in the process and connect his feelings to the original circumstances that provoked them, he became more able to validate himself.

By the end of Gordon's work, not only was he able to stay in the present moment and feel confident in his ability to manage his finances and his life, but he began pursuing photography, a hobby that he had dropped decades ago. Gordon reported finding pleasure from creative expression. He also began to regularly take time off from work to enjoy relaxing vacations with his wife. Before ending his treatment, Gordon had an experience that reflected how far he had come. "My wife and I went to the West Coast for two weeks! I haven't been away from work for that long in many, many years. I was able to really have a great time and not worry about the business. In fact, I'm planning on taking another two-week trip this year. I really feel I can trust myself and the universe. Life is good."

Linda's Story

Remember Linda, the black belt in karate I mentioned earlier? She often felt helpless, inadequate and frozen in fear. Linda was very self-conscious in social situations, anticipating that people would recognize her defectiveness and humiliate her. Her shame and fear were centered on her physical appearance. To anyone's eyes, her complexion was absolutely fine, but she thought it was horrible and agonized over it every day. Linda was extremely indecisive and was tormented by decision-making as well as by her appearance. She blamed herself for not having made better decisions about the care of her face and her shame and paranoia built to a crescendo of delusional proportions. This was when Linda finally sought therapy.

After first helping Linda stabilize with affect management skills and a referral for medication, we began to resolve traumatic memories with EMDR. As is often the case with people who have relied on dissociation and minimization to survive, Linda had endured an appalling amount of abuse and neglect. The extent of her trauma became apparent as she began to share with me stories of her childhood that she had dismissed and forgotten. As each tragic story was told, she wore a broad smile that was completely out of attunement with the emotions she must have felt.

As we proceeded with the EMDR work and Linda's self-doubt persisted, though at a much more manageable level, I encouraged her again and again to stay with the process. I was confident she would eventually round the corner and find herself on a new, positive trajectory.

As we approached the one-year anniversary of the emotional meltdown that had brought her to my office, Linda told me of her recent experience at a wedding. Leading up to the wedding, she felt some fear about her appearance and what to do, but she decided to not trouble herself about it. She also had no difficulty choosing outfits to buy for herself and her husband. These were all major shifts for her.

Shortly after she arrived at the reception, a relative she hadn't seen in years said loudly and bluntly in front of others, "Hey, remember how your brother used to always call you 'Big Ears?'" He repeated this inappropriate and insensitive remark again and again. Instead of feeling humiliated, Linda consciously shrugged it off. About an hour later, he said it again. This time it was even more apparent to her just how "weird" *his* behavior was. Despite these blatant invitations to feel shame, Linda had a wonderful time at the wedding. She danced all night long with many people, mostly at her initiative. Linda told me that she was twirling all around the dance floor and had the best time. Linda even invited a child with acne who was sitting alone to come up and dance with her and was pleased to see later that the child was dancing with her peers.

At some point, she noticed that her siblings were watching her and seemed to be talking about her. They were surprised to see that she had been drinking water, not alcohol. Having had an alcoholic father who was a "happy drunk," they had assumed anyone having that much fun must be drinking alcohol. Linda's fear and shame had reduced so dramatically that she was able to be carefree and spontaneous throughout the evening, and it wasn't alcohol or Prozac talking. These changes were her new, wired-in default position.

Over the next few months, additional EMDR work led to Linda finally feeling outrage for having been so mistreated in her life. This was possible because of having accessed feelings of self-worth and entitlement to proper treatment by others. Linda came to a recent session eager to tell me the following dream from the past week. As she entered her childhood bedroom, she sensed the presence of an evil force. Suddenly filling the window was a huge threatening face. Just as suddenly, the face crashed through the window. Linda immediately stepped forward and screamed at the face: "I'm not afraid of you! You can't scare me anymore!" And the evil face shrank away. Linda told me with delight, "That's the first terrifying dream in which I had a voice!"

Ricky's Story

Ricky's childhood was riddled with rejection and brutality from his father and peers. The exception to this painful childhood was his love of hunting out in the peaceful woods, which he shared with his father and grandfather. At age 13, Ricky found out that, because of a ban on assault weapons, he might not be free to pursue his hobby throughout his life. Being a minor, Ricky felt powerless to do anything about this problem.

Fast forward twenty years and you will find Ricky glued to the computer for hours, compelled to keep informed of the minds and actions of those who oppose the NRA. He seeks out the websites with the most polarized points of view, the most brutal opponents with the most incendiary language. Listening to such people reinforces Ricky's sense of contempt, outrage, hatred and fear. It reinforces his belief that, "I'm going to be trampled on if I don't fight." During the second EMDR session on the assault weapons ban, the following partial list of statements reflect the evolution of Ricky's perspective. Each statement was made when I asked him, after about a minute, "What are you noticing now?"

"The price of liberty is eternal vigilance . . . We have to be stubborn . . . I see their smug smiles when they won . . . I've got to push back . . . I won't compromise—they didn't . . . I have to whip up the people who are complacent . . . I always feel I haven't done enough and I don't know enough . . . I don't have to try and figure everything out on my own—there is the one website that has all the information I need . . . I'm spending more time trying to preserve my rights than enjoying them . . . There are organizations so that each of us don't have to do all the work by ourselves . . . I haven't been going to any websites to learn more about my hobby . . . *this all harkens back to a time when I felt trampled upon and felt powerless* . . . I'd forgotten that it's all about having a good time, not looking for threat around the corner . . . I don't have to be vigilant all the time, that burns people out . . . I can relax and enjoy myself . . . there's a time and place for action . . . I don't have to look for a fight or conflict."

At the end of this one hour EMDR session, I asked Ricky what he now believed about himself: "I don't have to go it alone. It's not me against the world. I have others I can turn to for support. I don't have to be Atlas holding up the world. I don't have to be an island. I'm safe now. I don't have to be wearing a shield and standing alone in the middle of an open field."

Ricky then told me that as a hunter, "When I'm calm and serene and aware and alert I take in the whole picture, rather than focusing in on only one small part of it. That's when I'm most effective." As each trauma is healed, Ricky's PTSD symptoms of impending doom and hypervigilance diminish further, allowing him to feel safer, calmer and more a part of the whole . . . wherever he is.

Ricky's story tells us a lot about what might motivate the most extreme, hostile and combative participants in "tugs of war" between groups of all sizes and over any subject. How many of us have experienced having our feelings and needs "trampled upon," leaving us to feel devalued and helpless? How many of us have unconsciously attempted to compensate for that sense of unworthiness and helplessness? While some of us might play out that need for power and respect on the small stage of our marriage or family life, others may project all those feelings of outrage, vindication and need for control on larger stages. The national and international headlines are filled with such stories.

Moving Beyond Trauma

Over the last few years, as I've learned from experience, I've discovered the importance of introducing my clients to mindfulness meditation, which I will discuss in Chapter Nine. Even though my clients and I do EMDR on future scenarios that are likely to push their buttons, we can never predict all the circumstances that could trigger old wounds. For this reason, as well as others, it is in the best interest of us all to cultivate our non-judgmental, observant self that can be aware of what is happening within us and between us as we live our lives. In other words, the mindfulness that is present during EMDR trauma work needs to be available as much as possible at all other times.

On the same note, while EMDR helps people heal trauma, develop adaptive beliefs about themselves, strengthen their adult self, develop better judgment and decision-making and be more fully in the present, it doesn't inoculate people against experiencing any further painful events. As M. Scott Peck said in *The Road Less Traveled*, "Therapy and love don't diminish risk or pain but support and teach courage."

An aspect of EMDR treatment that has inspired and moved me is the way many clients evolve, not just from intense distress to neutrality, but from distress to a deeply positive emotional zone. Once their emotional pain has dissolved, clients who had been feeling highly defective, inadequate and vulnerable may begin to generate layer after layer of self-acceptance, appreciation, compassion, pride and love. All of the intense pressure that clients withstand, as they face their greatest wounds and fears, transforms their sense of self from dense, sooty coal to a light-filled diamond. Peter, who I told you about at the start of this chapter, believed that he was weak when we began a recent EMDR session. That session focused on a physical attack by his father in front of other children. Within an hour he experienced the heart-felt realization that he was a strong and moral person, capable of empathy for and protection of those who are weaker than him.

A client of mine, Arlene, came to me in her mid-sixties, never having experienced therapy before. She finally decided she had to face the traumas that had been haunting her for six decades. During her second EMDR session, she faced the memory of being separated at age three from her mother and sibling after her father's sudden death. While living with relatives, she was molested by her grandfather. At the end of the session, following intense emotional distress, Arlene experienced a feeling of spaciousness and peace inside her chest. Then a striking awareness: "I'm bigger than all of that . . . *I am bigger than all that!*"

The ability of EMDR clients to re-access their capacity for positive emotions is a significant benefit. Optimal health, whether in childhood or adulthood, is not just being released from a relentless nightmare of disturbing emotions, but the ability to feel the full range of positive emotions. When clients are parents, their children benefit greatly from being in the presence of their parents' new-found joy, laughter and pleasure in being alive. Positive emotions are contagious and have a palpable impact on both the physiology and mental state of family members, particularly young developing children. Adults may know that enjoying their children is an important parental responsibility, but knowing it and *feeling* it are two different things.

Seeing clients leave my office following an EMDR session with growing feelings of self-worth, confidence and calm has been a gift to me as well as them. One such client told me recently that her chronically depressed father lamented woefully and cynically, "Does it *ever* get better?" Without skipping a beat, she answered, "Yes, it does." For years, people would say to me upon hearing that I was a social worker, "Oh, that must be so rewarding." It took my learning and practicing EMDR for my clients to achieve the goals they dreamed of and for me to truly feel rewarded.

In Southeast Asia there was a huge, spectacular, solid gold statue of the Buddha that was covered up with plaster so that war-time intruders wouldn't realize its worth and steal or harm it. Centuries later, a flood caused a crack in the statue and revealed something shining beneath. When the hardened material was thoroughly removed, the witnesses were astonished by the golden sculpture. Our true nature and its brilliance are also covered, but by layers of defenses, stuck emotions, symptoms and distorted beliefs that fool us into thinking we are something we are not. With EMDR, our inborn healing mechanism helps us to rediscover our True Self which, despite life's slings and arrows, has remained unscathed. The greatest thrill of practicing psychotherapy is in witnessing those who have known deep suffering rest peacefully in the comforting arms of their spirit and inner beauty.

CHAPTER FIVE

Self-Care and Self-Soothing

THERE ARE MANY DIFFERENT TECHNIQUES, exercises and resources that can help us stay in our optimal arousal zone and wisest state of mind. *Peace in the Heart and Home* is not a complete presentation of all that is available. This chapter and the ones on Physical Health and Mindfulness provide some of the best practices that I know and recommend. What I love about these self-care and self-soothing methods is that they are empowering, portable, legal, free and have no negative side effects. They can be used without concern for harmful dependency or overdose. And, as one client pointed out with glee, "They're not fattening!"

Before I share some of the more unfamiliar, therapeutic and potent forms of self-care, I would like to share the multitude of stress relief methods that are available in everyday life. The following is a partial list from a favorite poster of mine, 101 STRESS RELIEVERS (www.parlay.com):

- Ask for help
- Laugh at something you did
- Play with your dog
- Go fishing

- Stand up and stretch
- Listen to the birds
- Keep a journal of thoughts and feelings
- Call up an old friend
- Lie in a hammock
- Walk barefoot in the grass
- Stop and look out the window
- Look closely at a flower, leaf, blade of grass or tree trunk
- Plant a flower
- Smell a flower
- Take a child to the playground
- Do one thing at a time
- Take a deep breath—let it all out
- Take a leisurely stroll
- Take a long bath
- Take an herbal tea break
- Take the back roads
- Sing a song
- Eat an orange slowly, segment by segment
- Take time to watch the sunrise and sunset
- Go for a brisk walk
- Hug someone you love
- Put a cat in your lap
- Wear earplugs when it is noisy
- Practice yoga
- Sit by a fountain or stream
- Sit by a fire
- Watch a cloud or insect for five minutes

Some other activities that may alter your perspective and improve your mood include the following:

- Bake some cookies
- Put on your favorite music and dance
- Find a playground and go on the swings
- Watch cartoons you loved as a child
- Visit a pet store
- Look through baby and childhood photographs of yourself and your spouse, as well as those of your children

If you were to ask the average person, "What do you do to take care of yourself, to treat yourself well and recharge your batteries?" they might say one of the following: play a round of golf, go out to dinner, get my nails and hair done, get a massage, buy myself something I've been wanting, have some beers and laughs or play games on the computer. While these methods may provide a lift or escape, their impact is very short-lived. It's more a surface spray than a deep root-watering nourishment.

A strong indicator for mental, emotional, and social health is the ability to recognize the need for care and then provide it to oneself, as well as to reach out for care from another. Healthy practices also entail being able to accept help, respond when a loved one asks for support and recognize another's need and initiate care giving. In a later chapter I will explore in depth how one builds a secure, interdependent attachment bond with a partner. In this chapter I am focusing on the ability to care for oneself, psychologically and emotionally, which then also impacts the health of our body and our relationships.

In childhood, the most significant relationship we have is with our primary caretaker, followed by other caretakers and family members. Out of that flows our relationship with ourself and others. In adulthood, the most significant relationship we have is with ourself, which includes our relationship history. Out of that flows our relationship with others. Self-care is the capacity for mindful attention to one's state of mind and body and responding to that state, as necessary, to maintain our optimal functioning, decision-making and behavior.

Some of us are overly aware of other people's attitudes, emotions, behaviors and functioning. Consequently, we either try to control them or pressure them into changing. Such individuals may be considered high-maintenance or control freaks with a bottomless pit of expectations and disappointments. Often when we are so preoccupied with others' behavior and how they should act differently, it is in order for *us* to feel better and to manage *our* emotional state. Anxiously-attached individuals tend to see *the other* as the sole source of potential relief. They will invest huge amounts of energy trying to fix or change others or get them to respond so they can be at peace themselves. In other words, their happiness is overly dependent on the actions and behaviors of others.

Avoidantly-attached individuals tend to be at the other extreme. They don't permit themselves any hope or expectation at all that someone will come through for them and comfort them. Their relationship role is always as the reactor, not the initiator. In relational interactions, the concerns and emotional needs addressed are always those of the initiator. The avoidantly-attached have little clue as to what they need or feel, aside from the urge to placate and then steer clear of difficult people so they can focus on activities, possessions or their physical condition. They may even express bewilderment or contempt toward their partner for being so emotional, sensitive and needy.

When we are functioning at our best, we are attuned to and have a finger on the emotional pulse of both our own inner being *and* the state of those we care about the most, our significant others. This attunement is not a hyper-vigilant, anxious awareness, but instead a relaxed, alert and caring attention. It makes a huge difference in how we feel and how others feel in our company. It is the difference between a vice-like grip and a relaxed hand being held.

Well-balanced individuals have a competent and secure adult self that is able to provide their own affect management, self-soothing, self-validation, sound judgment and behavioral management *and* initiate requests for connection, comfort and support from others. In the chapter on Mindfulness, the Higher Self and Being, I will discuss at length our highest human capacities and how we can access and cultivate them. But for now I want to especially focus on how we can bring this Higher Self to the anxious, traumatized and defensive child parts of our personality.

When I refer to our relationship with ourself as being a foundational factor in our relationship to life and others, I am referring to our ability to relate to ourself with open-mindedness, honesty, compassion, respect, patience and kindness. It also means taking time to be with ourself, to reflect, to experience and process our emotions, to look at our life, to look at the natural world and to *see the whole picture so that our personal life and troubles neither dominate nor avoid the radar screen of our awareness.*

Before beginning to share the methods of self-care that I have found beneficial for many of my clients, let me say the following. If you ever find that an activity, technique or form of treatment makes matters worse, discontinue it immediately. Each person is unique and an approach that is helpful and safe for some people may not be for you.

Back of Head Scale

A basic requirement for self-care is the ability to recognize when we are losing touch with the present moment and to take measures to regain present awareness. When we zone out or dissociate we are more vulnerable to experiencing further trauma, because we are not alert and in a position to assess the safety of our environment. When we are not "all there," we are more prone to slipping into child ego states, use poor judgment and feel less capable of caring for ourselves. EMDR clinician Jim Knipe, PhD developed a technique, the "Back of Head Scale" (BHS), to help clients recognize their degree of mental presence.

Imagine an invisible line that starts about 15 inches in front of your face and extends to the back of your head. At the 15 inches end of the continuum you are fully aware of who you are and where you are and you feel yourself in your body. You are fully able to attend to events occurring in the present moment. When you are feeling that way, then you indicate that by stretching your arm out fully in front of you, with your hand in the "stop" position.

The other extreme of the continuum represents being lost in thoughts, another time and place or a general fog. That state of mind is indicated by bending your arm at the elbow and positioning your hand just past the ear, at the back of the head. Whenever you want to assess your degree of presence, put your hand somewhere in the space on that continuum between hand completely stretched forward and at the back of your head. Anytime your hand is about three inches from your face, you need to take measures to become more alert and connected to the present.

Grounding Techniques

There are a number of ways a person can regain mental presence and connection to his or her body:

- Stomp or press your feet into the ground so you regain your awareness of your body.
- If you are sitting, bring your full attention to your back, buttocks and arms being supported by the chair. Make sure you are

sitting erect, rather than slumped, in order to feel more adult and competent.

- *Briefly* put a frozen package from the freezer on your face and arms.
- Take a few sniffs of peppermint oil.
- One by one, put a number of objects in your hands and bring your attention to their shape, form, weight, texture and smell.
- Hold and stroke a favorite object that you find soothing.
- Toss a tissue back and forth from one hand to the other.
- Toss a ball back and forth from one hand to the other.

Healthy Defenses and Pacing Ourselves

Another aspect of self-care involves using healthy and appropriate defenses such as: humor, playfulness, seeking information, other perspectives, support and comfort, the ability to say "no" and asserting ourselves. It also entails consciously pacing ourselves and setting aside time for activities like exercise, social interaction, recreation, volunteering, creative endeavors, and especially, solitude, reflection and meditation. Some of these things, like exercise, meditation and socializing, will be done daily or several times a week. With the remaining, we may focus on one or a few at a time, perhaps pursuing different activities during different phases of our life. We can only do so much and have to make choices.

In contemporary society, people are drowning in a sea of endless stimulation, opportunities, activities, resources and choices. We all desperately need for our mental, physical and spiritual health to say "no" or "another time" far more than "yes." We must be the steward of our time and space; only we know what we already have on our plate. We need to significantly alter our balance of activity and stillness, doing and being. I will speak more about this in the chapter on Mindfulness, the Higher Self and Being.

Imaginary Resources

Our internal capacity for achieving stillness and a sense of calm security can often come from surprising sources. Sometimes during EMDR trauma processing a client's psyche will spontaneously provide a resource person to help the child through the disturbing memory. During one such experience, a client of mine found the actor Morgan Freeman appear before him. This "Imaginary Resource" then guided my client with his famous soothing, humane and wise tone of voice. In a number of other EMDR sessions, that same client found his adult self dressed in an orange sweat suit appear in the memory to provide parental encouragement, reassurance and loving kindness to his younger self.

We all have the capacity to use our imaginations or memories to identify resources that we can turn to for meeting our emotional needs. The resource could be someone we still have in our life who is warm and reassuring. The resource might be someone who is no longer alive, like a grandparent who always made us feel loved and safe. We can imagine being in the presence of someone who is very calming and loving like Gandhi or Mother Teresa. The resource could be someone from the movies, theater, literature or television who possesses qualities we admire or would like to possess such as equanimity, courage, dignity, perseverance or patience. The resource can come from nature such as a tall stately oak, a serene body of water or the relentless energy of ocean waves. It could also be a favorite place we have been to or would love to go to that provides us with feelings of calm, relaxation or safety. We could also recall anything that triggers feelings of gratitude, appreciation, awe, joy or love: a newborn baby, a giggling child, a star-filled night, the sound of spring peepers, the exhilaration of the music and movement in *Riverdance*.

Self-Taps

When we focus our attention on these imaginary resources, *using all our senses*, our body and mind respond just as if the events were actually happening in our external life. Once we begin to notice a shift in our body from tension to relaxation and calm, we can introduce some bi-lateral stimulation in the form of alternating left to right, gentle, slow, rhythmic self-taps with our palms on our thighs. As we alternate left, right, left and notice the calm feelings, we say to ourself, "I am calm" or "I am relaxed."

Other ways of doing this are the following. When we hug ourself, each hand is on the opposite upper arm and we can tap in this position.

(When the hands are raised fully off the upper arm, this is called a "Butterfly Hug," a method young children can be taught to self-soothe.) Or, when we are in public, we can hold our arms crossed on our chest, as people often do, and with our hands under each upper arm, gently press our fingers into each side of the upper torso. If we're sitting at a desk at work, we can tap the top of our thighs unobtrusively, providing ourselves self-soothing, helping ourselves to feel calm and in our adult state of mind. *It is important to note that these taps should only be done for about half a minute per use and only while focused on positive emotions and sensations.*

Imaginary Container

Another way of using the faculties of our right brain hemisphere is to create an "Imaginary Container." There are times when we're under too much stress and need quick relief so that we don't become overwhelmed. We can close our eyes and imagine a container that is big and strong enough to hold all those disturbing things that we can't deal with right now or all at once. Because it's imaginary, we can make it of any material, shape or size we want. This container meets the need of putting all the anxieties safely away, rather than having them shower from all over like a hail storm. Some people picture a rigid plastic container with a tight-fitting lid. Others may picture a dumpster or a large trunk. You could even picture a cave with panthers guarding it—whatever gives you confidence that your troubles are stored away and relieves you of carrying the burden. A new client of mine came up with the moving and powerful image of "God's pocket."

Next, you might want to imagine that the container has a vacuum hose attached so that you can always add more of your stressors without having to open the lid. You also imagine a valve with a spout so that, when you are ready, you can remove one item to work on. This imaginary container is not a garbage dump; rather, it's just a temporary arrangement so that you have the energy, attention and calm to handle what is manageable in the moment. You can address the most troublesome stored stressors at another time when you have the necessary resources including, if necessary, professional guidance.

Emotional Thermometer

Still another way of being proactive and integrating self-care into daily life is to use an "Emotional Thermometer." One's emotional state can be rated by imagining a scale from negative ten (the worst you could feel) to 0 (neutral) and then to positive ten (the best you could feel). People who are actively developing affect management skills can check their emotional temperature on a regular basis, perhaps on the hour. Whenever the temperature is near zero or entering the negative zone, they can use a number of different self-soothing strategies to bring their temperature back into the positives. It is best to provide self-care at the first sign of approaching the negative temperature numbers, before a negative state of body and mind becomes too severe and entrenched to respond to your efforts.

This is the adult equivalent of what good parents do for their children: they don't allow their children to deteriorate to the point where they are exhausted and inconsolable. They are attuned to their children's emotional and physical states and respond as often as necessary to keep bringing their children out of the negative zone and back into a positive state. Once children have been soothed and reassured, they are able to hop off their parents' laps and return to full functioning in the world. Most people are not mindful of the state they are in throughout the day. Therefore, it is highly beneficial to develop the habit of becoming more attuned and responsive to oneself.

People who are trying to create new self-care habits often wonder how to remember to use their tools and strategies. Luckily, there are a number of tickler systems we can use. We can leave brief notes on mirrors, refrigerators, car dashboards, computer screen-savers or any place we frequent throughout the day. The note can say, "Time to Practice Self-care" or could list the strategies we want to practice. One client of mine bought special washable markers and wrote her reminders directly on the mirrors and other surfaces. We can leave a voice message reminder on our cell phone that we never erase. We can write a specific self-care exercise on each day of our daily planner, just like any other responsibility we want to make sure we carry out. We can set our watch or cell phone alarm to signal self-care breaks. We can practice mindful breathing (see "breath awareness" in the Mindfulness chapter) every time we come to a red light, every time we are waiting for a webpage to load, every time we use the toilet, every time we wait in a check-out line. Use your imagination and I'm sure you will develop additional ideas that work for you.

Laughter, Smiles and Positive Emotions

In 1979 Norman Cousins wrote *Anatomy of an Illness as Perceived by the Patient* about his overcoming a life-threatening and incurable disease with the help of Marx Brothers films. Ever since then, there has been ongoing research into the connection between laughter and healing. Laughter has been associated with improved immunity as well as reduction of inflammation. You'll see in the next chapter, Physical Health, the significance of this. Additionally, laughter triggers the release of endorphins, the body's natural painkillers, and produces a general sense of well-being. Indeed, Cousins found that watching comedy made it possible for him to experience pain-free sleep.

While I wouldn't recommend distraction or humor as one's only tool, as part of a treatment plan they can be highly valuable, especially for those who get too caught up in their troubles. Humor can be more than simple distraction. One of the reasons laughter has a positive impact on our physical health is that it gives our internal organs a vigorous work out. Laughter helps reduce stress by suppressing levels of epinephrine and by putting things in perspective. When we don't take enough time away from our problems, we may miss the opportunities for laughter that could soften the sharp edges of life. Stand-up comics do not have a monopoly on humor. We all have the capacity for finding the comical and surprising in our daily lives. We may even take a put-down, consciously or unconsciously directed at us, and turn it on its head by enjoying its absurdity. By doing so, we deflect any harm and instead experience delight. If we don't take ourselves too seriously, if we are able to appreciate that we are all capable of mindlessness, goof-ups or "senior moments," we can have a good-natured, wonderful laugh at ourselves. G.K. Chesterton said, "Angels can fly because they can take themselves lightly."

I recall one time when I was renting a car with a remote door opener. I got so used to using it that I walked inside my building and tried to open my office door with it. Another time, when I first began to use voicemail, I actually forgot that I was checking a message. I got caught up in what the person was saying and tried to respond to her remarks. Each time I tried to interject a comment, the other person kept right on talking non-stop. I was flabbergasted at how rude she was being for not letting me get a word in edgewise. When she hung up before I got to say good bye, I really was annoyed. I told the office secretary about the disturbing call, saying how unlike Mary it was to act that way. Once it occurred to me what I had done, I laughed out loud. These two stories can still make me laugh whenever I remember them.

Not all conflicts need to be settled through serious discussion. Bernie Siegel, MD, author of *Love, Medicine and Miracles* and many other inspiring books, shared the following story from when he and his wife were bringing up their five children, four of whom were boys. The children were raising hell in the kitchen one day, so he said, "You may choose peace or you may choose conflict." His daughter answered, "I'll have pizza." Everyone busted out laughing and the problem was fixed. Bernie sent me the story in an email with the subject heading, "Pizza in the Heart and Home."

One of the conscious decisions we can make to help our mood is to gravitate towards optimistic and upbeat people because emotions are contagious. Even when we are not in such company, *choosing* to put on a full smile, that uses the muscles of the eyes as well as lips, actually has been found in studies to lift spirits. Again, I am not suggesting that we should disguise our emotions as a rule or that this replaces the need for acknowledging and experiencing one's full range of emotions. But it is one of the ways we can manage our emotions and increase the amount of time we are in a positive state of mind and body. Diverse fields such as psychoneuroimmunology, Positive Psychology, Buddhism and the Institute of HeartMath are recognizing the benefit to our physiology, mood and functioning of genuine positive emotions including compassion, gratitude, appreciation, joy, love and awe. These emotions can be increased through intention and awareness. Buddhist practice entails the cultivation of "loving kindness" and compassion for self as well as others. The recordings and books of Buddhists Thich Nhat Hanh, Pema Chodron and Jack Kornfield, for example, provide instruction and guidance in developing these qualities for self as well as all living beings. These teachers are highly respected, beloved and experienced and carry on wisdom traditions that are thousands of years old.

In order to care for ourselves we need to scan the environment for what feeds our soul, in the same way that a hummingbird naturally seeks out the flowers with the best nectar. Just as we can keep our senses open for beauty and what about reality pleases us, we can keep our mind open for anything that might lighten our mood or create harmony. Reading books such as *Random Acts of Kindness* and *Chicken Soup for the Soul* is another way of reminding ourselves of the goodness of people and the world. The reading matter, music and television shows we choose can numb us, further entrench our distressing emotions or instead reassure, inspire and comfort us. We need to be mindful of the choices we make in our daily life.

Productive Problem-Solving

The client who bought the washable markers has benefitted from having a sign on the bathroom mirror that helps her catch herself taking emotions too seriously. It says: "If you haven't found a legitimate reason to be anxious within a few minutes, then it's old garbage." She has found this saying very helpful in letting go of fearful, ruminating thoughts and then regaining her perspective in the present moment.

It is important to recognize that our problems are worsened by worrying or rehashing the story dozens of times. It's equivalent to hitting a home run and going around the bases fifty times—it's overkill. One of the reasons people spin their wheels with problems is because they are using only half of their brain. This is excessive rational analysis. Those with avoidant attachment may deal with their fears by worrying over the factual details. But, there are many aspects of life that our rational brain just can't wrap itself around, no matter how hard it tries. Those with anxious attachment are likely to drown in their emotions, with reason nowhere to be found. The ability to have access to *both* reason and emotion will be discussed in the chapter on Mindfulness.

One of the ways people cause themselves prolonged misery and lack of resolution of problems is by going in and out of the problem in a half-conscious way dozens, if not hundreds, of times a day. This habit can be replaced with designating a sufficient period of time a day, say half an hour, to explore the problem with full attention. For example, you may promise yourself that you will focus on the problem from 10 AM until 10:30 AM every day. Once you have fulfilled the half hour for the day, any time during the rest of the day that you catch yourself focusing on the problem, you say to yourself, "No more focusing on that subject today. I've already addressed it. I can think about it again tomorrow at 10 AM." Then you can put the problem into your imaginary container.

Measuring Progress

It is very important that you are able to recognize your growth so that you will feel encouraged, hopeful and motivated to continue your efforts. There are three key ways of measuring progress: frequency, intensity and duration. Let's say that one of your major symptoms has been feeling panicked that you are going to make a horrible mistake and others will reject you. At the start of psychotherapy and/or a daily extensive program of self-care and mindfulness practice, how often do you experience an episode like this? How intense is the symptom and how long does it last? Perhaps you have these episodes fifteen times a week and on a scale of 0 to ten, ten being the worst you could feel and 0 being calm, you feel ten when it strikes. Each time you have an episode it lasts for about four hours. This is your "baseline." Write it down in a journal in which you document the three dimensions of symptom experience on a daily basis.

I suggest that you refrain from preoccupation with changes from day to day. What is more important is the overall progress at the end of each week of self-care. After engaging in your therapeutic program for two months, you may find that your episodes are less frequent, down from fifteen a week to eight a week. The intensity may still be high, eight, but the duration is only one hour instead of four. You are moving in the right direction. The longer you persevere with your program, the more progress you will experience. *I can't emphasize enough how important it is that you integrate a minimum of an hour's worth of high quality self-care practices into your day, especially those of you who have been experiencing chronic stress.* If you are sick and tired of being sick and tired, the practices in this chapter will be the handles and steps that will get you out of the deep hole you've been stuck in.

Mindful Reminders

Author Peter Russell has provided another useful tool for self-care on his website, www.peterrussell.com. Russell, author of *Waking Up in Time: Finding Inner Peace in Times of Accelerating Change,* has a section on his site called "Mindful Reminders" where you can arrange to randomly receive either verbal or bell reminders via your computer to be mindful of the present moment or bring non-judgmental awareness to your breath, your body or some aspect of your thoughts and emotions. You can modify the settings for how often you want to receive a reminder, such as every fifteen minutes or every hour and a half.

As mentioned earlier, our imaginations can be used for good or harm. When our imagination is prone to creating disturbing, catastrophic scenarios, we die a thousand deaths. On the other hand, we can intentionally use our imagination to provide our inner children with compassionate connection, nurturing, reassurance and guidance. The human brain does not distinguish between an actual event and an imagined one. The brain releases chemicals throughout the body that correspond to the emotions that an imaginary experience elicits. If you picture a threatening scene, then stress hormones such as cortisol are likely to be released. If you picture a loving and soothing scene and bring your attention to the way you are feeling in your body, then chemicals will be released such as oxytocin, the bonding hormone. Our brain is our own personal pharmacy, open 24/7, and we can access it through the use of imagery.

Belleruth Naparstek's Guided Imagery Recordings

Psychotherapist Belleruth Naparstek has created the Health Journeys Guided Imagery series which is used in thousands of hospitals and clinics. Many clinicians, including myself, share these recordings with their clients. Recordings cover subjects such as self-esteem, sleep, weight loss, alcohol, pain, stress, depression and post-traumatic stress disorder.

According to Naparstek, research has shown that guided imagery can be very beneficial in relaxing, calming and elevating mood; lowering blood pressure, blood sugar and cholesterol; speeding up healing from surgical wounds; elevating the immune function; reducing pain and headache; inspiring and motivating; improving performance at work and sports; enhancing intuition and creativity; lowering anxiety and depression and reducing food and drug cravings. You can obtain these recordings at Naparstek's website, www.healthjourneys.com.

Imagery is very valuable in healing attachment trauma and providing restorative attachment experiences. There is no statute of limitations for filling the emotional void from childhood deprivation. Whenever I speak with clients about the emotions that haunt them, I picture a child crying in bed and the adult self closing the door, putting in ear plugs, telling herself, "I don't hear you, I don't hear you!" I imagine the child giving up, falling asleep from exhaustion and then waking up later to find herself still alone. And the crying starts up again. The fact that the inner child is still letting us know she is there through the expression of pain means she is still hungering for connection and comfort. Responding to her compassionately has a tremendous positive effect on the vulnerable inner child. Harder to heal is the child who has given up trying to get a response and gone from protest to despair to detached numbness.

Imaginal Nurturing

Psychotherapist April Steele has developed a form of inner child work called "Imaginal Nurturing." Clients are taught to connect with and develop a relationship with their insecure and lonely inner child. They use their imagination and senses to make the scene as vivid and realistic as possible. Clients can begin an imaginal nurturing session by asking themselves in a kind voice, "Who is in need of comforting right now?" and then bringing that child into the present with the adult. Imaginal nurturing is providing the child with a new, wholesome experience with a caring adult in the present day. *Imaginal nurturing can be performed by an individual at home because the focus is on a positive new experience rather than a potentially overwhelming one. EMDR focuses on a past trauma and so should only be done with the therapist.*

For a client's first experience with imaginal nurturing the therapist will talk directly to the child and in a slow, soothing voice say something like, "Little five-year-old, I want you to know that you are not alone anymore. The adult who is holding you right now is the person you grew up to be. And because you share the same body, you will always be together. She cares very deeply about you. See how her eyes are kind and her touch is gentle? You are safe now. You can relax now. You don't have to do anything to be loved, because you are lovable just the way you are." The client feels the child in her arms or on her lap, makes eye contact with her, attunes to how the child is feeling and asks the child what she needs to feel more secure and loved. Then the client responds imaginally to the child's expressed needs and longings. For example, the child might say, "I just need to know you'll always be there for me" or "Hold me close and tell me why you love me." As the child feels calmer and more secure, the client brings her attention to the good feelings arising in her body.

Imaginal nurturing can be done at the end of EMDR sessions to provide the child with the new lessons and self-beliefs that the client has taken from the experience. It can also be done as a stand-alone intervention in the therapist's office to help clients recognize the power they have to soothe their hurt inner child and manage their emotions. A third option is the following. In our daily lives, whenever we experience strong emotions, we can ask ourselves, "How old do I feel right now?" Each of us may have experienced certain ages of our childhood to be particularly difficult. Maybe age five, age nine and our mid-teens were the times we needed the greatest support. Each of these children may have unique needs that correspond with their stage of development. Five year olds may need lots of physical affection and tenderness. Nine year olds may long for the presence of an adult enjoying their ball games and noticing their strengths. Teens may need to have an adult who encourages them to make their own choices and understands when they experience disappointments. Each visit with an inner child may last less than five minutes and yet be quite powerful because it is providing the perfect antidote to the child's emotional state.

Anxiously-attached individuals begin to replace making demands and desperate bids for attention with self-soothing. They recognize disturbing feelings as an opportunity to provide love and support to their inner child. This gives them a sense of empowerment and self-validation. Taking responsibility for their own emotional state can result in better relationships with others who are relieved of the heavy burden. Those who are avoidantly-attached benefit from practicing imaginal nurturing because their inner child is being provided the loving attention, understanding, recognition and encouragement that breathe life back into their deflated sense of self-worth and competence.

In addition to caring for our younger personality parts when we are experiencing emotional distress, we can proactively meet with inner children on a daily basis to reassure each child of our availability and to strengthen our connection with them. For example, we can check in with a particularly insecure child every morning by saying, "Here I am again. I just want to remind you that you're not alone. I'm an adult and I care about you. If you need a hug, or reassurance or encouragement, just let me know. You're important and I want to give you whatever you need to feel safe and happy. If any person or situation feels overwhelming, remember, you can leave it to me, the adult, to handle. I have learned a lot over the years and I know how to protect you and deal with the world. And I intend to keep on learning better ways of handling difficult things, so that you can have a good life. You deserve that." Then ask the child how she or he is feeling, knowing you care. Then notice the good feelings in your body that come from this nurturing relationship.

Clients who practice imaginal nurturing notice that they feel much calmer in their body from the experience and that the children begin to feel good about themselves and hopeful about having their needs met. Each time an inner child feels a secure connection with the adult self, a sense of security gets wired into the emotional brain, while the circuits for the negative emotional beliefs begin to atrophy from lack of use. Compared to the methods my clients have used throughout their lifetime to deal with disturbing emotions, imaginal nurturing resonates deeply as being right on target. Just this past week, a sophisticated, yet haunted, woman in her sixties told me how pleasantly surprised she has been by doing the imaginal nurturing at home. She said to me: "When you first introduced me to it, I thought it sounded so silly. But I have to admit, using it has helped me to feel more adult, secure and able to handle financial matters that used to intimidate me."

I imagine the inner child as a dry sponge, dying of thirst for love, attention and protection. As soon as the adult self connects and attunes to the child, it is as though water fills those parched pores. The child absorbs the refreshment and feels relieved, sated and content. Practicing imaginal nurturing on a daily basis extends therapy from one day a week to seven, thus expediting the healing. When there are no insecure, deprived parts of our personality, there is no inner turmoil and we are able to focus on the present moment. Throughout my life I've heard people say with annoyance or disdain about someone, "Oh, she is just looking for attention." And I say, "What is wrong with that?" All beings—plant, animal and human—require and thrive on attention. Children need to learn that they are significant and worthy of positive attention. They need to know that they're not invisible, a nuisance or a mistake.

Children who have been treated in a way that makes them doubt their worth may develop a ravenous appetite for attention and try throughout their lives to get it met inappropriately, through clinging, whining, demanding, blaming, threatening, people-pleasing, over-achieving, giving or selling their bodies or turning to anyone who shows them the slightest attention. That is tragic and hugely self-defeating. Instead, relief can be found when our adult nurturing self looks inward and gives our inner children all the love and attention that they have always deserved and needed to thrive. Give to our heart's content.

While our society tends to equate nurturing with women, I have found my male clients willing and able to carry out and benefit from these nurturing experiences. Male children are just as in need and deserving of warmth, emotional support and protection as female children. Many men are loving, tender parents toward their children. Men who are on the path of owning and integrating their childhood emotional experiences appreciate the power and value of responding to their insecure child. A successful businessman I was seeing told me about sitting down to dinner at a restaurant with his date when he began to feel panic and anxiety. He immediately excused himself to go to the bathroom. There he entered a stall, closed his eyes and reassured the little boy inside of him that he was safe. A few minutes later, he returned to the table feeling again like a competent adult. And may I say, all without the use of addictive anti-anxiety medication.

Inner Child Work

Inner children need to be helped to realize that they no longer live in the past circumstances; that they are safe now, they have resources now; they are in the body of competent, caring adults who can make their own decisions now. Child parts that feel emotional distress from the past insecure bond and traumas need a relationship that provides protection, understanding and comfort. Child parts that developed to defend the child from contact with painful emotions need help in recognizing that a responsive adult is now available and that, while their efforts during childhood were tremendously helpful, their efforts are now making matters worse.

These protective child parts can be helped to see that the adult self now has more appropriate ways to handle difficult emotions and relationships and the young parts can finally get their own unmet needs met. Once relieved of their burdens, young parts may be freed up to paint, enjoy the swings or daydream. Some of my clients have found it a great relief to tell a child part that she doesn't have to be present when the adult is involved with difficult people and situations. The child can stay in the bedroom, for example, playing with toys, cuddling a stuffed animal or having a grandparent read them a storybook, while the adult takes care of adult matters.

Adults can care for themselves by anticipating the particular protector or hurt child states that are likely to come up throughout the day. That way, you can identify the earliest cues that a protective or hurt child ego state is kicking in. For example, you may recognize that a part of you is quick to self-sacrifice and placate others in order to avoid conflict. You may know that you are prone to self-criticism to make sure you don't engage in any behavior that might result in others rejecting you. You may have a tendency to feel guilty and inadequate. Each morning, you can prepare yourself by stating to yourself your intention to capitalize on these opportunities to re-parent your inner children. You can keep a journal of the situations that triggered your children's entrance and how effective you were in nurturing or redirecting them. To learn more about caring for your "Internal Family," I suggest you read *Introduction to the Internal Family Systems Model* by Richard C. Schwartz and visit www.selfleadership.org.

⚭ ⚭

I believe that some people who live with chronic stress and tension have so little experience of feeling calm and peaceful in their body and mind, that they may take the debilitated state for granted. They may not really know what they're missing. Other people may be highly aware that what they are experiencing is a serious problem, but have no reliable way to calm down aside from alcohol or drugs, recreational or prescribed. Being calm while half conscious or "out of it" is not the same thing as being calm while fully awake and aware. I believe that you will find a number of the techniques and exercises in this book effective in bringing you periods of rest and solace that you can consciously enjoy. The more you can reliably access inner calm, the more you will be able to recognize the contrasting state of stress and take necessary action to bring yourself relief.

Because the vast majority of us were not fortunate enough to have social and emotional security "wired in" during our formative years, we need to create the skills, resources and experiences that will alter our social and emotional brain circuits. While this involves a lot of conscious effort, it is well worth it. What I often tell my clients is this: "Think of this year as a major turning point and landmark period in your life in which you devote a great deal of time and attention to creating new habits and healing old wounds. Your efforts are going to result in new default settings that will make being alive far more enjoyable."

CHAPTER SIX

Physical Health

Most of us recognize today that our physical health and habits impact our mind and overall functioning. However, we don't sufficiently appreciate how much our mental, emotional and social health affects our bodies. Relationship trauma and chronic or severe stress play huge roles in the wide range of physical conditions that plague us. In order to enjoy optimal health, we need to deeply attend to our minds as well as our bodies.

I'm not denying that other factors impact our health and well-being, including pollution, infection, injury, poor diet, sedentary lifestyles, inadequate sleep, alcohol, drugs, tobacco, and genetic vulnerabilities. Nonetheless, our emotional state is an important contributor to our physical difficulties. To a large degree, our affluent society encourages the kind of lifestyle that creates emotional disharmony and resultant physical problems. Our frantic pace, consumer mentality, pressure to achieve and be self-sufficient, lack of social support, relationship disharmony and deprivation (past and present) and our disconnection from nature and our true self all contribute to a level of stress that, for most of us, threatens our health.

I find it significant that amid all the clamor about health care reform in the United States, nearly all the emphasis has been placed on how it will be paid for, with barely any mention of how to dramatically reduce our susceptibility to illness in the first place. So often we put all our attention on costly treatment in late stages of disease rather than in primary prevention. We seem to take for granted that our bodies will chronically malfunction throughout a good part of our lives. I don't believe it is inevitable to experience the degree of physical and psychological suffering that we do. Except in the case of old age, we need to view ill health as predominantly the result of an imbalance in our mind-body system—a miraculous creation capable of intelligently and simultaneously juggling millions of processes.

How big a role does stress play in physical illness? Physician, psychiatrist and neuroscientist David Servan-Schreiber reports that "Clinical studies suggest that 50 to 75% of all visits to the doctor are primarily related to stress, and that, in terms of mortality, stress poses a more serious risk factor than tobacco. In fact, eight out of ten of the most commonly used medications in the United States are intended to treat problems directly related to stress: antidepressants, anti-anxiety medications, sleeping pills, antacids for heartburn and ulcers, and medications for high blood pressure."

Mental health disorders impact not just the mind but the body. Depression can create aches, pains and restlessness in the body and interfere with sleep, energy, appetite, weight and the drive for sex, activity and even staying alive. One survey indicates that 90% of those with depression get treated through their primary care physicians, most of whom offer drugs and a few minutes of reassurance. If you have understood what I've presented to you in previous chapters, you will find these statistics quite disturbing.

Mind-Body Communication

How do our bodies and our mental, emotional and relational stress intertwine and affect one another? When we feel threatened and the stress response is triggered, our physiology abruptly changes to enable us to meet the crisis. The autonomic nervous system regulates the muscles of our bodies and the organs—heart, lungs, stomach and intestines. The changes that occur under stress are intended specifically to assist our bodies in fighting or fleeing.

That means other functions are shut down to redirect our energies to where they are most needed. One of the functions that is considered non-essential under these circumstances is the immune response. It is ironic that when we are under chronic or severe stress, our bodies become more vulnerable than ever. And to add insult to injury, the vast majority of the time that we become hyper-aroused in contemporary life, the stress response is not even an appropriate or helpful response.

An immune system that is shut down due to an overly-triggered stress response is more vulnerable to becoming dysregulated. Autoimmune, immune deficiency and inflammatory diseases stem from an imbalanced immune system. So, stress and anxiety are major factors in the majority of the illnesses we suffer, both physically and mentally. Chronic inflammation can lead to a host of diseases and conditions, including hay fever, asthma, allergies and hypersensitivities, psoriasis, bursitis, ulcerative colitis, irritable bowel syndrome, spastic colon, pelvic inflammatory disease, Crohn's Disease, lactose and gluten intolerance, gouty arthritis, rheumatoid arthritis, osteoarthritis, chronic obstructive pulmonary disease, metabolic disorders like Type 2 diabetes, osteoporosis, migraines, panic attacks, multiple sclerosis, lupus, Parkinson's Disease, cancer, Alzheimer's and atherosclerosis, or clogged arteries, which can lead to heart attack or stroke. Many of these diseases are chronic, systemic, debilitating and life-altering; some are life-threatening.

Marcelle Pick, an ob/gyn nurse practitioner and co-founder of the Women to Women Health Care Center (www.womentowomen.com), states that low-grade chronic inflammation is also the source of a wide range of common symptoms such as body aches and pain, congestion, frequent infections, diarrhea, dry eyes, indigestion, shortness of breath, skin outbreaks, swelling, stiffness, weight gain and obesity. Part of the stress response involves the release of cortisol throughout the body. When a person experiences chronic stress, the excessive release of cortisol can eventually result in cortisol deficiency and adrenal fatigue or imbalance. According to Pick, these factors, in turn, contribute to sleep disorders, digestive problems, low sex drive, stubborn weight gain, chronic fatigue syndrome, fibromyalgia, arthritis, hypothyroidism, premature menopause, eczema, hypertension and depression.

According to the National Institute of Neurological Disorders and Stroke, when something goes wrong with the autonomic nervous system, it can cause serious problems including blood pressure problems, heart problems, breathing and swallowing difficulties, and erectile dysfunction in men. Some disorders are temporary, but many worsen over time. When they affect your breathing or heart function, these disorders can be life-threatening.

The above-mentioned problems are clearly widespread nowadays. Racing heart and breathing and swallowing difficulties are found in panic attacks, which are a major symptom of anxiety disorders. Breathing difficulties are at the core of asthma. Hypertension affects one in four adults and is a risk factor in stroke, heart attack and heart disease. Erectile dysfunction has become a household term thanks to pharmaceutical companies who are capitalizing on the apparently large number of men with that difficulty.

What this suggests is that the same dynamics that contribute to anxiety and mood disorders, an overworked or imbalanced autonomic nervous system, contribute to the wide range of medical disorders that plague contemporary society. The blitz of advertising from pharmaceutical companies and the biologically-based health professionals, who rely heavily on medication as the key intervention for mental, emotional and physical disorders, will tell you there is nothing to be done except to take pills. Some people may have to subject themselves to a ghastly laundry list of potential side effects in order to derive that benefit.

The Dunedin Multidisciplinary Health and Development Study followed 1,037 participants in a longitudinal study lasting 32 years. The results were reported in the December 2009 issue of the *Archives of Pediatrics and Adolescent Medicine*, "Children exposed to adverse psychosocial experiences have enduring emotional, immune, and metabolic abnormalities that contribute to explaining their elevated risk for age-related disease." The researchers concluded that promoting healthy psychosocial experiences in childhood is essential in order to prevent age-related disorders such as cardiovascular disease.

There is no question that most of us have genetic vulnerabilities to disease. For some of us, the tendency might be for a condition such as attention deficit hyperactivity disorder, obsessive-compulsive disorder, bipolar disorder, depression, schizophrenia or alcoholism. Others are prone to cancer, diabetes, high blood pressure, heart disease or respiratory conditions. Sometimes, a family's history shows members of each generation suffering from a particular disorder or condition. It is the family's Achilles' heel. But what we need to recognize is that a genetic predisposition is not a genetic inevitability. A gene can become activated or remain dormant throughout a lifetime. Extreme stress and the absence of sufficient social and emotional support can be the determining factors between health and illness.

In the coming years, I expect that we will gain a much better understanding of the determining factors that enable people to experience full remissions, even when diseases appear to be entrenched. I believe that the individual's emotional integrity (left and right brain integration) and how much irreparable damage has already occurred to the person's body will be two of the key factors. My emphasis in this book, however, is on primary prevention—what we can do to prevent the development of health problems in the first place, whether they are troublesome, draining, disabling or life-threatening.

Most people and their physicians have no idea just how common it is for the body to become dysregulated and symptomatic due to unresolved psychological issues. So they only look for purely physical causes and medical interventions. I know of many people who have gone from doctor to doctor and specialist to specialist seeking solutions to ailments that were never understood as the aftermath of psychological trauma. I do believe it is important for people to have a complete physical to rule out or treat any condition or disease. However, I also hope that the information provided in this chapter will encourage those with "acting-out bodies" to consider the strong possibility that their bodies are trying to give them a wake-up call. Physical distress may be a blessing in disguise, an opportunity to identify and heal emotional trauma that has not yet been resolved. I hope that one of the major lessons you will take from *Peace in the Heart and Home* is to recognize a lack of peace in your body as a reflection of lack of peace in your heart and home, and that rather than just trying to snuff out fires, you be open-minded and courageous enough to seek out a qualified mental health professional who will help you identify and heal the earliest sources of ignition.

Even when there is a disease that can be treated with medicine, dietary changes, rehabilitation, rest or surgery, it is important, in my opinion, for the person to explore with a therapist what current and/ or past relationship stressors might be impacting his or her physical health. Managed care organizations might be at odds with my point of view. Whether the condition is physical or psychological, the pressure is to patch people up and send them out the door. While this may save money in the short run, in the long run the person is likely to relapse or develop different symptoms and conditions and require treatment again down the line. Or the anxiety that fueled the illness may be rerouted to another family member who will become symptomatic. A family is a system that recycles unprocessed emotions, but I'll get into that in a later chapter. I believe that working intensely with a therapist who is knowledgeable about attachment, trauma and family systems is an extremely worthwhile money, time and energy investment when years, if not decades, of low-grade or severe physical and emotional suffering are replaced with a future of thriving and optimal functioning. True healing work is a gift that keeps on giving.

Too many physicians and medically-oriented mental health professionals have no understanding or appreciation of how insidious and pervasive psychological trauma is and how much suffering it causes for millions of people in their everyday lives. Instead, they see people with severe mental illness, like bipolar disorder, psychosis and borderline personality disorder, as the only ones really in need of extensive psychological intervention. Some refer to all other therapy clients as "the worried well," which to me is a failure in understanding and empathy. Some medical personnel still perceive psychotherapy as being for exceptional, crazy people. The last time a doctor said this to me, I responded, "The people I work with in my therapy practice are just like you and me." The reality is that most of us will need psychotherapy services at some time in our lives, because life is difficult and it is wise to seek help when we are stuck. I have no qualms about telling my clients that I have benefited from participating in psychotherapy.

The Expressive Voice of the Body: Seven Stories

People who seek psychotherapy for psychological, behavioral or relationship problems tend to experience a wide range of bodily complaints. I'd like to share several anecdotes to demonstrate the wide range of ways the body can express emotional issues a person may have difficulty processing consciously. These stories call to mind the research of Hoppe and Bogen and their observation that "Alexithymia, [the inability to put words to feelings] and somatization disorder [the conversion of emotional conflicts into bodily disease] may reflect left-right dissociation." I'm providing quite a few anecdotes because I believe that the vast majority of people don't recognize what their bodies are really telling them. The way I see it, our emotions are music and our bodies are instruments that play the discordant tunes. But if we don't know how to read music, we just think the instrument is defective.

Marty: "Something is Wrong With Me"

My client Marty came to me because of turmoil in his marriage. In addition to his emotional and relationship difficulties, Marty had a history of physical ailments. Each ailment started in a subtle way, escalated as time went on and didn't abate. For a full year he went from doctor to doctor, ranging from alternative to traditional orientations, trying to resolve a chronic digestive system disturbance that involved abdominal cramping, bloating, diarrhea and passing gas. Each health professional had a different diagnosis and recommendations, but in retrospect, it seems clear that he suffered from irritable bowel syndrome. Marty became obsessed with his condition and plagued by feelings of confusion, anxiety, helplessness, isolation and fear of being humiliated.

One morning, Marty woke up full of dread. He had made plans with his wife to drive two hours to a major New York City museum where bathrooms were hard to find. Following the event, he had promised to attend a gathering at his brother's home, which was a 45-minute drive from the museum. Then he faced a two-hour drive back home. Before even leaving the house, Marty had to use the toilet about eight times. Anxiously, he wondered how he would ever make it through the day without a disastrous accident.

Yet, throughout the entire ride to the museum, the museum exhibit and the drive to his brother's home, Marty had no urge to use the bathroom. Once he got to his brother's home, however, where he had easy access to a bathroom, he found himself in the bathroom at least a dozen times over the course of a few hours. During the entire ride home, he again experienced no urge to use a toilet. How did Marty's body turn on and off like that and spare him the humiliation that seemed inevitable?

That period of Marty's life was not the only one in which he suffered physically and mentally. He also told me about the year in his life when he was plagued with an extensive and ugly skin rash that wouldn't go away, despite regular visits to a dermatologist. What was extraordinary about this experience was that the rash never appeared on Marty's face, neck or hands, so it was invisible to others. Nonetheless, Marty was obsessed with his devastating condition and felt helpless, anxious and ashamed about it—just as he had with his digestive disorder. Again, how could Marty's body give him such strong signals that "something is wrong with me" and yet spare him the ultimate humiliation of others discovering his dark secret?

In many ways, Marty's childhood family was stable and to out-siders seemed normal. There was no domestic violence, substance abuse, divorce, physical abuse, sexual abuse, physical neglect, or frequent moves. At community events, Marty's father was jovial, sociable and well-liked. Marty's mother was sweet and gentle. People adored her. At school, Marty seemed happy-go-lucky, a self-starter who got excellent grades. Yet, under the surface, he suffered greatly and nobody had any idea what his daily home and emotional life were like. Just as Marty's physical symptoms were hidden from others' awareness, so his painful emotional reality was known only to him.

At home, Marty's father was very moody, controlling, perfectionistic and unable to empathize. He often expressed anger, disgust, distrust, disapproval and disappointment in family members. Marty's mother, meanwhile, was distracted, child-like, emotionally unavailable, passive and prone to dissociation. Whenever Marty tearfully pleaded with his father to understand him and allow him to participate in age-appropriate activities, his father was incapable of providing understanding and support. Almost every request Marty made of his father was met with resistance and refusal. The few times his father did relent, his tone and words implied that Marty was selfish and undeserving. When Marty cried alone in his room after arguments with his father, his mother was nowhere to be found. When he cried at the dinner table, his mother was distracted and unresponsive. When his parents had their recurring futile arguments and Marty cried and begged them to get along, they were too out of control to stop and comfort him.

In our work together, Marty was able to process the pain, loneliness, shame, helplessness and fear these experiences had caused him. The integration of his emotional history into his conscious awareness was the end of the right and left brain hemisphere dissociation. Marty's body no longer had to express for him something that was hidden and denied. His physical symptoms vanished. Marty's experiences were a major lesson to me in the power of the psyche to deliver a physical condition that reflects the person's emotional drama, to fine tune its presentation, and to alert the person to the presence of something deeply out of whack.

Gary: Who's in the Driver's Seat?

You may recall our previous discussion of polarized ego states, in which conflicted parts of our personality try, each in their own way, to protect us. Gary was an extremely hard-working lawyer whose bent over posture seemed to reflect the burdens he always carried. Gary could never give himself permission to rest, play or ask for help. His life was one endless string of responsibilities and chores. The words he spoke and the lifeless tone of his voice also revealed how discouraged and long-suffering he was. The part of his personality in the driver seat of his life was a tyrant, pushing him to be constantly productive.

Eventually the chronic stress took its toll, and Gary had a stroke while only in his forties. Once that occurred, it gave Gary the opportunity he had never allowed himself before to take it easy. Now the previously dominated part of Gary's personality that had wanted to rest and be free of pressure was in the driver's seat. It had taken a medical crisis for a change in his lifestyle to occur and for him to stop saying "yes" to demands and to start saying, "not now." Gary was unable to handle the same mental and physical challenges and pace as previously, yet he didn't instead capitalize on the freed-up time to create a new, fulfilling and balanced life that would include friendship, reflection, pleasure or creativity. He had swung from one polar extreme to the other: from over-functioning to under-functioning, both of which are unhealthy. It's always tragic when a person has to wait until his body sets limits for him, rather than knowing, respecting and asserting his own legitimate psychological needs.

Catherine: A Migraine Tug of War

After 35 years of a painfully lonely marriage, Catherine was struggling with whether or not to leave her husband. The insecure child part of Catherine feared that she could never make it on her own. The adult in her knew that she was competent, that her husband had never invested in the relationship and had refused to join her in therapy and that to stay with him would be sacrificing any chance of happiness. Ever since her children had left home, Catherine began to suffer migraines. Her husband continued to ignore her except to express contempt. In therapy, as Catherine began to face the decades of pain and helplessness that she'd dissociated from and that had led to major depression, her migraines began to disappear.

However, when Catherine began to take steps to separate from her husband, she suffered a severe migraine that stopped her in her tracks. Her sister, meaning well, suggested that maybe the migraine indicated she really didn't want to divorce. Catherine stopped taking steps to separate, and the migraine subsided.

As Catherine reflected on this pattern, she realized that the part of her that felt fearful and caused the migraine was a small child who lacked the judgment and perspective of her adult self. Once again, she began to take steps toward separation. At a later therapy session, as she discussed her fears about her future, she immediately felt a vice-like tightening in her head. When I asked her what words that bodily sensation would use if it could, she said, "Don't slide back! Don't give up on yourself! You'll regret it if you do!" Catherine and I realized that her migraines reflected the internal conflict between the adult part of her that advocates being true to herself and the compliant girl who sacrifices herself by always doing what others expect of her.

From that point forward, the more that Catherine vividly imagined reassuring the inner child that she no longer had to live by the rules of the past, the less she experienced migraines, the more her adult self was in charge of decision-making and the greater self-worth, self-confidence and determination she experienced.

Ellen: The Mind-Body Shouting, "Enough! I Can't Take Anymore!"

Ellen grew up in a household in which both of her parents were anxious and out of control. Her father was extremely irrational, narcissistic, judgmental, insensitive, controlling and aggressive with his wife and three children. Both parents were physically abusive to the children as well. The tension in Ellen's home was so chronic and intense that by early adulthood, she became an alcoholic, developed irritable bowel syndrome, stopped getting her period and was diagnosed with adrenal fatigue.

After a series of panic attacks, Ellen experienced what felt to her like a seizure. Ever since then, her body felt both numb and as though an electrical current were running through it. Her vision, hearing and sense of balance also became distorted. These chronic symptoms were extremely disturbing to her. Additionally, Ellen experienced two episodes of severe withdrawal symptoms from changes in her anti-anxiety medication, resulting in visits to the emergency room.

When Ellen came to see me, her sense of shame, guilt, anxiety, fear and helplessness were severe. Yet, because of her intense sense of loyalty to her parents, she held them entirely blameless. Over the course of a few years of working together, including EMDR work, Ellen developed a much more appropriate and adult perspective on herself and her relationship with her parents. She now is capable of self-compassion, self-pride and self-validation. She can now assert herself, even with her father. She is off anti-anxiety medications, maintaining sobriety and no longer has irritable bowel syndrome. She continues, however, to struggle with fatigue and the disturbing sensory phenomena. Ellen had been in therapy previously throughout her adult life, but the treatment had been limited to drugs and talk. No one had ever told her that there were other, more deeply effective methods of addressing her problems.

Ellen's life is a lesson and incentive to us all to seek trauma-oriented treatment as early as possible. The longer we suffer from unresolved trauma, the more the various systems of our body get dysregulated and exhausted, the more dysfunctional neural networks get entrenched, the harder it is to recalibrate and heal our systems.

Nonetheless, Ellen continues to make great strides. Currently, she is in the midst of a second family crisis in a few months. First a drug-addicted relative died and now her beloved mother is in the hospital. In the past, surrounded by highly dysfunctional family members, Ellen would have absorbed their emotions and become filled with panic, guilt, shame and helplessness. Today, she is able to be in their presence, observe them objectively and be aware of feelings of anger, disgust and disappointment along with the urge to shake them and say, "wake up!" Much of the time, she is able to feel centered, calm and confident while her family members mindlessly spew emotional venom. While she doesn't breathe in their pain, she *is* compassionate and has loving feelings for them; so she is not shut down and numb, an important distinction. At times, she is able to firmly point out to her father what he needs to do, for both the family's sake and his own, and her father has taken her seriously and responded to her suggestions.

When Ellen shared this information with me, I told her how impressed I am with how well she is managing these challenging people and situations. I told her that it's one thing to access calm and one's center when meditating alone in one's room or at a spiritual retreat, but another thing entirely to sustain one's sense of self, composure and power in the midst of rampant unconsciousness. It is a reflection of how far she has come.

Susan: The Picked-On Child

Another client of mine, 20-year old Susan, grew up with parents who were both depressed and highly critical. Mealtime was painful for Susan, as her parents found a thousand little ways to judge her. Susan's mother had grown up the victim of her brother's constant teasing and tormenting. When Susan visited with relatives, she dreaded seeing her uncle who always managed to bring her to tears with his teasing. The reason Susan had sought therapy was because she had picked at her skin to the point that she felt compelled to wear clothing that would cover what *to her* was ugly and deeply shameful. In the summer, Susan refused to wear a bathing suit, shorts or a tank top—only long pants and long-sleeved shirts. Susan's compulsive behavior, which played out on her body, perfectly reflected the daily attachment trauma of being picked on.

Susan told me that she had been scratching her skin since kindergarten and that her stepsister and father also had this habit. Her mother was a perfectionist and chronic worrier who had to have her hair and make-up perfect before leaving the house. Susan hoped that therapy would help her to feel more self-confidence, direction and drive. She also hoped to be able to find a boyfriend so that "who I am matters to someone."

A major part of my work with Susan was doing EMDR on a number of memories in which she was helpless, humiliated and made to feel inadequate. Besides painful experiences with family members, there were other traumatic experiences like experiencing unwanted kissing and touching by her teacher when she was a young teen. At the start of that EMDR session, Susan was feeling guilt, shame and powerlessness and believing, "I'm stupid and weak." By the end of the session she was fully feeling, "I am strong and able to protect myself." She told me, "I can tell who respects me—if someone doesn't respect me, why should I trust or respect them? I will decide what I want. Others don't have the right to step over that line."

By the time we had healed the traumatic memories and related current triggers, Susan had discontinued picking her skin and felt self-worth and self-confidence. In the summer, she began to wear a bathing suit, shorts and T-shirts. She had also begun to carry out plans to move out of her family home and transfer to a college where she would live on campus.

Barbara: "I Can Handle Anything"

As a child, Barbara was highly sensitive to her mother's emotional pain. She did everything in her power to make her mother happy. She wrote her mother hundreds of love notes to cheer her up. She entertained her mother with songs and dances. She ignored any problems of her own and wore a smile. But, no matter how hard she tried, the results of her efforts were always fleeting. In adulthood, Barbara made a career out of being compassionate and responsive to anyone in need. Wherever she looked, Barbara saw a worthy cause that aimed to alleviate suffering or provide encouragement and support to the disheartened. She invested huge amounts of time and energy volunteering and received a great deal of recognition for her selflessness. Barbara had a big heart for everyone but never asked for anything for herself.

Over the years, Barbara experienced migraines and other physical pain, was diagnosed with breast cancer and then developed heart problems requiring multiple surgeries. She never saw any connection between her sensitive heart, self-sacrifice and physical ailments. Each time she overcame another medical challenge, she was relieved and saw it as proof that she was resilient and could handle anything. Barbara's doctors never helped her look at the big picture and explore what might be contributing to her pattern of physical vulnerability.

Barbara's goal in therapy was to find the recipe for ending her husband's complaints and misery. She had no interest at all in exploring her own feelings, needs or patterns. In her eyes, her only problem was that her husband had a problem. As a result, Barbara was not able to make use of therapy. She continued to experience tremendous stress, which put her at high risk of developing further life-threatening health problems.

Sharon: The Battle for a Child's Soul

Sharon grew up in a home with a father who constantly spoke about evil and righteousness and judged Sharon's behaviors as shameful. Her mother was loving toward her but unable to control the cruel behaviors of other family members. Whenever Sharon saw dark shadows in her bedroom, her father told her it was the devil, which terrified her and consigned her to a lifetime of seeing threatening dark shadows and black hooded figures. In early adolescence, Sharon's older sister repeatedly told her: "Boys only like you because you are a slut." Sharon remembers having been a cheerful and bubbly little girl, but as her father and sister became more and more irrational and hostile toward her, she felt more and more shameful and unworthy. The more Sharon's mother saw good in Sharon, the more her father and sister saw evil in her.

Sharon began to abuse alcohol and drugs. Over the years, as her emotional pain persisted, she became promiscuous, developed anorexia and then bulimia and shopped compulsively. Sharon also engaged in long-distance running, often tuning out pain that indicated injuries. Sharon used dissociation as a major strategy for managing her painful emotions. She later developed panic attacks, severe migraines and vertigo. She also developed RSD, Reflex

Sympathetic Dystrophy or Complex Regional Pain Syndrome, which involved severe and chronic pain in her limbs.

When I met Sharon, she told me, "I'm always trying to find that calm I'm missing. I always want to make sure everyone knows how insignificant I felt as a child. I want validation, reassurance and comfort. Nobody ever listened or heard me. I can go into a black hole. What gets me mad is—'won't somebody come and pick me up'?" Based on Sharon's extensive symptoms, I diagnosed her with PTSD, major depression and somatization disorder, which is a chronic condition in which a person has multiple medically unexplained physical symptoms.

Sharon had seen other therapists before and experienced talk therapy. In our work together, Sharon eagerly used the affect management, mindfulness and imaginal nurturing strategies and resources I introduced her to. She was enormously courageous as she processed powerful and painful emotions in EMDR sessions. As a result, not only did she dramatically alter her self-image and self-confidence and discontinue her self-destructive behaviors, but her physical symptoms, including the RSD, disappeared. The bubbly, enthusiastic person she had once been returned in full force and she expressed great joy and self-love as she reconnected with her true self.

Eight months after therapy ended, Sharon wrote me a letter that ended this way: "Well, it's hard to put into exact words how proud of myself I am! The kids see me really happy, really peaceful. The lessons that are being learned, by us all, are incredible. We appreciate the simple things, the uncomplicated things that life now gives us. The three of us are easily and simply happy. So, all in all, I feel Wonderful!! I feel normal! I deal with everyday B.S., just like everyone else. I work, just like everyone else. I'm tired and I struggle just like everyone else. I cry, like everyone. I laugh always, because I don't blame myself for everyday 'hard' situations. I smile because that's life and I'm A-Part-of-It!!"

Sharon's story reminds me of the current plague of mysterious conditions that torment and exhaust so many women. Reflex Sympathetic

Dystrophy, fibromyalgia, chronic fatigue syndrome, chronic Epstein Barr Syndrome, chronic pain, multiple sclerosis, Lupus, and Rheumatoid Arthritis are so prevalent nowadays. They seem to be the equivalent of the paralysis, tics, hallucinations, sensory distortions and body pain that Freud saw in Victorian women patients whom he diagnosed with hysteria. If you look at websites by both medical and lay groups, it is clear that they have no idea what is at the root of these widespread ailments. What *is* clear is that the victims feel helpless, overwhelmed, panicked, afraid, confused and in despair. This sounds to me like what a lot of children experience in their families of origin but have to dissociate from in order to survive.

I must acknowledge here that not all people with chronic emotional distress or childhood trauma develop these tormenting health problems. There is still a great deal for us to learn about the various factors that contribute to or shield us from physical and mental dysfunction. Just the same, when people do have medically unexplained severe or recurrent physical complaints, by looking at their attachment and trauma history, I believe we will probably find ample justification for later development of physical and psychological distress. The recognition of the traumatic history is not just an excuse or explanation. It provides a framework and direction for therapeutic intervention. As Sharon's case indicates, there is potential and hope for overcoming these mysterious and distressing conditions and progressing, not just to a non-symptomatic state, but to a state of optimal well-being.

Healing Approaches

At this point I'd like to mention the work of neurologist Robert Scaer, MD, author of *The Trauma Spectrum: Hidden Wounds and Human Resiliency* and *The Body Bears the Burden: Trauma, Dissociation and Disease*. For 20 years, Dr. Scaer served as Medical Director of Rehabilitation Services at the Mapleton Center, a division of Boulder Community Hospital in Colorado. Many of his patients suffered from severe and chronic pain disorders, such as RSD, that had been precipitated by minor motor vehicle accidents at speeds as low as 10 to 15 miles per hour. What should have been simple, short-term whiplash, mushroomed into complex, long-lasting physical and psychological symptoms and what Dr. Scaer came to call Whiplash Syndrome. Eventually, Dr. Scaer began exploring the backgrounds of these patients and discovered that the majority of them had been victims of multiple traumatic experiences or severe child abuse.

These dramatic findings led to Dr. Scaer's study of the role of traumatic stress in mental illness, chronic diseases and baffling syndromes. Dr. Scaer sees psychological trauma as pervasive in the average person's life. He is a strong advocate for interventions that connect directly with the body, particularly Somatic Experiencing. Somatic Experiencing (SE) was developed by Dr. Peter Levine, author of a book I highly recommend, *Waking the Tiger: Healing Trauma: The Innate Capacity to Transform Overwhelming Experiences*. SE is a gentle therapy for resolving and discharging unresolved survival energies generated by trauma. The clinician first helps the client access a state of strength and then has him or her gradually attend to the nuances and edges of the nervous system activation. Like EMDR, SE is a body-oriented trauma treatment that focuses on body sensations, accesses the body's wisdom and is highly regarded among increasing numbers of mental health professionals.

Another innovator in the realm of mind-body medicine, David Servan-Schreiber, is an advocate of natural healing methods such as actively developing "heart coherence." Dr. Servan-Schreiber, a physician, psychiatrist and neuroscientist, was a founding member of the Board of Directors of Doctors Without Borders and director of The University of Pittsburgh's Shadyside Hospital Center for Complementary Medicine and is a certified EMDR instructor. He is also the author of an excellent book entitled, *The Instinct to Heal: Curing Stress, Anxiety, and Depression Without Drugs and Without Talk Therapy*. More information can be found at www.instincttoheal.org.

In Servan Schreiber's book he quotes research from the Institute of HeartMath in Boulder Creek, California (www.heartmath.org) that supports the idea that a key path to physical and emotional health involves developing heart coherence. HeartMath's research says that the heart has 40,000 neurons, called "the little brain in the heart," which communicates back and forth with the emotional brain. The emotional brain is linked to the autonomic nervous system, which controls the physiology of the body: heart rate, blood pressure, appetite, sleep, sexual drive and the immune system. To heal stress, anxiety and depression it is necessary to act on the emotional brain. Based on his extensive knowledge and experience, he strongly recommends using methods of healing that act on the body rather than rely only on thought and language. *The Instinct to Heal* is devoted to seven such methods, including heart coherence and EMDR.

HeartMath researchers describe coherence as a highly efficient state in which the nervous, cardiovascular, hormonal and immune systems are working efficiently, orderly and harmoniously. Research shows that when we activate this state, we experience greater emotional stability, mental clarity and improved cognitive function. When our heart rate variability, or cardiac rhythm, enters a state of coherence, the rhythm is optimal and the message it sends to the emotional brain, is "Relax. All is well. There is no need to activate the stress response." Heart coherence has been shown to lower stress and protect against depression, high blood pressure, heart disease and a variety of aging processes. By contrast, when our heart rate variability is reduced and chaotic—the common pattern for most of us—the rhythm communicated to the brain activates the fight-flight reaction, which sets off a cascade of physiological and chemical changes in the body. These changes, especially when recurrent and chronic, result in stress, anxiety and depression.

The good news is that we can develop heart coherence through optimal breathing, one of the few autonomic functions that is within our conscious control. Our lungs, heart and brain create a feedback loop that can be influenced through mindfulness of the breath combined with thoughts and images that generate feelings of gratitude, compassion and love. Servan-Schreiber says, "The results experienced by men and women who have discovered coherence and practice it regularly are almost too good to be true. The control of anxiety and depression, the lowering of blood pressure, the increase in the hormone DHEA, the stimulation of the immune system—what these preliminary results suggest is not only a slowing down of the aging process, but a turning back of the physiological clock. However difficult to believe, the nature of these results matches the nature of the physical and psychological damage inflicted by stress. If stress can cause so much harm, I am not entirely surprised that inner mastery can do so much good."

There are a number of ways to develop an optimal breathing pattern, most of them quite simple. One is yoga, an age-old method of self-care and self-actualization. Another, more contemporary approach to cultivating mindful breathing that Dr. Servan-Schreiber describes and some of my clients have found very helpful is a product called emWave Personal Stress Reliever, created by HeartMath. You can find a wealth of information about the science of the heart, stress and optimal well-being at www.heartmath.org and about the emWave at www.emwave.com.

The scientifically-researched emWave is basically a portable bio-feedback device. It is useful for those who like an approach that assists with motivation and discipline and provides immediate, tangible feedback. I have purchased a few emWaves that I lend to clients so they can practice entering and maintaining heart coherence. With the feedback they receive, they come to recognize when they are in coherence. Once they reliably can sense that physiological state, they often don't need further reliance on the device, although some of my clients have chosen to purchase their own.

Practicing mindful breathing, while focusing on positive emotions, just 20 minutes a day can be very helpful in recalibrating the nervous system and helping to regulate sleep, appetite and mood. For those who have experienced chronic stress, I recommend practicing the breathing 20 minutes three times a day for a total of an hour. Because this intervention has no negative side effects and so many benefits, I recommend doing more rather than less, especially if your body has suffered decades-long excessive stress. Our nervous system needs serious help in getting out of the automatic rut of anticipating threat.

Concluding Thoughts

It is quite appalling and tragic that billions of dollars a year are invested in solutions that provide so little benefit, create so many side effects, treat only the symptoms and fail to identify and heal the root causes. Between our lives being so harried, there being such a confusing information explosion and our inclination to look for easy answers, we are not taking advantage of the solutions that require courage and discipline and truly are effective and long-lasting. Not only do the strategies that Dr. Servan-Schreiber and I recommend significantly reduce suffering, but they also elicit states of mind, body and emotion that are optimal.

I believe it is our destiny and that we human beings deserve not just to stop limping through life, but to thrive, feel joyful passion about being alive and use our energy to be creative and nourish each other. Is any pill ever going to be able to do that for the vast majority of us, reliably and without disturbing side effects? If the day ever comes that such a pill is manufactured, I suspect Rod Serling of the Twilight Zone will have written about it and the consequences will somehow be perverse.

CHAPTER SEVEN

Intimate Relationships

THE GOOD NEWS ABOUT OUR love relationships is that there is
a rapidly emerging scientific theory to explain what takes place
between intimate partners. There is also an effective therapy approach
that corresponds with that theory. The patterns found in happy, secure
couples versus insecure couples are highly predictable and understandable when you have the proper map to guide you. There *is* a method in
the madness—and better yet, a method out of the madness. Let me tell
you about it.

The very emotional needs we instinctively tried to get our parents
to meet, long ago, are the same ones we consciously or unconsciously
long for our adult romantic partner to fulfill. Adults who are in touch
with their instinctual attachment longings and needs will be looking for
connection in the form of accessibility, responsiveness and engagement.
Or put another way, they will expect their partner to be available, attuned
and emotionally present and to respond in a way that is comforting. If
we've been lucky enough to have had a secure attachment experience

with our parents, we will feel whole and valuable and our partner will be the frosting on the cake. Because we had our basic emotional needs sufficiently met in childhood, we are unlikely to feel panic and go into defense mode when our partner at times behaves poorly, invalidates our experience or isn't immediately available. We will intuitively know how to soothe ourselves and repair the bond with our partner. Trust, safety and love will be regained over and over again. Our life will be a balanced blend of satisfying relationships, activities and solitude.

When we are accustomed to being responded to by our parents and experiencing repair of breaks in harmony, we will not find it comfortable, familiar or desirable to be in a relationship with someone who is overbearing, rejecting, indifferent or undependable. We will be drawn to someone who is attentive, sensitive and responsive while, at the same time, able to request and receive support in return. When our partner's caring behavior is "good enough," just as with "good enough mothering," then there is a feeling of psychological safety. We feel heard, understood, empowered, supported, respected, valued and loved, which reinforces our positive beliefs about ourselves, others and life. This makes us appreciate our partner and life and able to give back with a generous spirit. The mutually nurturing pattern of interaction is a "secure attachment cycle."

Unfortunately, the majority of us did not receive "good enough parenting" or suffered too much trauma to feel secure. That means the people we are attracted to and the way we deal with our emotions are inevitably a recipe for disaster. Not only are we *not* going to get the frosting; we're not even going to get the cake. Worse than that, we eventually get gruel. In adulthood, as in childhood, the person we depend upon the most turns out to be both the source of our greatest longing and our greatest pain. It's not exaggerating to say that we turn out to be each other's "designated tormentor." The relationship becomes more a marriage of two sets of defenses than two authentic selves. Marriage and life then become not for the faint of heart.

In the beginning of an intimate partnership, there is almost always a powerful sense of hope and promise: *This* is the person who is going to, well . . . bring me the happiness I've always dreamed of. For the partner with an anxious-preoccupied attachment style, who has lived with the undying hope that love, connection and validation could be obtained, if she just tried hard enough, there is finally a sense of fulfillment. For the avoidantly-attached partner, there may be the unconscious recognition that, "Here finally is someone who is pleased with me, who sees me as good enough and who won't expect much of me because she is willing to do all the work of keeping us connected. Here is someone who won't be disappointed in me and who will do enough feeling, investing and risking for both of us."

In the early months and even years of many relationships, there may be few signs of the challenges that lie ahead. Difficulties might not emerge until the couple starts having children. Often, threads of frustration, disappointment, hurt, doubt and loneliness may be so insidious and feel so familiar that we don't fully recognize or question them. If we do question what's happening, we may do so in an unproductive way and/or our partner may fail to understand or appreciate our concerns. But at this stage in the relationship, our ability to forgive and forget may be strong enough to overshadow our doubts and fears. For others, especially those with a fearful attachment style, major problems are woven into the relationship right from the very start. The relationship is chronically tumultuous and yet, somehow, the partners can't let go of each other. For them, to be in relationship is to be in misery; blanketed by perpetual storm clouds and relieved by the occasional glimpse of blue sky. Being clenched in an emotional wrestling match is the story of their lives.

Keeping Up with Change

Throughout human history, the majority of couples were an integral part of an extended family or small community. Each partner had access to others who could provide social support, connection, stimulation, friendship, comfort and advice. This helped provide stability to a marriage. By contrast, in contemporary society many couples are overworked, over-scheduled, isolated and live far from extended family, often in housing developments that lack any sense of community. This puts more pressure on each partner to meet the other's social and emotional needs. The smaller the support system is, the more intense the marital bond, the higher the expectations and the greater chance of conflict. When expectations are inevitably not met, the key question becomes, "Will the partner be able to express his or her vulnerable feelings about the unmet needs; feelings such as sadness, hurt, loneliness and fear?" Unfortunately, partners are more likely to respond to relationship conflict with one of two extremes: nagging, demanding, blaming, criticizing and attacking *or* burying the feelings and needs.

Another current contributor to relational conflict is our increasingly complex, heterogeneous, democratic society. Until very recently, there was a hierarchy in family life with the male adult in charge and the women and children conditioned to be compliant. There was less overt conflict within a family because women and children knew they were powerless and learned to dismiss, ignore or keep their opinions, feelings and needs to themselves. If a man was overwhelmed by disturbing emotions and events, he was entitled to release his frustrations on his wife and children as well as on enemies of the larger community. There was no expectation on the woman's part or in society that things could or should be different. Likewise, in certain cultures elders have been perceived as having greater wisdom and deserving of greater respect and decision making power than younger generations. The more rigid, simple and accepted the social pattern, the more stable the society. Stability does not necessarily mean that a pattern is conducive to the well-being of the group's members, just that the pattern is predictable and steady.

The process of social evolution has produced democracy, which has extended rights to a much wider portion of society, making it possible for more people to be valued, respected and empowered. The price of a democratic society, however, is more internal conflict and less stability. Today, in most homes and marriages, there is the expectation that women have equal rights and decision-making power. I believe that a major reason there is so much marital strife and divorce nowadays is that we are in the midst of a major unprecedented social experiment.

Now, more than ever before, people, especially women, expect that their marriage will be much more than a social contract to share their material resources, distribute household responsibilities, raise children and be there for each other in sickness and old age. Since the various liberation movements of the 1960s, people have been trying to create something that they never witnessed or experienced before—democratic marriages that respect the feelings, needs and concerns of *both* partners—"life, liberty and the pursuit of happiness" *within* a marriage.

Not only are both partners deemed equals, but also deserving of having more than their tangible needs met. They now feel deserving of psychological fulfillment, as well. This is very new. This new challenge may result in many casualties in the early stages of mastering the evolutionary leap, but the process is worthwhile as we seek to function at a higher level of psychological and spiritual maturity. Instead of a large-scale war between two different external cultures, this cultural "war" is going on within our individual homes.

How Couples Try to Cope

While these and other societal dynamics are shifting rapidly, the average marriage is rife with frustration and deprivation for *both* partners. Women now are more vocal and outspoken when they feel disappointment and dissatisfaction in the marriage, but their style of expression is typically aggressive, inefficient and self-defeating. Most men are newcomers to the idea of emotional needs and so are at a loss as to what their wives are looking for from them and what their own emotional needs are. While their wives are looking for "software" such as warmth, sharing and caring, men may be attempting to prove their love through "hardware" such as being an invulnerable "rock" and reliable provider, doing chores around the house, staying out of trouble and giving practical advice.

As mentioned earlier in this book, avoidantly-attached spouses tend to be in the passive, reactive, self-reliant, distancing role and to minimize problems and needs—both their partners' and their own. Think independent cats. By contrast, the anxiously-attached spouse is in the pursuing, attention-seeking, demanding, entitled role and feels compelled to deal with problems, emotions and needs. Think affection-starved dogs. Frustrated anxiously-attached spouses may eventually shut down and withdraw and become what are called "burned out pursuers." Fearful-attached spouses may alternate on a daily basis between making demands and distrustfully withdrawing. So, while on our wedding day we may have visions of equality, mutuality, responsiveness and fairness, putting them into practice can be extremely hard, especially when we have had no emotional history of living that way and intimacy triggers so many unresolved fears and unhealed wounds.

When the honeymoon is over and spouses face each other with all of their unacknowledged fears and unfinished emotional business, most partners are unprepared to cope. They had hoped, consciously or unconsciously, to feel connected, known, understood, loved, respected and supported. Instead, they find that their partner is critical, rejecting, nagging, dismissive, unavailable or shut down. Feelings of psychological safety vanish and defensive behaviors escalate into a damaging "negative attachment cycle." The person they once perceived as their safe haven and source of comfort has transformed into someone hurtful, repulsive or threatening. Partners increasingly question whether they've chosen the right person, whether they will ever be able to get their needs met and whether they should cut their losses and abandon what clearly appears to be a sinking ship.

The various coping mechanisms partners rely on while the relationship is deteriorating inevitably make matters much worse. Coping strategies may include shutting down, porn and Internet addictions, keeping longer work hours, abusing substances and other compulsive behaviors. It also can include what are called "triangles," investing in other relationships to keep the marriage in a holding pattern. The third party could be a lover, Internet relationship, child, best friend, elderly parent, therapist or minister. The third party could even be sports, a pet or even a house. I've heard of cases in which once the couple finished building their dream house, they divorced.

Using these kinds of problematic coping strategies, marriages may hang on by a thread for years. By the time a couple finally finds the courage to seek professional help, there can be so much hurt, hopelessness, disconnection, distrust and anger that they may perceive the relationship as doomed and not worth trying to resurrect. While the therapist may believe that the couple could create a secure bond through couples therapy, all it takes is one member of the couple losing hope and motivation for the plug on the marriage to be pulled. It's sad for the therapist to witness the end of a marriage when she has hope that, with courage and hard work, this relationship could grow into something better than either partner had previously experienced.

Some partners may not be capable or willing, at this stage of their life, to take the risks necessary to try and build trust and security. Sometimes the history of pain experienced with a partner is too overwhelming and the person seeks a new lease on life. Some couples have worked bravely in therapy but, despite the best efforts of the couple and their therapist, one or both partners decide that the changes are not substantial enough to continue in the marriage. Divorce *does not* mean that the members of the family will now have no chance for experiencing security or fulfillment. How the couple navigates the separation and divorce process will have a great deal to do with both the practical and emotional experience of this transition. An adversarial path is not inevitable. The couple might select a process such as mediation or a collaborative law practice which work for the best outcome for all family members. Information on these alternatives can be found at the following websites: www.acrnet.org for the Association for Conflict Resolution and www.collaborativepractice. com for the International Academy of Collaborative Professionals.

Also, if the couple is able to insulate their children from conflicts both during and after the divorce, this will be the single biggest predictor for the children's functioning as they transition from one household to two. All individuals, couples and families are faced with challenges of some type. Whatever difficult reality we are faced with, whether or not of our own choosing, we always have the capacity to choose our approach and responses to that challenge. Fortunately there are many professionals trained to help individuals and couples with this transition.

What helps us rise above life's trials, whatever they may be, is processing our own and our children's emotions mindfully and with compassion. It is in any human being's best interest to acknowledge their full range of emotions, including anguish, hopelessness, anger and hatred. This, of course, must be done in the proper setting and at an appropriate time. When we are able to experience a safe holding environment while our emotions flow, there is a greater likelihood we will be able to eventually experience acceptance, self-compassion and maybe even compassion for the person who has hurt us. If we find that we become stuck in anger, hatred, revenge or aversion, therapy such as EMDR may be very helpful in enabling us to move through these difficult feelings into acceptance. Despite the pain of an unwelcome life passage, we may ultimately experience a sense of growth and new possibilities. The chapter on Mindfulness and Being will speak more about cultivating this special state of mind which entails seeing the whole picture with curiosity, clarity, courage and compassion.

Advice for Couples

There are many ways nowadays for couples to find out what behaviors contribute to a solid, satisfying marriage. There are articles, books, audio and DVD programs, weekend workshops, conferences and websites. Relational therapist Terrence Real has written an excellent book: *How Can I Get Through to You: Reconnecting Men and Women.* Information about his books, CDs and workshops can be found at his website, www.terryreal.com.

Clinical psychologist and researcher John Gottman (www.gottman.com), is renowned for over three decades of couples research to discover what makes marriage succeed—or not. He has written many books for the public and offers couple workshops and retreats. Based on his findings, he makes the following major recommendations to couples:

- Seek professional help early.
- Edit yourself rather than expressing every critical thought.
- Bring up problems gently and without blame. Avoid criticism and contempt.
- Husbands: Accept influence from your wife.
- Refuse to accept hurtful behavior from one another right from the beginning of the relationship.
- Learn to repair and exit arguments before they get out of control. (Some useful strategies: Change the topic, use humor, make a caring remark, make clear your common ground, back down, show appreciation or take a twenty minute break.)
- Focus on what is good about your spouse and your relationship; show appreciation, admiration and acknowledgement.

- Do not withdraw from your spouse; isolation is damaging to physical as well as emotional health.
- Avoid criticism, defensiveness, stonewalling and contempt. The most damaging behavior of all—and most predictive of divorce—is contempt.

Interestingly, Gottman found that anger and conflict are *not* predictors of relationship failure. As long as criticism, defensiveness, stonewalling and contempt are avoided, couples can express anger and disagreement and still enjoy long-term satisfaction. In fact, the happiest of couples often have issues and problems that they learn to cope with but never resolve.

Shortly I will describe the emotional dynamics that get in the way of our carrying out the best of relationship advice, and then I will suggest strategies for overcoming those obstacles. But first, I would like to share some insightful quotes from philosophers, authors and therapists that also point us in the right direction. These quotations and many more can be found at www.smartmarriages.com.

"What counts in making a happy marriage is not so much how compatible you are, but how you deal with incompatibility."

— Leo Tolstoy

"The first duty of love is to listen."

— Paul Tillich

"The success of marriage comes not in finding the 'right' person, but in the ability of both partners to adjust to the real person they inevitably realize they married."

— John Fischer

"Love seems the swiftest, but it is the slowest of all growths. No man or woman really knows what perfect love is until they have been married a quarter of a century."

— Mark Twain

"Once it's established that we are a team, I can demand of you and expect you to demand of me. Life without pain is an addiction and the fantasy of perpetual happiness is like the 'delusion of fusion.'"

— CARL WHITTAKER

"To keep your marriage brimming, with love in the wedding cup, whenever you're wrong, admit it; whenever you're right, shut up."

— OGDEN NASH

"Love doesn't sit there like a stone, it has to be made, like bread, remade everyday, made new."

— ANONYMOUS

"Success in marriage doesn't come through finding the right mate, but through being the right mate."

— BARRETT R. BRICKNER

"A first-rate marriage is like a first-rate hotel; expensive, but worth it."

— MIGNON MCLAUGHLIN

"People do not marry people, not real ones anyway; they marry what they think the person is; they marry illusions and images. The exciting adventure of marriage is finding out who the partner really is."

— JAMES L. FRAMO

"The concept of two people living together for twenty-five years without a serious dispute suggests a lack of spirit only to be admired in sheep."

— A.P. HERBERT

"In the consumer culture of marriage, commitments last as long as the other person is meeting our needs . . . Most baby boomers and their offspring carry in our heads the internalized voice of the consumer culture—to encourage us to stop working so hard or to get out of a marriage that is not meeting our current emotional needs."

— BILL DOHERTY

"One advantage of marriage, it seems to me, is that when you fall out of love with each other, it keeps you together until maybe you fall in love again."

— JUDITH VIORST

"Chains do not hold a marriage together. It is threads, hundreds of tiny threads which sew people together through the years. That is what makes a marriage last—more than passion or even sex."

— SIMONE SIGNORET

This last quote, one of my favorite on marriage, comes from Eckhart Tolle's book, *The New Earth*:

"Never before have relationships been as problematic and conflict ridden as they are now. As you may have noticed, they are not here to make you happy or fulfilled. If you continue to pursue the goal of salvation through a relationship, you will be disillusioned again and again. But, if you accept that the relationship is here to make you conscious instead of happy, then the relationship *will* offer you salvation, and you will be aligning yourself with the higher consciousness that wants to be born into this world."

Why Him? Why Her?

One of the most astounding dynamics in human relationships is how the unconscious intuition of our brain's right hemisphere is able to act as radar to find us just the right partner to provoke and recreate our childhood attachment relationship. The person we are attracted to—what we call "chemistry"—is someone with that perfect combustible mix of familiarity, hope and challenge. When we experience the attraction, we have no clue how much this person is going to help us continue our unfinished work with our family-of-origin. And yet this is absolutely what is occurring. It's like when you draw a partial circle, about 300 degrees around—your urge is to complete it, to have closure. Therapists may refer to this phenomenon as a "reenactment" or a "repetition compulsion." I'd like to share a few examples of our uncanny ability to find a mate who has the capacity to elicit our most significant childhood longings, frustrations and fears.

Amy and Carl

Amy, married with no children, came to therapy because she was extremely anxious about her pets. Her husband would acquire animals and because of his schedule, she ended up providing most of the care. (I've seen this dynamic a number of times, in which one partner keeps providing the other partner with animals or projects to take care of, resulting in neglect of the couple's relationship and their personal health.) Amy was obsessed with the safety of these animals, even though she didn't particularly love them, and incessantly worried that they were in danger due to her not being responsible enough.

Months into our work together, Amy told me that before she and her husband had married, Carl had been arrested for attempted robbery. Normally an upstanding, conscientious individual, Carl was desperate for money because he was going bankrupt caring for all the animals he had rescued from being destroyed. Amy told me that from the very first conversation with Carl, which was on the phone, she sensed that this was going to be the man she would marry. Yet, at this point she knew nothing of his preoccupation with saving animals.

Both Amy and Carl felt a tremendous sense of responsibility for the welfare of vulnerable creatures. Their childhood histories provided ample evidence for why they should feel this way. Starting at age five, Amy was the only family member who expressed any fear about her mother lying on the couch day after day. Amy's mother spoke and looked as if she were dying, but whenever Amy sought validation or reassurance from her father or older siblings, they dismissed her concerns. Since she failed to get support from her father, she began to pray to God that, if she kept her room perfectly neat, he would keep her mother alive. This was the start of obsessive-compulsive disorder for Amy. Additionally, once when Amy was a young child, her mother briefly left her in charge of watching her baby sister. Accidentally the baby fell off the table. Amy's mother said half-heartedly, "Well, let's put her in bed and we'll see in the morning if she makes it." Amy stood in the doorway for hours, her eyes glued to her sister. Her mother never called a doctor or reassured Amy.

Carl was raised by a mother who took in stray animals and foster children. She was obsessed with helping those who were vulnerable and yet, she herself was a weak reed. She was depressed and suicidal. Against this background, the teenage Carl was in a restaurant one evening with his parents when his father realized he'd forgotten his heart medication. Carl went back home to get it, running as fast as he could. But when he returned to the restaurant, his father was dead.

In childhood, both Carl and Amy experienced powerful feelings of responsibility for the safety and well-being of others. In their marriage, however, Amy was the one who owned and expressed all the fears, while Carl was the one who dismissed and minimized them. So, just as in childhood, Amy's fears were not taken seriously and Carl's attachment figure was emotionally overwhelmed. And again, as in their first attachment relationship, one person was anxious, in pain and hypersensitive to her emotional needs and the other was emotionally detached. This time around, Carl is in the role of the dismissive attachment figure, while Amy is in the role of the need-deprived child. Repetition compulsion, reenactment: the past permeates the present.

Tom and Melinda

Tom and Melinda came to therapy when their marital conflict escalated for the first time into physical aggression. Melinda complained that Tom was like the "Spock" character in *Star Trek*—cold, distant and more attached to his cell phone and computer than to her. She was especially disturbed by his procrastination in helping with projects that were important to her. Tom complained that Melinda's emotions, problems and demands took up so much space that there was no room for his concerns. The more Melinda expressed pain and anger, the more Tom distanced himself from her. The more he detached, the more she expressed pain and anger. Those times when he did come forward to comfort her, she angrily and coldly pushed him away; so Tom felt he was in a Catch-22 situation. Melinda had a fearful attachment status; she couldn't trust that Tom really cared or that she was deserving of care.

During therapy sessions, Melinda revealed that as a child her family never took interest in her development. She was allowed to stay alone in her room, watching television and wasting time. She wanted so much to be able to develop interests and accomplish things, but she was the family's scapegoat. She was verbally and physically abused and then ignored.

Tom grew up with a father who was compulsive about being productive. Tom and his siblings were expected to be high achievers in school, sports and work. Family vacations were spent doing work on their house. Tom was never allowed to relax and play. In his adulthood home, Tom was repelled by work projects of any sort. At work he had a high-stress position that put relentless demands on him, to which he couldn't say no. When Melinda pressured him to get involved in projects at home, he felt compelled to procrastinate. Both Melinda's demands and his job demands thrust Tom back into his childhood emotional state of being pressured and overburdened. For Melinda, Tom's unavailability and reluctance to help her with her projects elicited her childhood feelings of abandonment and rejection.

A Touchy Subject

Another scenario that elicits childhood wounds is the following. Many men rely heavily on sex as their way to feel and express love and closeness and to re-access their emotional aliveness. They are more action-oriented and less comfortable expressing their love verbally. Some avoidant men may only feel safe expressing anger, frustration or sexual desire, a rather limited emotional repertoire. Some men are very in touch with their yearning for physical touch and closeness, instinctively knowing it will soothe their anxious body and mind. Often times these kinds of men will marry the very person who is aversive to touch, perhaps because of having been sexually abused or exploited. The more the man pursues the woman, the more she feels unsafe, ashamed or like an object. The more she withdraws or shuts down, the more the man feels rejected, unlovable and restless.

I should point out now, before I go any further, that some marriages are calm and low-conflict because the reenactment of attachment trauma and drama are being played out with someone else such as a child, relative, ex-spouse, lover, friend, neighbor, co-worker or boss. But reenactments are not even limited to human relationships; we can act out our emotional life stories with a pet, an addictive substance, the courts or politics. In these cases, the major attachment relationship invested with emotion and meaning is not the marital pair. Sometimes the members of a couple are disconnected from any painful emotions and co-create a fantasy of having a perfect marriage and family. In such cases, you may find in time that one of their children acquires a substance addiction, another a mental illness and perhaps a third a life-altering medical condition or physical disability. Those emotions are going to register somewhere within the family system. Like *The Picture of Dorian Gray*, hidden in the attic, the eternal Adonis in the living room is too good to be true.

But in most couples, at least one member is consciously in distress over the inability to get their attachment needs met by their partner. When our painful childhood emotions and core beliefs about ourselves and others get triggered by our current insecure attachment bond, the past infiltrates the present. We all have a tendency to choose partners whose ways of defending themselves from their sensitivities, vulnerabilities and wounds puts salt in our own sensitivities, vulnerabilities and wounds. We, in turn, blindly put salt in the wounds of our partners whenever we defend ourselves.

I call this dynamic "interlocking wounds and defenses." I sometimes will pull from my desk drawer a "Chinese finger trap" to demonstrate for my clients how they keep themselves stuck through the way they defend themselves. For example, the more he shuts down, withdraws and drinks, the more she criticizes, blames and nags. The more she criticizes, blames and nags, the more he shuts down, withdraws and drinks. The only way to get free from the finger trap is to do what is counter-intuitive, a simultaneous relinquishing of defenses; universal disarmament of emotional nuclear weapons. As anyone who has been in an intimate relationship knows, when the amygdala registers threat, it is the emotional equivalent of a nuclear bomb.

Understanding Attraction

I've given much thought to the question of why we are designed to be drawn—like a moth to a flame—to the very person who is most likely to resurrect all our childhood anguish. It seems like a cruel hoax to play on two wounded souls. The following are conclusions I've arrived at to explain the underlying value of the repetition compulsion. I am not implying that the conclusions are based on science or fact. These "explanations" are provided as ways for us to reframe these reenactments as potentially beneficial, rather than reflecting futility, punishment or hopelessness.

First, creating security out of the worst case scenario is like Rumpelstiltskin's accomplishment of turning straw into gold. To be able to win acceptance and compassion from someone who has been critical or withholding is so rewarding, especially when it couldn't be accomplished our first go round with our parents. It means so much more than if it were given freely without a fight. Life sets us up with the opportunity to be grand prize winners. If we can master this, everything else is a piece of cake.

Secondly, when we are attached to someone who provokes our greatest hurts and fears, the only way to overcome the destructive pattern and create a secure bond is by cultivating our Highest Self. These admirable human traits include: courage, open-mindedness, curiosity, reflection, honesty, self-awareness, patience, tolerance, compassion, diligence and foresight. Viewed another way, if our emotional needs were easily met by our mate, there would be no motivation to become more conscious. There would be no incentive to grow, to stretch beyond our comfort zone, to develop our capacity for love. We could get away with shooting from the hip or going through life mindlessly. Our interlocking wounds are like the irritating sand that creates the oyster's pearl.

A third explanation for why we are designed to be attracted to someone who we will become allergic to might be the following. Incompatibility stretches us to develop tolerance of differences and empathy for others whom we might otherwise be quick to judge or reject. Developing tolerance and empathy in our relationships is a microcosm of what we need to do globally to increase the chances of harmony between cultures, religious and racial groups and nations. Each couple is a small-scale version of Israelis and Palestinians, Protestants and Catholics, Bosnians and Serbs or Tutsis and Hutus.

Here is one last explanation. Just as a plant's roots reach for water and a sunflower's head turns its face to the sun, an anxious person seeks the autonomy and reasonable calm of the avoider, while the avoider is drawn to the emotional expressiveness and desire for connection of the anxious person. We seek our missing half. In order to thrive, plants need water *and* sun. For humans to be whole, they need contrasting ingredients: reason *and* emotion, autonomy *and* connection. For humans and marriages to thrive, they need to be competent at and comfortable with *all* four ways of being.

Each partner of a couple represents opposite traits, defensive behaviors and emotional states. For example, one partner may be saint-like or a martyr, never angry, always loyal, overly responsible and adaptive, prone to guilt and self-doubt, ever-patient, selfless and oblivious to her own needs. She might even feel that no one else is qualified or devoted enough to provide the level of care necessary to hold the difficult partner together. She may have an undying belief that she has the key to making the suffering, disapproving one happy. She may not be able to tolerate the other's disappointment, anger and judgment and may feel compelled to do anything to avoid provoking those responses. She may strive to be perpetually cheery and bright in the hope of lightening her partner's heaviness.

At the same time, the high maintenance partner feels highly entitled, angry and impatient and is demanding, critical and controlling. He can't tolerate any frustration. Anything less than perfection triggers disappointment and a temper tantrum. In this scenario, the martyr is reenacting the role of the parentified child while the high-maintenance one is reenacting the role of the angry, suffering and demanding parent or sibling.

There are other common patterns. For example, one partner may always pursue love and attention from the other partner who is indifferent, cold and focused on tasks. Or, one partner may be mischievous, irresponsible and teasing, while the other partner is gullible, easily hurt and overly serious. Or one partner may be sensitive and overly protective of the children, while the other partner is eager to toughen the children with challenges and callousness. In still another pattern, one partner carries the full load of adult pressures and responsibilities, while the other pursues personal interests and pleasures or suffers from chronic physical ailments that prevent her from doing her share.

In all these cases, instead of the polar positions being wrestled with and integrated internally, they get wrestled between two people. What you then have are two caricatures instead of two whole human beings. We need to recognize that these are complex issues that we each need to negotiate within ourselves. You might ask yourself:

- In what situations is it wise to be patient, accepting and passive?
- In what situations is it wise to take action or express disapproval or anger?
- Am I able to be adaptive *and* set limits or expectations?
- Am I courageous enough to ask for my needs to be met *as well as* compassionate enough to respond when my partner is in need?
- Am I able to pursue interests and develop skills *as well as* invest in relationships and reflect on emotions?
- Can I admit my own sensitivities, embarrassments and fears and have a sense of humor that doesn't hurt others?

- Can I manage my own emotions and be playful and light-hearted?
- When my children are in need of nurturing, empathy and guidance can I offer it?
- When my children are in need of discipline, expectations and limits can I provide it?
- Do I have a balance of being conscientious and enjoying myself?

Being in a relationship with a polar opposite partner makes it easy for us to hold onto our rigid positions, but it also causes problems that cannot be resolved until we become whole. The more we can own the complexity of issues within ourselves, the less likely we will feel in conflict with, and alienated from, our partner. *Again, the solution to relational peace is personal wholeness.*

A new client of mine, Diana, has been the spokesperson for all disturbing emotions in her 25-year marriage to a husband who is known as eternally happy and fun to be with. While she loves Alan, she has also been devastated by his inability to empathize whenever she feels sad, afraid or angry. He can't come through for her because he has disowned these emotions. All these years, she has taken his insensitivity and unresponsiveness personally, as a reflection of her own unworthiness. I explained to her that people with avoidant attachment possess a Teflon coating that enables emotions to instantly slide off into an unvisited burial ground. Discovering for the first time that Alan's behavior is a common defense strategy for dealing with painful emotions came as a great relief to Diana. She said to me, "I feel sadness and compassion for him now that I know he has pain that he can't deal with either."

I should point out at this juncture that, a pitfall all therapists must be careful for, is judging a client's partner or their marital dynamics based solely on the views and experiences of the partner we are seeing individually. Unless the other member of the couple is present, the most we can do is make an educated guess based on the input of the client *and* our knowledge of attachment dynamics. It is very common for partners to misinterpret their spouse's behavior and intentions and without the other partner there to provide their own experience and perspective, a therapist would most likely have a skewed version of reality. Often when a client's partner does participate, even once, his or her experiences can be elicited from the therapist. As a result, a new understanding and appreciation can begin to develop as to his or her motives, fears and unmet needs. There are always two perspectives as well as a larger one which takes into account both partners' perspectives.

The Painful Trap

Most individuals don't realize that their partners are suffering as much as they are. There are those who don't want to let their partner's pain register because it reinforces their sense of shame and inadequacy. In some cases, avoiders have become so effective at being oblivious that they truly miss the signals of pain sent by their partners. Other avoiders may see their burned out, despairing partners in bed day after day and misperceive them as just being physically tired or even irresponsible.

Most members of a couple look at their partner, who is distant, guarded, putting on a fake smile, irritable, frantic, angry or judgmental, and see no sign of the fear, shame, helplessness, hurt, loneliness and confusion that are in his or her heart. Neither person has ever had an adult strong enough to lean on, and the discovery that now, in adulthood, the person they are most depending upon for support is distant or aggressive is too much to bear. All of the unexpressed anger, frustration, horror and disappointment from childhood bursts through the floodgates toward the partner.

It may be the equivalent of two children in a home without sufficient parental connection and support. The children rival each other for the limited resources. Each deals with his or her frustration and deprivation by blaming and attacking the other. Because it's not safe to direct anger or express hurt to the ones who are truly responsible, the parents, that means innocent parties are going to get the brunt of the displaced emotions. Then because each person is acting so hurtfully, the other person feels justified in attacking back. They have their perception and belief of the other being bad confirmed. So, I think this may be what happens in some marriages and it is quite a tragedy for both members of the couple and for their children who bear witness.

It is next to impossible to repair the rupture between partners as long as each person's defenses or protective parts are allowed to run the show. As discussed in an earlier chapter, certain protective parts were developed during childhood and so their judgment is poor and their perspective limited. Sometimes the feelings that we experience when we are being triggered aren't even feelings we experienced as a child. Sometimes the feelings are ones that a new protective part feels entitled or empowered to have in adolescence and adulthood, such as hatred, outrage, indignation or defiance. These emotions may be understandable in the context of childhood trauma, but in the adult relationship, the reaction is often overblown and therefore destructive. Unfortunately, if the choice is between building trust with the other and being a righteous victim, the protective part is going to err on the side of being a righteous victim. Better to be safe than get burned again.

Psychiatrist Maurice Nicoll said, "Life is a drama of the visible and invisible." Psychology and spirituality author J. G. Bennett similarly observed, "We tend to see ourselves primarily in the light of our intentions, which are invisible to others, while we see others mainly in the light of their actions, which are visible to us. We have a situation in which misunderstanding and injustice are the order of the day." What keeps partners stuck is this fact that we are far more aware of our own intentions, efforts, hurts and frustrations than those of the other person. We neglect to see our behavior from the perspective of the other and we assume the other *should* be able to understand our suffering without us having to spell it out and reveal our soft underbelly. This, in a nutshell, is the source of conflict and disharmony in all relationships, whether between husband and wife, parent and child, two cultures or two nations. Without understanding and compassion for the other as well as ourselves, we are doomed to work at cross-purposes and bring each other down.

This brings to mind an image that I recently acquired, thanks to a stimulating conversation with a local clergyman. When we were talking about human beings and their potential for getting along peacefully, he asked whether I could foresee a time when "the lion will lay down with the lamb." I immediately thought how perfect a metaphor this is for intimate relationships. Both partners, consciously or unconsciously, experience themselves as the vulnerable, threatened lamb and the other as the threatening, harmful lion. The reality is that each partner is both a lion and a lamb. We are more able to recognize our own vulnerability and to perceive our fighting, fleeing or freezing as necessary against such a threatening lion. As I see it, it is the challenge for each member of a couple to discover the lion in oneself and the lamb in our partner. When we accomplish that, the lion and the lamb will lie down together.

What is often tragic in relationships is that both parties are putting out so much energy and effort with the belief that what they are doing is the most appropriate thing to do to get their needs met and to make the relationship work. Often people don't recognize how much their partners have been sincerely trying. They accuse the other of not really caring. It's adding insult to injury when you spin your wheels and then are told you're not trying or caring. Not only are your efforts *not* helping, they are instead bringing out the worst in your partner. The failure is in the strategies and our perceptions, not our hearts. Stephen R. Covey was asked after a speech about how to forgive someone who has committed adultery. He said the question made him think of the old prayer, "Oh Lord, let me forgive those who sin differently than I do." Or, we might say, in the context of the relationship dynamics I've been discussing: "May I forgive those who defend themselves differently than I do."

There was a therapist who had a client who was very unhappy in her marriage and divorced her husband because he was so cold, distant, unresponsive and passive. About a year later, the same therapist was meeting with another woman client who came in one day to report how happy she was since she found a new lover. She described him as being caring, engaged and supportive. When she mentioned his name to the therapist, the therapist recognized him to be the ex-husband of the other female client. In one relationship, the man's defenses were elicited by the wife, and in the new relationship, the woman was experiencing what the man was capable of when not feeling threatened.

It is very common for people to end a marriage believing that their spouse was the major cause of the marriage's failure. We rarely realize that each of us is just going to bring our childhood insecurities and defenses into the next intimate relationship. It is only a matter of time before the new relationship begins to hatch its own unique triggers to each partner's childhood wounds. The lesson here is that all adults need to become experts on their own emotional history and how it is playing out in their adult relationships.

Managing the Rough Waters and Staying Afloat

It takes one's Adult Higher Self to see the larger pattern that is strangling both individuals simultaneously and to rein in the defenses. Being able to identify the negative cycle or Chinese finger trap is the crucial first step in climbing out of the black hole. When both members of the couple can really see how their defensive behavior affects the other emotionally in a "chicken and egg" cycle, then they will be motivated to deescalate the negative cycle and begin to learn a new way of dealing with emotions and expressing their needs. It also takes our Higher Self to recognize that attacking our partner is not the way to vindicate and heal our inner wounded child. This is a lesson religious groups, racial groups, tribes and nations, all groups that have experienced victimization, betrayal, hostility or genocide, also need desperately to learn.

Instead of being overly-focused on what's wrong with our partner (which I admit is tremendously tempting), we need to be proactive, gutsy and mindful enough to identify our own emotional reactivity and the meaning and sources of those reactions. As soon as we regain our composure and self-awareness after having been blindsided, we can ask ourselves, "When as a child or adolescent did I feel this very same way?" or "What did I experience as a child or adolescent that would have justified my feeling or acting the way I just did?" The emotions, body sensations and beliefs we just felt are like a divining rod that points to the place to dig. Here, if you look with curiosity, you will find something of value. By reflecting on what you find and seeing how it relates to the lightening strike that just occurred, you can return to your partner and repair the rupture by sharing what you just discovered. When this new information is presented in a heartfelt way, your partner is likely to begin to appreciate your painful predicament and how it could have triggered such an extreme response. You are more likely to receive empathy.

This is the same process as the "floatback technique" done to identify traumatic memories for EMDR work. In the following example, my client didn't experience an acute emotional hijack as much as ongoing distress in relation to her husband. Molly complained that she felt trapped when her husband constantly checked in to see what she was doing. She wished he would give her more space so she could have some peace. Molly felt nervous in her stomach and felt, "I'm trapped and can't protect myself." She often felt the urge to flee. When she reflected on when as a child she felt the same way, she recalled being 9 years old and one of her mother's creepy live-in boyfriends suddenly came into the shower with her. The understandable feeling of threat Molly felt as a child was piggy-backing on her relationship with her husband, day after day, without her realizing it.

I also want to point out that some of our emotional hijacks might be because a dream, goal or value that we developed to compensate for our painful past is being blocked or stymied, unwittingly, by our partner. An example of this is the following. Donna's mother was very cold and businesslike. Every night at bedtime, her mother told her to do her bathroom routine and get into bed. There never was any bedtime story, loving words, hug or kiss. In adulthood, Donna wanted desperately to make bedtime a warm and tender time for her child, so she never would feel unloved and lonely. Unfortunately, her husband Larry was jealous of the special attention Donna showered on their child and he kept pressuring her to join him in the living room. Every time this happened, Donna reacted with hostility toward Larry, which made him all the more jealous and possessive.

In the midst of a full-blown amygdala hijack, it is extremely unlikely that we will be able to use any of the sage advice we have heard or read about healthy relationship behavior. A hijack will most likely result in a survival reaction—fight, flight or freeze. Fight is blame, criticize, demand, yell, defend or pursue with relentless speech. Flight is withdraw and lose ourselves in work, electronic pastimes and other activities. Freeze is cave in, shut down, stonewall or go numb. A famous psychiatrist was once asked for his definition of a good marriage. His answer made me laugh: "A good marriage is when only one person at a time is insane." Yet, at the same time, it is sad that when we or our partner get hijacked and defenses kick in, we are perceived as either insane or heartless. More likely, we are genuinely feeling afraid, panicked, hurt, helpless or ashamed.

If you are self-aware enough to recognize that your emotions are exploding off the chart and you are able to pull back, the best bet is to hold off on any immediate action, including words. Instead, take some time alone. Tell your partner, when you leave, that you are coming back and that you are committed to the relationship. Then, while meditating, walking or doing some task that requires little attention, clarify for yourself what is going on inside of you.

Wait until your agitation, fury or pain has subsided before approaching your partner again. When you feel calm enough to talk with your partner, emphasize what you experienced and what was triggered, rather than making judgments and assumptions about your partner. Leave it to your partner to share what his or her motivations and intentions were.

It's important to put this plan in place with your partner at a time when you're *not* in crisis, so that neither of you feel abandoned when the other has to take a "time out." You can explain that you may need to take some time away for the welfare of the relationship—a half hour or more—to better understand and deal with the strong emotions that have arisen. You may want to suggest that your partner do the same during his or her times of sudden, strong emotion.

The best ways to reduce the risk of hijacks that I know of include the following: EMDR on the original traumas and the current-day triggers, mindfulness meditation practice, building heart coherence with mindful breathing and developing relationships with our inner hurt and protective child parts. Also valuable are sufficient sleep, daily exercise and a more spacious lifestyle, by which I mean reducing our schedules to a less stressful pace. *Doing the above involves a lot of mindfulness, time, commitment and effort, but the alternative is a lot of physical, emotional, mental and relationship distress. Take your pick.*

During periods of calm, it can be useful to do a "psychological post-mortem" on your major arguments and share with your partner the emotional meaning behind your behavior. It requires courage and diligence to look beneath our defenses to discover the authentic motives and emotions that caused our reaction. It involves expressing, in a heartfelt way, the fear, shame, helplessness, hurt, loneliness and sadness under-neath the anger, frustration or apparent indifference. It means sharing the childhood emotional context that gets triggered to give meaning to one's strong reactions.

In order for this process to work, the partners have to take turns putting their concerns on the back burner so that each person can be fully heard and validated, without the "Yes, but" that so undermines our sense of being heard, understood and supported. This last point is very important and can be challenging to carry out. It may help to agree that one person will remain the "speaker" until he/she feels fully heard and understood by the "listener," before you switch positions. For best results, the understanding must be at an emotional level, not simply rational.

The more conversations partners have in which they share their losses, vulnerabilities and insecurities and receive understanding and reassur-ance, the more trust they develop and the more quickly they will be able to deescalate or disarm future hijacks or arguments. Sometimes repair will be done in a bumbling fashion, yet still be effective. As security grows, repair can be done more elegantly, with a sudden changing of gears and a quick offer of self-insight, reassurance, physical affection or shared humor.

It is important to know that conflict, misunderstanding and injury are inevitable in relationships and don't have to be destructive. The key is whether or not the couple can repair frequently and adequately enough to maintain feelings of trust and security. Growth requires disequilibrium, not perpetual balance. If a couple never experiences conflict or crisis, that may indicate a lack of emotional investment, self-awareness, honesty or courage. The couple may have the mis-guided belief that conflict is a sign of trouble in the relationship, and so suppress any awareness or expression of dissatisfaction. They may be withholding their feelings and needs for fear that the relationship isn't strong enough to handle them. Some of these couples last a lifetime but connection may come at the cost of physical health, autonomy, genuine connection, personal integrity or growth. One member of the couple may be doing a great deal of appeasing and subjugating to keep the peace. Another possible outcome is that the partner who has been suppressing feelings will one day—without warning—up and abandon the relationship. The one left behind will say, "I don't understand, he never said anything was wrong."

The majority of couples will probably need professional assistance in negotiating the treacherous waters of insecure attachment. The earlier help is sought, the greater chance of bringing about positive results before one or both partners get too discouraged. Also, the sooner the attachment bond becomes secure, the less damage will be done to each partner's and their children's emotional, mental and physical health. Creating security out of a lifetime of insecurity is a mighty challenge for us to master. Once powerful emotions come into play, problems can escalate fast. It's hard for me to fathom how people can create and sustain a secure bond without competent guidance. There are so many land mines.

EFT: Emotionally Focused Therapy for Couples

The most effective couples therapy approach that I know of is Emotionally Focused Therapy for Couples (EFT). This powerful approach has made a significant contribution to my understanding of marriage and family life and is a treatment that I am seeking to master. I do want to point out, though, that much of what I've written in this chapter does not necessarily reflect the perspective of EFT, but rather comes from my own personal and professional observation and experience.

EFT was developed by clinical psychologist and researcher Sue Johnson, a recognized leader in the new science of love and relationships. She is Director of the Ottawa Couple and Family Institute and the International Center for Excellence in Emotionally Focused Therapy (ICEEFT.) Therapists who have trained in EFT can be found at www.iceeft.com. The website also offers two wonderful resources by Sue Johnson. The first is a book, *Hold Me Tight: Seven Conversations for a Lifetime of Love*, which she wrote to help couples understand the process of identifying their negative cycle and then holding effective conversations that create empathy, connection and a secure bond. Dr. Johnson followed the book with a DVD of the same title. The DVD of *Hold Me Tight* shows three real couples being guided by Dr. Johnson through the "conversations for connection." This is a highly valuable resource because we have the opportunity to see what healthy, security-boosting intimate relating looks like—something we rarely see in TV, movies or our circle of family and friends.

EFT is based on John Bowlby's attachment research, which found that humans and higher primate animals appear to have an innate need to feel attached to and comforted by significant others. As I've explained previously, this need applies to adults as much as children. We all need to know that we have someone to whom we are special, someone who will be there for us in times of need. Although we have these attachment needs and longings, the painful experiences most of us have had in childhood result in fear, distrust and hesitancy to share our soft, "primary emotions" when we experience them. This is especially the case when we feel them in relation to our key attachment figure in adulthood—our spouse or partner. These primary emotions may be fear, shame, inadequacy, self-hatred, helplessness, despair, loneliness or a sense of being overwhelmed. Instead, we tend to express what are called "secondary emotions," such as anger, frustration, annoyance or coldness. While these emotions feel much safer to *us*, they can be very threatening to the recipient.

In the EFT process, couples are helped to identify first their secondary and then their primary emotions and the painful impact and interpretations that the partners' defensive behaviors provoke in them. Throughout the process, both partners experience the therapist's non-judgment, validation and empathy which provide support as partners venture outside their emotional comfort zone. This also helps each person begin to see the other in a new light and appreciate the other's experience.

With the therapist's help, partners begin to see how they have co-created a circular dance of defenses that keeps both trapped and deprived of basic needs. Typically, these needs are for safety, security, comfort, connection, protection, acceptance and respect. Gradually each member begins to explore the layers of emotion, feelings and meaning that they have been experiencing in relation to their partner's behavior. Each is encouraged to take risks in admitting and sharing with the other, face-to-face, the experiences of isolation, abandonment, betrayal, loss, deprivation, inadequacy or rejection that they have been feeling in the relationship.

As the partners become better able to articulate their emotional experience in the relationship, they are guided to take the risk of asking directly, and in a more heartfelt way, for their needs to be met. When a partner speaks in this non-threatening, genuine and vulnerable way, with eye-to-eye contact, it tends to evoke in the listener an inherent capacity for understanding and compassion. Increasingly, partners are able to communicate in this honest and open way as well as listen to each other from the heart, rather than taking words at their literal or surface meaning. The couple becomes more fluent in the language of the heart.

Sometimes substantial progress in EFT cannot happen until the couple addresses one or more "attachment wounds or injuries." These are events in the couple's history in which one member felt devastated by the other partner's behavior. For example, a woman who has just given birth is stunned and crushed when her husband says that he has to go back to the office for the rest of the day. Or, a husband, who has shared with his wife a deeply humiliating event at work, feels betrayed upon hearing her repeat the story to a girlfriend in a light-hearted manner.

EFT helps the wounded partners explore and express how these traumatic events impacted their self-image, emotional state, physical state, view of the relationship and future needs and decisions. The wounded partner expresses to the partner what she needed at the time; he in turn, expresses his feelings upon hearing how much his behavior impacted her. Once the injured partner senses that her partner is genuinely moved by her emotional experience, and that his apology is from the heart, she can put the injury to rest. This is a very sensitive, subtle process that cannot be rushed.

In the last stage of EFT work, the couple tells the story of how they got stuck and how they were able to evolve to a place where they can trust and depend upon each other. This capacity to articulate a coherent story reflects their new ability to understand the emotional meaning of their experiences. As we saw in previous chapters, integration is the key to resolution, security and health. With the creation of a secure and trusting bond, the couple is now able to resolve the issues with which they have perennially struggled, from parenting and finances to in-laws, sex and division of chores.

A securely attached couple will know how to do what EFT calls, *The Four Rs: Request, Receive, Respond* and *Reach*. We need to be able to request comfort and support from our partner in an efficient and non-threatening way. Both partners must make requests, not just the one who has sought attention all along. If avoidant partners don't identify and express their own feelings, concerns and needs, it is problematic for a number of reasons. First, avoiders need to acknowledge that, as human beings, they have psychological needs like everyone else. They need to overcome any feelings of shame and fear of being seen as weak or defective. They need to be able to feel entitled to having their needs met and their emotions understood and appreciated. They need to take more responsibility for identifying and owning their own emotional issues and take more initiative in addressing them. Then their partner is far less likely to complain "I wouldn't have to be a crank if you were a self-starter."

Those who have been avoidant need to find the courage and put in the time to reflect and be mindful of their inner world and how their relationships impact them. To be healthy is to be fully aware, willing to face all of reality, not just what is rosy or neutral. By acknowledging needs and concerns of their own, avoiders help provide a balance in the relationship so that they don't always feel like the recipient of complaints and the partner doesn't get stuck in the role as the perpetually dissatisfied critic. Avoiders need to set limits and let partners know when their expectations are too much.

It is just as important for avoiders' spouses (who are usually anxiously-attached) to have the experience of putting their concerns on the back burner, to know that it isn't always about them. They need to recognize that their partner has feelings, needs and complaints too. Anxious partners need to experience being the one who is needed and leaned upon. It helps them to rein in their intensity and self-preoccupation and to experience the strength and pride of knowing that they can come through for their spouse.

The second "R" is the ability to receive comfort and support when our partner offers it. This means trusting that the care is sincere and being fully emotionally-present in order to absorb it. Especially when the comfort is physical—a tender hand on the shoulder, hand, knee or face, a full-body hug or cuddling—the benefits are tremendous, both to the relationship and to each partner's physical and emotional well-being. Physical touch is a natural tranquilizer and underutilized in a society where the medicine cabinet is where we reach instead. Physical touch releases oxytocin, which has been found to increase feelings of tranquility, love and connection as well as reduce stress, anxiety, depression and cravings. Recently, a highly anxious client of mine told his wife that the simple act of her sliding her hand into his hand just melted him inside.

Third, we need to be able to respond and provide attention, comfort and support when our partner asks for it. This means really seeing our partner as deserving and human—neither a rock nor a bottomless pit. We need to be able to be in synch with our partner when he or she is experiencing strong emotions. If our partner is upset, that is not the time to make a humorous quip. If our partner is expressing delight over something meaningful that has just happened, that's not the time to express bitterness and cynicism. Not experiencing attunement with our partner will most likely trigger the pain of childhood emotional deprivation, the thousands of times we were not heard, understood or cared about. Reason, logic, philosophy, advice and flippant remarks may work fine at the job, in the locker room or with acquaintances, but they can be poison in intimate relationships, especially when sensitive feelings are involved.

We need to be able to catch ourselves entering defense mode and abruptly switch gears into caring mode when our partner expresses a problem or need. Doing so is highly effective and efficient, saving our partner a great deal of hurt and ourself a great deal of aggravation and frustration. When our response is right on target, we are able to move forward with great ease. As Jean-Jacques Rousseau said, "What wisdom can you find that is greater than kindness?"

Last, we need to be able to reach out to our partner and initiate support when we perceive he or she is in need. Our partner needs to be on our radar screen. This last ability is sorely lacking in contemporary society with our crazy, non-stop schedules. I can't tell you how many couples I've worked with who, when asked how their week was, replied "busy" and then admitted that they barely saw or interacted with each other. Having new forms of communication, like text-messaging, that make it possible for us to easily get in touch with each other, anywhere, anytime, may give couples the false sense that they are connected. I cannot emphasize enough: When it comes to our most important relationships, we must make full use of our eyes, hearts and arms to keep our love alive. Anything less will result in a flat or frail connection. When we aren't deeply connected with our loved ones, it leaves us vulnerable to creating substitute relationships with food, alcohol, drugs, gambling, possessions, cyber-relationships, affairs and countless other forms of false connection.

It is important to know that when a partner is abusing alcohol or drugs, that addiction must be treated before the couple can make progress. As long as someone is self-medicating, he or she will not be in a position to access emotions or experience true empathy. Likewise, if domestic violence is involved, couples therapy may be initially unsuitable. An assessment will need to be done to determine whether it will be beneficial or detrimental to have the victim speak openly in front of the abusive partner. The violent partner may be referred for individual therapy and anger management prior to couples work in order to provide safety.

In other cases, a member of a couple may be suffering from a mental health problem that interferes with the person's capacity to benefit from couples therapy. Such individuals will need to also engage in individual therapy. For example, someone with Post Traumatic Stress Disorder may have powerful emotions and entrenched self-beliefs that prevent the person from perceiving themselves, their partner and their current situation accurately, no matter how much feedback and reassurance the other partner provides.

Another mental health obstacle to effective couples therapy is a severe personality disorder. Those who are sociopathic or have a severe case of narcissistic personality disorder will be manipulative, cold and unable to experience empathy. They may exploit sensitive information provided by their partners for their own self-serving purposes. On the other hand, I have seen many people who have initially behaved coldly and indifferently become warm and compassionate and vulnerable through EFT treatment. There is a big difference between being avoidantly-attached and being sociopathic. It is important for a therapist to make the judgment as to whether both partners have the capacity to change and to care.

Any couple in which a partner is actively engaged in an affair, whether known to the partner or not, will most likely experience limited progress. As long as people have that safety net and maintain the delusion that they can get their needs met by someone else without having to take personal risks or make changes, they will not be investing in the marriage or therapy process. An affair, whether in person or on the Internet, is not a committed relationship and so there are no conflicts to negotiate. Trust comes from working through conflict between competing needs and emotionally-driven perspectives and creating solutions that reflect empathy and respect for both partners. It is only when the going gets rough that people find out whether someone will really be there for them, will really respond to their needs. While I don't have facts to substantiate this, I would suspect that, once an illicit lover becomes a legitimate partner, the relationship goes South.

For these reasons, affairs may involve fondness, passion, connection and even intimate sharing, but they are not based on trust. Affairs, in my opinion, are never benign because the emotional dramas that ensue can wound individuals and destroy family connections. Additionally, affairs can create triangles that recreate childhood trauma in the most astonishing ways. I know of a case in which the woman's relationship dynamics with her lover and husband were a complete psychological reenactment of a childhood traumatic triangle. To not explore the meaning inherent in these relationships is to ignore a potential emotional and therapeutic goldmine. In order to capitalize on the opportunity for full healing that couples therapy can provide, the relationship with the third party must come out of the closet and be placed squarely on the therapy agenda.

Sometimes an individual has a unique situation that makes bringing up the affair in couples therapy extremely difficult.

- If you believe that revealing the affair would devastate your partner's trust in you to the point of giving up on the marriage.

- If you want to end the affair but a part of you feels compelled to continue the relationship.
- If you want to commit to working on saving your marriage, then I propose the following.

Rather than doing couples therapy at this time, begin individual therapy with an EMDR-trained therapist. The compulsive relationship may very well be a reenactment of a childhood attachment relationship and, by resolving that trauma, you will most likely be able to get unstuck and move forward. Then you can ask your spouse to join you in strengthening the relationship with couples therapy.

I believe that couples who wish to thrive, as a couple *and* as whole human beings, will be evolving in the following directions through the mindful efforts described in this book. Anxiously-attached partners will become less aggressive, demanding, verbose and impulsive and more soft, vulnerable and receptive in their approach. They will edit their own speech and leave ample space for their partner to find and express his or her experience. They will become more able to recognize and communicate to their partner what they appreciate in their partner and in their life. They will take responsibility for self-care, managing their emotions and getting treatment for their childhood traumas. They will balance their legitimate need for relationship connection with developing interests, friendships and the pleasures of solitude.

Avoidantly-attached partners will be venturing into new terrain— their emotional world, past and present. They will be moving in the direction of more emotional awareness, presence, engagement and responsiveness. They will be less guarded and less fearful of focusing on problems. They will be more able to reflect, tolerate emotions and identify and express their own perspective and needs. Some avoidantly-attached partners will no longer corner the market on a forced optimism; they will be able to own and express doubts, concerns and negative emotions without fearing they will make matters worse. They will be able to recognize their need for connection and request support as well as give it. They will send clearer and louder signals to their partner that they value their partner and relationship.

Both partners will become more curious about their partner's perceptions and emotional experience. Both will be less quick to assume they know each other's motives. Both will be able to share their most vulnerable emotions, meaningful experiences and significant losses, regrets, hopes and dreams. They will use physical touch to soothe and comfort each other. They will be aware of their partner's fears and sensitivities and make efforts to avoid triggering them, if possible, and provide reassurance when they can't be avoided. The previously anxious partner will feel connected, supported and valued. The previously avoidant partner will feel effective, understood and valued. Both will have earned a secure attachment.

Whatever investment we make in becoming a more evolved, whole and emotionally mature partner will benefit us, our children and our community, as well as our partner. We are all inextricably joined, whether we realize it or not. When it comes to our intimate relationships, what goes around comes around. Mistreating or neglecting our loved ones is equivalent to poisoning our own water supply. We are all drinking from the same emotional well. Any social or physical organism is unhealthy to the degree that parts of it remain vulnerable and unattended. The security of a couple, family or world is in proportion to the security of its most vulnerable member. So, when we choose to walk the tightrope of emotional risk-taking with our partner, paradoxically, we build a more secure home-base for both of us, as well as greater security for those around us.

CHAPTER EIGHT

Family Life

As we embark on marriage and start our own families, most of us are at the height of our hopes and positive intentions. Our love for our partner and excitement about our future together propels us onto a current that feels strong, clear and vital. The photographs of our wedding day and, later on, holding our newborn babies, capture the looks of love, devotion and hope on our faces. Some of us may be conscious of a desire to do things differently and better than our parents. Others of us may not have given more than a few moments thought to the subject. Thanks to the media, it's hard for anyone to be ignorant about the challenges of family life and high risk of divorce. Yet somehow, between the confidence of youth, the power of love and the instinct to carry on the human race, we take our leaps of faith.

Afterward, as the days turn into months and then years, life gets complicated; we get caught up in the web of details and demands upon us. As a result, our capacity to see the big picture, and our role in it, becomes clouded. The less mindful we are of this big picture, the more likely we are to fall into an emotional trance that radiates from our families of origin.

The Ghost of Attachment Past

Just as couples can reenact childhood fears and wounds through their relationship, parents can misperceive their children and respond to them, unknowingly, in the context of their attachment style and old emotional scenarios. Take Arlene and Roger, for example. As they raised their son, Derek, Arlene felt compelled to protect him from any emotional pain. While she was totally unconscious of her own childhood emotional deprivation and pain, she was powerfully preoccupied by, and hypersensitive to, her child's emotions. Arlene demonstrated an anxious attachment stance toward her son and his emotional well-being. In the meantime, Roger, who also was unaware of his own childhood pain, perceived Derek as needing to be toughened up, so he wouldn't be selfish or weak. He demonstrated a dismissive style toward Derek's emotional needs and put all his emphasis on building their son's physical skills and interests.

Arlene was preoccupied with emotions and Roger was preoccupied with the body. The more Arlene tried to protect and nurture their child, the more Roger undermined Arlene's attempts. The more Roger was insensitive toward Derek, the more frightened for Derek Arlene became and the more she criticized and tried to control Roger. The more Arlene pampered Derek and criticized Roger, the more Roger felt unloved and unimportant to Arlene.

The part of Arlene's personality in the driver seat perceived Derek through the eyes and heart of her childhood self. The part of Roger's personality in the driver seat was the part who was ashamed of the child he had been, vulnerable and needy. Neither parent saw the true Derek before them, but rather a projection of their own unresolved childhood memories. Despite their best intentions and efforts to care for him, Derek was exposed to parents who felt misunderstood and unsupported by each other and who were giving him mixed signals about himself, his emotions and his needs.

Unmet emotional needs from childhood can play out in families in a number of ways. In their early years of marriage, Ethan was the pursuer in his relationship with his wife Delores, who was timid and tended to withdraw. The more distant she became, the more irritable and controlling Ethan would become, which drove Delores further away from him. As the couple had children and Ethan lost hope that he would ever connect with his wife, he began to insist that his children do things and go places with him. If they resisted, he would get very upset until they gave in. As the children got older, son Steve managed to always be out of the house because of after school activities and visiting friends, so he was unavailable to do things with Dad. Middle son Arnie had ongoing battles with Dad and never relented. Youngest child Francine placated Dad and kept him company so he wouldn't be lonely and miserable. Each child handled the stressful demands differently. Steve's strategy was flight, Arnie's was fight and Francine's was freeze and submit.

When Francine was in her late teens, she had a boyfriend, Vic, who was very possessive and clingy. He panicked when Francine began to talk about breaking up because of his flirting with other girls when she wasn't around. Ethan didn't like Francine dating Vic and pressured her to break up with him. Francine felt torn between two males who were both demanding of her presence so they wouldn't feel alone and abandoned.

Understandably, Francine became highly distressed and her behavior became erratic as a result of these demands, which left no room for her to have her own needs met. Finally, she had a manic episode, was hospitalized and diagnosed with bipolar disorder. When I met Francine a year later and she told me of her symptoms and difficulties, they made perfect sense in the context of her relationship history. I believed that *eventually* she would be capable of functioning fine once she learned how to recalibrate her nervous system, manage her legitimate emotions, heal her traumas, validate herself and create mutual relationships. As Francine attended college in another state, and I was seeing her during the summer break, we were only able to start this process. I did, however, refer her to an EMDR therapist near her college.

Here's another family story that shows how parents' emotions impact their children. Gary and Tamara had a daughter, 16-year-old Karen. Gary brought Karen into therapy because she was severely under-functioning in school and was beginning to self-mutilate. Gary was in a panic over Karen's academic deterioration. For years, he had been engaging his daughter in intellectual debates to strengthen her cognitive ability. He was prone to giving long-winded sermons to Karen about the importance of education. Gary knew personally how not taking school seriously could severely affect one's future and he couldn't tolerate any cue that Karen was not focused on academics. In the meantime, Tamara was having regular clashes with their other daughter, Lisa. While each parent was anxiously-preoccupied with one of their children, they were avoidantly-attached to each other.

The more Gary had Karen under a microscope, the more powerless and inadequate she felt. The more scrutiny she underwent, the more she felt compelled to lose herself in music and the computer. The more she relied on distraction and escape to cope, the harder it was for her to maintain attention and concentration in school.

Gary and Karen had a few EFT sessions together in which they connected in a heartfelt way that was new for them both. However, Gary's fears got the best of him and he was impatient for Karen's grades to improve. He decided that his daughter had Attention Deficit Disorder and should be immediately assessed and treated for that specific condition. Any family relationship work would have to be put on the back burner. Gary ended Karen's therapy with me and found a therapist who specialized in ADD treatment. He said that he hoped to bring Karen back to me in the future to address Karen's depression.

Even if Karen's attention and academic performance issues are resolved, she will not have learned how to be aware of and express her emotions in her key attachment relationships. The emotional lessons she will have absorbed from her relationship with her father will erupt somehow, sometime in the future with a boyfriend, husband, child or other attachment relationship. The lessons Karen learned and might reenact include: "I'm only valuable if I'm smart," "My feelings and needs don't count," "I'm powerless" and "I can only be safe if I'm alone and shut-down."

There are many ways that childhood wounds and insecure attachment can get played out in our adult family; what I am sharing is just a sampling. Here's another story from my therapy practice. Candy married Ron, who had an adolescent daughter, Harriet, from a previous marriage. Candy was furious and mortified that Ron was so tolerant of Harriet's selfish and abusive behavior. Candy felt unprotected by Ron who dismissed her concerns. Candy told me that this situation was probably the most disturbing experience currently in her life.

When I asked her if this situation reminded her of another time in her life, Candy couldn't think of anything. And yet, just fifteen minutes earlier, Candy had off-handedly told me about a time in her early teens when she babysat and the child's father kissed her and touched her breasts. Candy told her mother what happened, but she made excuses for the man's behavior and seemed totally unconcerned about her daughter's feelings. When Candy pleaded for her mother's understanding and comfort, her mother said, "If you don't just forget about this and your father finds out, he'll practically kill the man and end up in jail. Is that what you want?" Despite having just told me about her mother dismissing what was clearly a frightening and disturbing experience, Candy could not put two and two together: that at least some of her outrage at Ron and Harriet belonged to her mother and the man who had violated her.

Further Variations of the Family Attachment Dance

In the early stage of many marriages, it is common for the anxiously-attached, intensely expressive and engaged wife to shower positive emotions—love, admiration and desire—on her avoidantly-attached husband. This type of attention makes the husband feel safe and valued. Then, when the couple has their first child, the wife shines the high beam of her love onto the child. While the powerful attachment to the baby is appropriate and healthy, the marriage can begin to take a backseat in the family, with the husband feeling like "chopped liver." The slow or sudden drop-off of positive attention can unconsciously trigger the husband's memories of emotional deprivation.

Without consciously processing and expressing to his wife his feelings of hurt, sadness, inadequacy, loneliness and being unlovable, the avoidant husband is at risk for developing compulsive behaviors to compensate for or forget about the loss. This could take the form of compulsive spending, working, Internet surfing, flirting, drinking, pot smoking or throwing himself even more passionately into sports as a player or spectator. As the husband becomes more and more distant and detached, the wife's anxious attachment switches further from her spouse to her child. When she does connect with her husband, it's likely to express negative emotions like disapproval, annoyance, frustration or anger.

If my description of attachment relationships sounds a bit one-dimensional, I want to point out that over time, an individual can experience many variations in attachment style and behavior. Over the years of a long-term relationship, the couple may start with one partner being the pursuer and the other being the withdrawer, and then at some point, the defenses reverse. Over the course of adult life, we can have a number of different attachment dramas with our parents, our adult partners, our young children, our grown children, our elderly parents and ourselves. In one relationship we may be an "anxious pursuer," in another an "anxious critic," in another an "anxious caretaker," in still another, an "avoidant distancer" or "placater."

Having either directly or vicariously experienced all these different ways of being with emotions and significant others, we can unconsciously reenact an array of attachment patterns. Furthermore, in different adult relationships we can end up playing the emotional and defensive scripts of several people—our young child self, adolescent self, mother, father or sibling. We even act out how we wish we had handled childhood challenges and how we wish our parents had treated us. It's also important to recognize that insecurity and security are on a continuum, rather than being an on/off phenomenon. We experience degrees of insecurity and degrees of security.

One of the most important things to know about family life and human relationships is that *the meaning and solution to conflict and problems are found more in the process, emotions and beliefs than the content.* When there are tensions between partners, the topic could be money, sex, lifestyle, chores, in-laws, time, activities or parenting—it doesn't really matter. They may argue over the most stupid or minor things if the matter is reminiscent of an earlier wound or if they are already upset and primed for expressing discontent. Usually the real issues in an argument are fears of abandonment, disconnection, rejection, betrayal, deprivation or being seen as unlovable, inadequate, insignificant or undeserving. It always comes back to three questions: *Are you there for me when I need you? Will you respond to what is important to me? Are you really listening and caring?*

When it comes to parent-child interactions, I realize that sometimes a cigar is just a cigar. There is a legitimate need for parents to teach, guide and discipline their children. It's also important to be able to enjoy, interact with and not put too much pressure on a child. But, more often than not, the energy flowing between a parent and child has a lifelong theme or "flavor" to it that overshoots the mark. Often, a parent's childhood wound and core belief about self and other are being replayed, and the parent may be trying to avoid feeling that old hurt again.

Parents may be chronically anxious about their children when it comes to psychological needs, physical safety, food, sleep, fitness, sexuality, friends, the opposite sex, appearance, rules, doing their homework, achievement, cleaning up their messes, helping the family or sharing activities with a parent. Other parents may express anger over these same matters. More than likely, the emotionally-laden issues underlying the subject have to do with the parents' fears, unmet needs, sensitivities or core beliefs about self and others. A parent's chronic anxiety, fear or excessive trust, permissiveness, support and devotion can be just as harmful to a child as anger, contempt and hostility.

The underlying dynamic might be the parent's overwhelming sense of responsibility for a vulnerable person's welfare, protection or problems. Such parents may want to spare their children from ever feeling deprived of support and concern and themselves from ever feeling guilt or shame. The parents' sense of self-worth may be centered on their ability to be a competent caretaker. A parent may perceive the child as especially vulnerable or not capable enough and therefore at risk of suffering. A parent may be afraid the child will make a catastrophic mistake that will ruin his or her life. A parent may have a powerful need to feel connected and belong. They might fear that their children cannot tolerate the pain of loneliness and rejection. As a result, the parent may be overly involved in the child's life, overdo socializing and deprive the child of solitude and independent play. Whatever form the anxiety takes, it can usually be traced back to a parent's early hurt or deprivation.

Unconscious Parenting: The Impact on Children

Some parents put enormous pressure on their children to be high achievers, have the absolute best education and present a polished front. These parents may be following in their parents' footsteps, not being able to tolerate imperfection in their children and not being able to appreciate the child's unique self. They may be allergic to feeling shame and fearful of others' judgment being harsh and unforgiving.

In adulthood, these grown children may go to the most elite colleges, work for the most esteemed businesses, live in the most prestigious communities and take the most impressive vacations. Like other addictions, the need to achieve and acquire only becomes more desperate over time, as each fix loses its effect. Unfortunately, what has been created is a "pseudo-self," a shimmering veneer hiding a deep emptiness, strong doubt about one's worth and a constant fear of being found out to be an imposter.

Sometimes, our protective parts try to make sure our children never feel ashamed, judged, controlled or burdened. We may go overboard being the non-judgmental, easy-going, undemanding parent we wish we had had. We find it easier and feel safer interacting with and fostering a bond with our children than our spouses. The children may be getting, not only their own share, but the other parent's share of love, acceptance, understanding, support and attention. With our spouse, in contrast, we express the opposite attitude of hostility, rejection and lack of empathy. Our spouse may be at the other extreme of the continuum and be hyper-vigilant for any behavior in the children that might bring shame or rejection to the family. We will each have identified with our parents' beliefs about others and use the hypercritical strategy. We play it out with our spouse, who in turn plays it out with the children.

While we may be able to recognize the harm done to a child by an aggressive, critical, demanding, rejecting or emotionally overwhelmed parent, it may be more difficult for us to see the harm that can be done when a parent is excessively supportive, protective or over-functioning. A parent who is overly responsible, giving, initiating and engaged can actually smother and suffocate a child's self-development. It's like a larger tree that blocks the younger tree from the sun.

Such children may not have sufficient opportunity to experience the sense of competency and satisfaction that comes from working out their own problems or having sufficient room to reflect, discover their own interests, dreams, opinions, emotions, needs and voice. They may not be given the chance to ask their own questions, determine what matters to them and what kind of response they need from their parent in order to feel supported. They are too often in the passive, receptive, adaptive position. Children need to be given ample opportunity to explore and articulate their inner world and determine which ways they can best express it in the outer world. They need their parents to provide a balance of being a sounding board and provider of information and direction.

A parent who is allergic to any reminder of control, disapproval, conflict or emotional intensity can prevent their child from experiencing discipline, working through conflict or tolerating a parent's negative emotions. Without conflict, the child doesn't learn how to repair a rupture or gain confidence that the parent's love is strong enough to weather a storm. Additionally, such children may learn that it is not okay to express any negative emotions, or disagree with their parent because their parent has to be seen as all good. When children withhold parts of their experience to protect their parents' self-image and sense of self-worth, they will feel shame about the emotions they do have and aren't supposed to have.

Here's another variation on that theme. When children are encouraged by adult family members to glorify or idolize a parent, this unrealistic image can create difficulties for the child in adulthood. When your parent is portrayed as a saint, hero or martyr,

- You are not allowed to own or express any anger, hurt, criticism or complaint
- Those repressed emotions and behavioral impulses may end up erupting at your spouse or child
- Either you, your spouse or your child will never seem good enough because the parent is such a tough act to follow

- You may feel compelled to express extreme praise and adulation of others, rather than being authentic
- You may feel that you have to be strong and perfect and hide your shameful weaknesses rather than recognize them as a sign of being human
- If your parent suffered, for example as a Holocaust survivor or other trauma victim, you may feel "What right do I have to complain?" Any problem you have seems trivial in contrast
- Or, you may have a sense that, "I can't afford to have needs or relax when others have accomplished or suffered so much."

A great deal of marital conflict can stem from each parent aiming to protect their child from hurts they had experienced in their own childhoods. Because the parents' strategies are polar opposites, each parent feels undermined in protecting their child by the other parent. Typically, each parent is barely cognizant of what is motivating their emotions and behaviors. The following case is an example of how this can play out over the years.

Dottie's vision of family life was to have the kind of dinnertime conversations that would foster her children's sense of being truly known, understood and valued. She wanted more than anything for her children to have their parents' full attention and interest in who they are and what was most important to them: their experiences, emotions, beliefs, perspectives, concerns and dreams. Her husband Larry's major concern about family life was that nobody would dominate or bore him or his children. He didn't want anyone else's sensitivities to get in the way of his right and need to be heard and recognized. He also wouldn't tolerate anyone seeing him as the bad guy and would insist on his being fine just the way he is.

Dottie spent years nagging Larry to join her and the children at the dinner table. Larry insisted on eating in the living room while watching television and reading the sports section. Eventually, many years later, Larry relented but he was very stiff and uncomfortable at the table. Often when Dottie began to tell stories from her day, Larry pressured her to get to the point and spare him the details. Dottie felt that cutting her anecdotes to the bare bones took all the pleasure out of the telling. She felt hurt and deprived and expressed her outrage. Larry thought she was being oversensitive and felt justified in his behavior. Dottie also would become upset that Larry took every potentially rich conversation and turned it into a joke. This would often result in her becoming confrontational and critical of Larry in front of the children. Larry in response would be defensive and dismiss her concerns.

Eventually in couples therapy, exploring their memories of their childhood homes, Larry recalled that he hated dinnertime because his father would bore him to death with drawn-out stories from his workday. He also recalled with hurt and bitterness the mealtime memories of his parents fawning over his sister because she was so fragile, and yet being quick to judge him harshly because they didn't see him as vulnerable or in need. Dottie recalled that as a child, her mother would flit around the kitchen inefficiently and barely ever sit down. Throughout dinnertime, her father would angrily and repeatedly complain, "Lena sit down, Lena sit down!" She could feel her father's upset at not having his wife at the table. Dottie also remembered that her parents never showed any interest in her inner life—her thoughts, feelings or experiences. Conversations were very functional and devoid of anything meaningful to Dottie.

Neither Larry nor Dottie felt heard or understood by their parents. Larry tried to protect himself in adulthood by avoiding the dinner table, insisting that others edit their talking, keeping things light and being defensive. Dottie, on the other hand, tried to protect herself by criticizing Larry, coming to the defense of her children, showing far more interest in what the children had to say than Larry and painting herself and the children as victims of Larry's bad behavior. As is so often the case in family life, a perfect storm was created.

This family's story shows us how important it is for each parent to recognize what childhood experiences had hurt them the most and what needs were unmet as a result. They need to be able to share with their partner these emotion-filled stories so they can have a deep appreciation of their raw spots, fears, hopes and needs. They need to understand why what their partner is trying to do is so meaningful and why they get so passionate about not being undermined. When a couple is able to empathize with each other, they are much more able to see the other as non-threatening, provide reassurance and behave in ways that support both partners' emotional needs. When a couple can operate on this level, their children are spared the bloody emotional mess that ensues when parents are working at cross-purposes.

Emotional Contagion

Children are highly sensitive to their parents' emotional states. It is wired in from birth as a survival mechanism so that they do their part to contribute to the attachment bond. Many of my adult clients recall how they were impacted by sensing their parents' misery, bitterness, sadness, chronic grief, helplessness, shame or fear. Sometimes the emotions that an adult experiences and expresses in their adult relationships are the emotions they unconsciously absorbed from their parent. For example, defining experiences from my client Leo's childhood were the times he listened at the top of the stairs while his mother grilled his father about where he had been. She was certain he was cheating on her, but for years he denied the truth. While Leo's siblings slept, he was riveted to this surreal middle-of-the-night drama. In adulthood, Leo became a federal investigator and in his marriage felt such suspicion and paranoia about his wife's loyalty that he couldn't stop himself from grilling her. His distrust, of course, played into her feelings of shame and inadequacy from her own childhood relationships.

When, on the other hand, a parent's prominent emotional state is positive, that too is contagious. When parents have a secure enough attachment with each other and both parents genuinely feel good about themselves and their lives, their children will absorb the feelings of trust, security, serenity, warmth, enthusiasm and joy. When parents are conscientious about repairing their inevitable ruptures, the children witness a return to harmony that reassures and soothes them as well. The children are able to sense at a gut level whether a repair was born out of appeasing, dismissal and the impulse to avoid facing fears or was born out of genuine processing of emotion, leading to understanding and warmth. Likewise, children can sense whether their parents are truly happy and at peace because human bodies and emotional energies speak louder than appearances and words.

I've found that many adults' anxiety stems from having been highly sensitive to their parents' or younger siblings' pain and having felt helpless in comforting them. Part of a child's incentive to help a parent is open-hearted compassion and part of it is because they can't get the love and care they need until their parent is at peace. It is tragic when roles reverse and a child takes responsibility for their parent's emotional well-being. These children will devote huge amounts of mental and emotional energy to trying to comfort and please their parents, with an undying determination and hope. Even when parents' disown or shut down from their emotional pain, the child is able to feel it.

For example, my client Cathy's depressed mother would always dismiss Cathy's concerns whenever she asked her mother what was wrong. While her mother's words denied any problems, her mother's non-verbal vibes cried out that she was a victim and martyr. Cathy's emotional intuition *knew* something was wrong and when her mother denied it, the child filled in the gap with all the feelings she was sensing and imagining. Then *Cathy* was left to carry and obsess over all those emotions without any support. Because Cathy couldn't receive comfort from her mother or experience a sense of competency in comforting her mother, she invested her emotional energy into her cat. Unlike her mother, her cat didn't lie, didn't appear to be unhappy, didn't judge Cathy as being too clingy and was able to give and respond to love. Her cat became her primary attachment relationship. At the same time, Cathy developed a hypersensitivity to the welfare of all cats and eventually was traumatized when her cat died.

At age 30, Cathy couldn't bear the thought of moving out of her childhood home and the obstacle was the image of her mother suffering without Cathy being there for her. Ironically, she saw her mother clearly in distress only a few times in her life. The one who consciously, deeply and chronically suffered was Cathy. Cathy had no hesitation in saying, "I would much rather suffer than see my mother suffer."

As a result of her therapy, including EMDR work, Cathy was able to overcome lifelong depression, fear, shame and guilt. After moving out of her childhood home, Cathy told me, "I'm surprised at how well I've adjusted living away from my family. I've been feeling quite comfortable in my new home. There really was no reason to have felt so afraid."

Being "My Brother's Keeper"—at Age 3

Often a parent who relies on dissociation and detachment to survive, in effect, abdicates responsibility for raising the children. While the children's physical needs are met, their emotional needs are ignored. When the child has any disturbing emotions, the parent dismisses them and the child eventually learns to not focus on her own needs. The parent may give accolades to the older child for being responsible for a younger sibling, even if the age difference is only one year. Sometimes the younger one becomes the caretaker, because she doesn't reveal as much vulnerability. The child's self-worth and identity, then, becomes tied to being a responsible caretaker. This praise alternates with subtle or explicit blaming and devaluing remarks like, "Why weren't you paying attention? Look at the mess he made!" or "You're the older one, you should have told him not to touch that razor in the bathtub." This can result in the "parentified child" feeling responsible not only for their siblings' behavior but for their happiness and very life.

Unlike the parents, these children have not developed adequate defenses and so are devastatingly aware of their siblings' pain. The look of sadness, helplessness and confusion on a sibling's face gets branded into a child's heart and unconscious mind. Guilt, fear and excessive empathy and loyalty rule these siblings who grow up to feel compelled to take responsibility not just for siblings but for *anyone* who appears to be struggling.

These anxiously attached, other-preoccupied caretakers often suffer both physical and emotional distress and chronically feel they aren't doing enough for others. After decades of living this way, the roles may reverse as their anxiety, overwhelm and emotional deprivation culminate in collapse, the inability to function and the need for someone else to take care of them. The pendulum has swung from over-functioning to under-functioning and, perhaps, their partners will now have to take on the work of two people. For example, those with chronic debilitating conditions, such as mentioned in the Physical Health chapter, may be "parentified children" who have finally burned out.

High-Maintenance and Low-Maintenance Children

In many families, there is both an anxiously-attached child and an avoidantly-attached one. Some anxiously-attached children feel that another is all-deserving and they dismiss their own needs. Then there are the anxiously-attached children who are stuck in entitlement—"it's all about me." Such anxiously-attached children act out—insisting on getting their way, getting their fair share, and generally dominating time and attention with their complaints and demands. Such children are high-maintenance. Avoidantly-attached children, in contrast, will be low-maintenance—highly cooperative self-starters who are extremely adaptable to every situation and never complain. While this works well for the social groups they are part of, it often is at the expense of the individual's sense of self, need fulfillment and long-term physical health.

It is very common for parents of anxiously-attached children to become intimidated and manipulated by their demanding, complaining youngsters. A terrible imbalance can develop in which the anxious child gets a disproportionate amount of family energy and attention while the avoidant child, who never complains or gets angry, gets overlooked and neglected. Anxious children can be highly jealous of any attention given elsewhere, even though they are getting far more than their share. The anxious child never feels sated, no matter how much is given. The avoidant child, meanwhile, shoves her unmet needs and feelings of inadequacy, anger and resentment underground, possibly to erupt much later in life in physical health problems or anger and hostility toward anyone he or she perceives as entitled, arrogant and bossy.

In some families, the parents feel guilt or a fear of depriving their child of what they need to feel secure. They may have difficulty distinguishing a need from a want. Such parents may be very familiar with imbalanced family relationships and take on the role of the appeaser and subjugator. They are selfless and their every behavior sends the message that their child is far more important. They are hyper-vigilant, emotionally reactive to the child's emotions and quick to give in so they and the child won't have to feel upset. Parents may derive satisfaction out of knowing they are all-giving and very responsive. Often, people who know how it feels to be deprived, abandoned or misunderstood fall into this trap, creating a child who is self-centered. So they keep giving in to bad behavior and inappropriate demands. The parents and their avoidant child may take on the attitude of, "It's just easier to do it myself than to deal with the aggravation of trying to get the high maintenance one to respond," which only reinforces the negative cycle.

Over time, parents, out of feeling exhausted and controlled, will begin to express more and more anger toward the child. This then reinforces the child's insecurity, leading to even more intense rigidity, complaining and demanding. Instead of the parents feeling helpless and hurt by their own parents, they've recreated the pattern with them being ruled by their child. Such children may be diagnosed with oppositional-defiant disorder. The parents often do not realize how their own fears and behaviors shaped their child's expectations of relationships. This family dynamic is very common and it is critical that the negative cycle be corrected early on as it is harmful to all involved. This is a situation that calls for professional intervention.

My client Beth grew up surrounded by insensitive, cruel family members and relatives who totally lacked empathy. Her feelings were always dismissed. Beth developed the habits of minimizing her feelings, smiling broadly and persevering in difficult situations without complaint. She never expressed anger or frustration. Beth grew up to be tremendously loving of animals and spent over three hours a day caring for her pets. She was very careful to make sure she responded to their need for security and support. It was a lot of work, but she always felt the joy the animals gave her made it worth the trouble. Also, Beth overcompensated for her perpetual feelings of fear by facing physical challenges that would have intimidated most people. She was a fearless downhill ski racer.

When Beth was pregnant with her first child, Lydia, and throughout the first years of Lydia's life, the child was exposed to her mother's high anxiety and fear. Lydia, like her mother, alternated between being fearless and feeling panicked. Because six-year-old Lydia had the courage to ride confidently on a huge horse, Beth didn't take Lydia's fear and panic seriously when it was expressed. When Lydia screamed out in fear about going into the basement or in disappointment over not getting to watch another show, Beth saw this as meaningless drama. Just as Beth had always covered her fear and disappointment with a big smile and the fortitude to push forward bravely, she responded to Lydia's distress with smiles and insistence she had no cause to be upset. Beth was out of sync, out of attunement, with her daughter's emotional state. Without realizing it, she was replicating what she experienced. The more that Beth disregarded and invalidated Lydia's (and her own) vulnerable feelings, the more angry and abusive Lydia became. Lydia's response to insecurity was the opposite of her mother's. Beth suppressed her emotions and needs, while Lydia blasted her emotions and needs. Whether the person is six-years-old or fifty-six-years-old, anger and hostility often are the outside manifestation of panic, helplessness and desperation to get a loved-one to pay attention and respond with empathy and support.

Parents of children like Lydia will need, among other things, to set boundaries while at the same time acknowledging and empathizing with the child's strong emotions. Anxious children need to have their emotions validated without the parents caving in to their unreasonable demands. Being a martyr benefits neither the parents nor the child. The parents need to recognize that setting limits strengthens their children's sense of security and helps them build their capacity to tolerate frustration. Life is full of frustration and children need to know how to cope with reality. When children experience that they are more powerful than their parents, it is actually an anxiety-provoking scenario. Children need to know that their parents are strong enough to not be overpowered by someone who bullies and to make sound judgments for the family's welfare.

While limit-setting is essential, to do so without responding to the child's emotions will result in an escalating battle of wills that damages the family's emotional climate. Parents need to provide soothing by calmly and warmly acknowledging their child's fears, using eye contact and, if the child is receptive, touch. They need to help their child articulate his or her feelings and needs. To do this well, we need to put ourselves in our child's shoes, imagining what might be going on inside and wondering out loud if we understand right. The more we understand our own emotional motivations, the more we can empathize with others.

Equally important, anxious children need to learn how to ask for reassurance that they matter and that their parents will be available and responsive without depriving others of having their needs met. They especially need help in learning how to self-soothe. For example, a child may be helped to develop a "safe place" and use the "Butterfly Hug" to calm themselves. There are EMDR therapists who specialize in working with children and can help them develop a few dependable skills or tools. Additionally, children can respond to EMDR trauma treatment more rapidly than adults with entrenched trauma neural networks acquired over decades. EMDRIA has a special interests group devoted to working with children and adolescents. Information may be obtained by going to www.emdria.org and looking up Special Interest Groups under "products and services." Also, the EMDR Institute, www.emdr.com, has a therapist directory in which you can seek names of those in your state who specialize in working with children.

Parents need to reconnect with their low-maintenance, avoidant children and make clear that they matter too and the parents are going to be more attentive and available from now on. Children who chronically witness parents indulging or fighting with a demanding sibling are as deeply impacted as the child who is in the spotlight. Each child needs a balance of receiving attention that is neither too intense nor diffuse. Parents need to have enough mindfulness to see the big picture, especially how their own behavior might be perceived by young, impressionable onlookers.

I'd like to speak more about the long-term lessons learned by the low-maintenance siblings of anxiously-attached children. In my practice I often work with adults who suffer from depression and/or anxiety as a result of the lessons they learned in homes like I've just described. One of the most powerful lessons is that it is safer to shrink into the wallpaper and not express yourself. Speaking up only leads to chronic conflict, criticism, hurt feelings, banging your head against the wall, anger and hostility. When you express yourself, you never win; you never are heard, understood or responded to. So there is no point in trying. This is called "learned helplessness."

When your needs are frustrated, and you believe there is nothing you can do about it, this creates feelings of resignation, sadness, hopelessness, resentment, bitterness and depression. In their attachment relationships, these avoidantly-attached individuals may expect the bare minimum and, once again, be in a relationship with someone who feels deprived, entitled and who has a bottomless pit when it comes to getting their needs met. They may go all out in other endeavors that seem safe and likely to pay off, such as work, sports or, ironically, caretaking others in need outside the family. They may over-function at work and in the community to compensate for the inner sense of inadequacy and powerlessness. They may be respected as the strong, level-headed and dependable leader. The pressure and anxiety that is chronically felt in the body, however, can eventually result in physical ailments, minor or major.

Another scenario for such grown up siblings may be feeling defeated, deflated and low-functioning across the board and wondering why they never follow-through with any of their goals. They may struggle with poor concentration, procrastination and behaviors that undermine themselves and others. Such individuals believe at the gut level: "I'm not important, I'm not good enough, I'm weak and I can't succeed." Their bodies and minds feel leaden and lethargic. They may find themselves attracted to porn sites to wake their bodies up. This becomes a compulsive fix and lifeline.

Grown up high-maintenance children experience difficulties on the other side of the continuum. They will need to change their focus from a stranglehold on relationships to developing their self-soothing skills and connection with the larger world and its nourishing bounty. I will address at length the opportunities for both the grown-up avoidant and anxiously attached children in the book's final chapter.

Other Forms of Yin and Yang in Family Life

Speaking of balance, each human being needs a balance of connection and autonomy. Too much connection and we lose ourself. Too much autonomy and we are isolated and unsupported. Either extreme is harmful to our health. Some parents err on the side of being too unavailable. They provide plenty of the material basics but are either clueless about emotional needs or are too overwhelmed with their personal lives or own arrested development. Other parents are too overwhelmingly present and engaged. Some partners come from diametrically opposed households. The one from an intrusive, enmeshed family environment now overvalues solitude and independence. The one from a lonely, isolated family environment now overvalues togetherness and sharing. Or they both come from the same extreme environment but one bought into it while the partner rebels against it.

In some families, two opposing value systems live side by side. One parent may corner the market on being relaxed, low-pressure, easy-going, non-judgmental, avoidant of facing problems, irreverent, impulsive and fun-loving. The other parent may corner the market on being concerned, serious, sensitive, and focused on problems, feelings, responsibility, discipline and improvement. Each parent perceives the other as harmful and needing to change. The indulgent parent runs no risk of being the "bad guy" to the children. The other parent becomes the bore, villain or kill-joy. (Picture Robin Williams and Sally Field in Mrs. Doubtfire.) You can imagine how these opposing values could play out in a family, reinforcing insecurities as each parent counteracts the other end of the continuum and confusing the hell out of the children.

Over the course of years the roles may switch so that each partner experiences being the protector and the enemy. Instead of each parent grappling with these complex issues and being able to relate to the child according to the situation rather than a rigid position, the issue gets balanced and addressed by divvying it up between two people. This leaves little room for the spouses to experience empathy and connection. This is where the "Venus and Mars" kind of talk comes in.

When we edit out certain emotions from our repertoire, it is more likely that we will be attracted to someone who will be very at home with experiencing and expressing that emotion, to a fault. We might never allow ourselves to acknowledge or express anger. We might be allergic to guilt or shame. We may tell ourselves we never feel helplessness, vulnerability or fear. Well, then our best friend or partner or child will probably be the spokesperson for those emotions. We'll end up experiencing them at arm's length, vicariously. The emotion will blare at us from the outside. We'll end up having to deal with those emotions one way or another.

This is also the case with behavior patterns. I once met a very composed mental health professional who in her adolescence was attracted to all the acting out peers at her school, even though she herself was obedient and reserved. In adulthood, she spent her workdays being ever patient listening to those who were having trouble emotionally or behaviorally. Yet, she actually revealed without blinking an eye that she didn't ever want nor need support from others. This is a classic example of avoidant attachment.

A common dynamic in families is that of blatant and latent problems. One parent or child may have numerous and obvious symptoms that make it clear that he or she has unresolved issues and needs help. The other parent or child may in contrast seem quite stable and rational. He or she may have only minor difficulties, such as physical ailments that are not affecting others or not recognized as significant. Often, when the symptomatic person has made great strides in therapy and is no longer expressing enough emotionality for two people, the other person's unfinished business begins to either gradually arise or suddenly erupt in response to some trigger.

Intergenerational Dramas

Often, family dramas and issues are played out over several generations. Children absorb their parents' emotions and then act them out in their own families. For example, Miranda's parents, Sara and Frank, had an unhappy marriage. Frank constantly spoke to Sara in an impatient and demeaning way, out of frustration with his wife's emotional coldness toward him and greater loyalty to her mother. Sara was preoccupied with her mother because the latter was shut down—having been traumatized from the loss of her own mother when she was ten. Sara never felt visible and significant to her mother. Frank was jealous and discouraged Sara's contact with her mother and her rare efforts at being more independent. Throughout her childhood, Miranda witnessed her father's misery and bullying and her mother's silent tolerance of it. Miranda sensed her mother's sadness, helplessness and longing for connection with her mother.

In adulthood, Miranda had little respect for her husband, Ricky, and didn't hide it. While she ridiculed her husband, she adored her mother, Sara. As for Ricky, he felt unloved and sometimes expressed this with anger and irritability. He eventually became resigned to never being understood or cared for. Miranda and Ricky had a daughter, Brenda, who, like her parents lacked a solid sense of self-worth. When she was in her twenties, Brenda moved in with her grandmother, Sara, who was now a widow and no longer living with a critical and controlling husband. Brenda always spoke glowingly and lovingly of her grandmother. Yet, after Brenda moved out five years later, Sara revealed in a rare moment of openness that during the time Brenda lived with her, Brenda said directly to her elderly grandmother, "Don't ask me to do anything for you. If you want me to go to the food store for you, I'm not doing it. I'm going to sit here and talk on the phone with my friends."

Every member of this family had experiences that generated feelings of being unlovable, undeserving or helpless to get love and recognition from the one person from whom they sought it. Each family member dealt with their painful feelings in a different way. Grandmother Sara helplessly wished to be with her mother while being submissive, distant and detached with grandfather. Grandfather Frank attacked his wife in a twisted attempt to get the love he felt deprived of. Miranda criticized or ignored Ricky at the same time she neglected herself and strove to make her mother feel valuable. Like her father, Miranda was critical of her spouse. Like her mother, Miranda was preoccupied with connecting with her mother. Ricky was like his mother-in-law, long-suffering and submissive to his spouse. In public, Brenda put her grandmother on a pedestal but in private she put herself on a pedestal at her grandmother's expense.

The distorted views each family member had of others led to extremes of adulation, contempt or indifference. Family members were unconsciously divided into "the entitled, worthy and lovable" and "the unentitled, unworthy and unlovable." Miranda was preoccupied with her mother's unverbalized, but palpable, sadness and pain. At the same time she was dismissive of her husband's feelings of discontent and her own emotional needs. Grandmother Sara experienced being overlooked by her grieving mother, criticized by her love-starved husband, devalued by her entitled granddaughter and over-valued by her compassionate daughter. While Sara was the recipient of intense love and concern from her daughter, it couldn't touch the part of her heart that Sara had needed in childhood for her mother to touch. And had Sara's mother been emotionally present to attune to and respond to her daughter, Sara would never have tolerated mistreatment from others or sent out signals of pain that her daughter felt compelled to answer.

Almost every family has their own "intergenerational drama" with distinctive themes and ways of managing disturbing emotions. You might find it valuable to discover your own. It's important to recognize that, while we can't undo what happened in the past, we can be mindful in the present and manage our current emotions appropriately, so that others don't end up breathing them in and acting them out in their own relationships. The more mindful we become of the larger picture, the more likely that we will invest our energies in the most productive directions. We may recognize that we've been excessively and exclusively watering a person whose heart is like a sidewalk or a bottomless pit, a person who never waters him or herself. We can then turn our watering can over ourselves and over another family member whose heart is soft, loose soil and has been endlessly waiting for a drop of love.

A family's "expressive style" can also be handed down over the generations. Some families let it all hang out, let their emotions fly and tell themselves "this is a good way to clear the air." Nothing is hidden, nobody has to guess what's going on; everybody gets to be heard. In another family, the parents make a set of rules, explicitly or implicitly, that command: "We don't confront each other. We don't say anything negative and we never complain, because nothing good comes out of conflict. We always focus on what's good and what we are grateful for." Each family pattern is an extreme reaction to fears about conflict, secrets, being heard, being hurt.

The truth is, we all need to know that we can express ourselves and be heard, that we don't have to be alone with our feelings, and that others will express themselves in a non-threatening way. We all need to know that family members will openly acknowledge and appreciate what is right and what pleases them, as well as express what is wrong and what upsets them. We need to know that we can be open with each other and still have boundaries, so that we don't become overwhelmed by others' problems. Finding this middle way is essential if all family members are to get their basic human needs met.

Cultivating Curiosity and Compassion

When a family member behaves in ways that are troubling or alarming to us, it's important that we exchange judgment for curiosity as soon as possible. At first, anger or fear will probably kick in, with the worst possible interpretation of the other's motives and likely consequences. Along with the strong emotions is often a corresponding urge to take decisive action right now. This is when a pause button can be very helpful. For the sooner we can regain our composure and Higher Self, the better our thinking and decision-making will be. We need to look beneath the surface, beneath the outward behavior, to understand what hidden need this behavior is meeting.

For example, some experts believe that when parents face the problem of compulsive texting by adolescents, they should simply lay down the law and throw the phone away. When a person is spending dozens of hours a week doing anything in a driven fashion, you have to consider that the behavior may be a compulsive way of either avoiding or managing disturbing emotions. So, if you take away one defensive strategy, another will most likely replace it. In an article I read about a compulsive texter, she stated that she had to keep her cell phone on all night long because, what if someone tried to reach her and couldn't connect, couldn't get a response? Once again, this sounds like insecure attachment, someone who knows how it feels to not be able to connect when in need and someone who has learned that she is responsible for taking away others' pain. No matter how many friends she responds to, her own feeling of insecurity will not be soothed. It won't scratch her itch. This is the early manifestation of what in adulthood will become rescuing animals, taking in far too many foster children, overprotecting children or sacrificing one's own health to save others.

It is also important to become aware of what kind of family behavior we tend to automatically feel compassion for—and what kind of behavior we're quick to judge. Many families have unconsciously created "heroes" and "villains." For most of us, it's easy to feel compassion for any victim of a family member who regularly relies on anger, control and aggression to handle their fears and needs. That family member may be seen as an innocent martyr or saint, deserving of sympathy and love. But how often do we feel compassion for the angry, aggressive person in the family?

While there is no doubt that aggression must be replaced with the courage to share vulnerable feelings, it is also important to recognize the suffering of the angry person. Anyone who has a pattern of defending himself or herself through the expression of anger is perennially perceived as the "bad guy" and the one who is wrong and sick. Since the bad guy never clearly reveals his or her hurt and helplessness, there is no evidence that he either needs or deserves compassion. Onlookers will most likely feel sorry for the victim while feeling disgust, disapproval and anger toward the angry aggressor. Being stuck in the "bad guy" role in the family, and not knowing how to inspire others to care, is a very painful place to be. These "fighting" family members need help just as desperately as those who freeze or flee.

Likewise, it is important to recognize the role of the "victim" in enabling the abuse. Those who are perceived by others as innocent victims and entitled to be angry rarely express anger or set limits. Children cannot be expected to advocate for themselves. However, when the victim is an adult, there often is no recognition by others of how inappropriate it is for him or her to be passive, tolerant and helpless. The self-worth of adult victims has been so beaten down over their entire lifetime that they feel more like helpless children than competent adults, which is why they remain stuck. Often children, in childhood or adulthood, will try to "rescue" their victimized parent. But this is a futile effort that is exhausting and may result in anxiety, depression or impaired physical health. The adult victim must take responsibility by seeking professional help to develop an *internal* sense of self-worth, entitlement and self-efficacy and truly transform his or her life and relationships.

Investing Our Energy in the Right Places

Stephen Covey, author of *The Seven Habits of Highly Effective People* and *The Seven Habits of Highly Effective Families*, discusses a valuable concept known as the "emotional bank account." In our relationships we make deposits when we do something supportive and we make withdrawals when we cause hurt. One withdrawal can counteract several deposits. This is an important point because a family member may be doing many positive things that demonstrate their love and devotion for another, but at the same time withhold a basic emotional need or stomp on a raw spot. When we are given mixed messages like this, we're left feeling a lack of confidence in our family member and what we mean to him or her.

As explained in the chapter on Attachment, it is normal to have ruptures in our relationships and we have to develop some tolerance for that. However, when the ruptures occur too often or are related to our deepest needs or wounds, our basic sense of security and trust is compromised. What is so tragic is that many parents and spouses put out tremendous energy and effort to give and respond to each other and their children, but their withdrawals create major setbacks and keep resurrecting their loved ones' doubts, fears and defenses.

In order to shift our relationship's emotional bank account in the direction of trust, we need to do what is counterintuitive and requires our Better Self. Instead of dismissing our family member's upset or blaming them for their own unhappiness, we need to express curiosity about what they experienced. We need to use our imagination and heart and walk in their shoes so that we can experience and express empathy. Truly understanding your family member's inner world will create a repair that is genuine and effective and can even bring you closer than before the injury occurred. Experiencing true understanding will be more conducive to happiness than more mundane deposits like being taken to a favorite water park, being given a DVD player or being allowed to have a sleepover party. It's for this reason that painful events in life do not have to be dead end streets, but can be seen as opportunities for genuine connection and growth. It all depends on who shows up—our defenses or our mindful Higher Self.

I've given much thought to what are the most significant advantages or resources children could have that would make them feel rich in the present and more likely to thrive in the future. Some children live in a neighborhood full of peers to play with, others have no one nearby. Some have aunts, uncles and cousins who get together with them often, others barely know their relatives. Some children have siblings, others don't. Some enjoy entertaining or intelligent conversations with their parents, others don't. Some get private lessons to cultivate their skills and talents, others don't. Some live in cities full of diversity, stimulation and culture. Others live in rural settings with plenty of fresh air and natural beauty. Some have had the experience of traveling to or living in other countries, while others have never left their small town. Some have had a church to belong to with guiding values and familiar, kind faces, while others have had no explicit direction or community.

Each one of these and other resources could just as likely be a source of pain as support, depending on the unique circumstances. I had a deeply frightened, depressed and self-destructive adolescent client who had traveled throughout the world and yet, when I asked her to imagine a place where she would feel safe or relaxed, she had great difficulty identifying one. She finally thought of a place which was walking distance from her home. While she had wonderful opportunities, the fact that she was predominantly raised by housekeepers while her parents were unavailable took a heavy toll on her self-worth and sense of security. I've also worked with individuals who experienced much mental cruelty at the hands of their aunts, uncles, cousins and grandparents or saw their relatives drunk, out of control and violent.

Some parents have made huge sacrifices in order that their children could excel in their area of talent and work on goals such as Olympic gold. While on the one hand the child is being given much encouragement and support in their area of interest, what happens when the child doesn't meet up to personal or familial standards? Knowing how much family members have given up so that the one individual could know success and fame, this could be a tremendous burden for a young person to carry. As children, they can't be expected to understand the repercussions of such an arrangement. I wonder how much a parent's own need to manage recurring feelings of shame, insignificance or vengeance plays into the creation of a shining star?

Every member of a family has the same psychological needs: safety, comfort, closeness, protection, encouragement, acceptance and respect. Some parents invest a great deal in their relationships with their children, while the relationship with their spouse is tense, hostile or almost non-existent. Any neglect, mistreating or undermining of one family member is going to be felt throughout the family system and will cause repercussions in the present as well as in the next generation. Family therapy practitioners call this the *intergenerational transmission of pain.* We need to keep uppermost in our minds what messages and lessons our children are taking from our behavior, which speaks louder than any words. As Robert Fulghum said, "Don't worry that children never listen to you, worry that they are always watching you." Albert Schweitzer also had this to say, "Example is not the main thing in influencing others. It is the only thing."

In some families, tremendous thought, time and energy are poured into achieving, developing skills and talents, or renovating their houses. While these, in and of themselves, are valid and worthwhile pursuits, when they are substitutes for being in touch with our inner life or nourishing intimate relationships, they can be equivalent to putting beautiful paintings over a crumbling wall. It seems to me that our first order of business is to remodel our emotional brains and relationships and be concerned with the Feng Shui of our psychological homes. Children breathe in the emotional states of their family members and the parents must be responsible about monitoring, managing and, if necessary, healing their emotional distress or numbness.

"A Man's Reach Should Exceed His Grasp or What's a Heaven For?"
Robert Browning

Throughout this book, I am presenting a vision that points us in a direction that will bring us greater peace and fulfillment. This vision is an ideal to bring to fruition in our daily life, as best we can, without the expectation of achieving perfection. We are, after all, human beings.

So what are the essential conditions that best nourish developing human beings? Priest and educator Theodore Hesburgh said, "The most important thing a father can do for his children is to love their mother." Psychologist Steven Stosny has said, "Research has shown a child who sees his mother mistreated is more damaged than if the child himself is abused." I believe that children need to witness *both* parents treating the other with respect and kindness. This doesn't mean they never disagree or argue. It means that they avoid destructive criticism, contempt and shutting out their partner. It also means that they show genuine affection toward the other and concern for whatever is important to their mate. They don't relegate their spouse to the bottom of the totem pole. Neither do they put their spouse on a pedestal.

Whatever way a couple relates to each other and to their child is going to create the wired-in template for the child on how to be in an intimate relationship. If a child doesn't have parents who can talk about their own and the child's vulnerable feelings, but instead rely on defenses, the child will carry that legacy into his or her adult relationships. In his research on attachment, psychoanalyst Peter Fonagy reports, "Children who have been taught to tell stories that include mental states demonstrate a greater frequency of secure attachment. Being able to understand and consider the mental states of oneself and others has been shown to decrease dependency on defensive strategies." This means that we need to help our children develop the language to observe, identify and express what they experience internally—beliefs, hopes, emotions, feelings and intentions. Our ability to put words to our mental states and their mental states, fosters their ability for reflection, empathy and wiser perceptions and decisions.

In addition, psychologist Louis Cozolino says, "With increased nurturance and support, stress hormone levels decrease; physical comfort and soothing talk with caretakers helps the brain to integrate experience." Just as adult members of an intimate relationship need to be accessible, responsive and engaged, children need the same from their parents. Children need to know that they can connect with their parents and that their parents are really paying full attention and not just going through the motions. Children need to feel confident that their parents will take their needs and concerns seriously and come through for the child.

As between members of a couple, the quality of the interaction between parent and child is more important than the content. In communicating with loved ones, we must be aware of nonverbal communication: our facial expressions, tone of voice, posture and being in sync with their emotional states. We must avoid any insensitive behavior, including mocking expressions, snickers, eye-rolling, sneers, gruffness, inappropriate laughing, or cold detachment. When our partner or child is feeling upset, that is a time for us to soften our voices, slow the pace of our speech, make eye contact and provide reassuring gentle touch. We need to remember that touch, when done for the benefit of the one we love, is a natural tranquilizer.

When there is conflict between parent and child, or between siblings, we need to quickly recognize that beneath the anger are probably feelings of hurt, sadness, powerlessness or fear. Just as with our adult partner, we need to be curious rather than judgmental and to repair ruptures with our children by processing the emotions, perceptions and beliefs involved. We need to give our children ample opportunity to express what was going on for them and validate their emotions, even if we disapprove of their behavior and set consequences for it. Just letting things blow over is not sufficient. We need to take every opportunity we can to cultivate our children's emotional intelligence.

We also need to develop a kind of "second sight" with family members. We need to be aware of not only what we intend by our remarks to a child or spouse, but how they might actually be receiving them. Sometimes family members will not give us any feedback to help us recognize and correct our behavior. We need to reflect more on whether there is any possible negative interpretation of our comments and/or nonverbal communication. We need to broaden our perspective to include the hearts and minds of others, imagining what it is like to be them in relation to us.

This means that often, it is far better for parents to be quiet and attentive than to speak. Giving children space to express themselves helps them clarify their perspectives and needs and develop their sense of self. At the same time, listening well helps us get a better understanding of who these young people are who are in our keep. As an example, for years in conversations with my family, I had a knee-jerk reaction of defending anyone whom I heard being judged. My kids now make a joke of it, "Yeah, Mom, everyone has good intentions." On the other hand, whenever someone was spoken of as having it all together, I would predictably point out that "everyone has issues." It only occurred to me recently how invalidating my response was to the person speaking. Now, my intention is to just listen, ask questions to better understand their perspective or make a remark that is supportive of their experience.

While we need to be responsive to the opinions, perceptions and feelings of our children, we must also be comfortable with being leaders and exercising our legitimate and valuable authority as parents. Today, family life is too often ruled by children, from their material desires to their extracurricular activities. While it is important to encourage our children's physical, artistic and social development and be present to provide moral support and recognition, it is also important that we not wear ourselves out. In previous generations children had no say, no rights. In recent generations, there seems to have been a pendulum swing to the other extreme in many homes. While developing critical thinking and practicing decision-making are important for our children, they should never be permitted to be the ultimate authority in a family. Parents are the architects of the family, and most children respond well if parents state their positions calmly, respectfully and firmly, and provide a brief, age-appropriate explanation of their decision-making. It is more important that parents demonstrate mature leadership than win a popularity contest.

Getting Help

We also need to take good care of ourselves. Children need to learn that the world doesn't revolve around them; others have needs too. Children need parents who are thriving, not martyrs. In fact, this probably is the number one factor in children's thriving—that they have parents who are mindful of their own emotional, mental and physical states and take whatever steps necessary to prosper. The quality of our family life follows from our own degree of well-being. We mustn't dismiss or minimize chronic states of depression, insecurity, anxiety, overwhelm, anger or distrust. We must take advantage of the opportunities now available to resolve these problems. Keep in mind that emotions in families are highly contagious. Whether family members deal with our emotions by absorbing them or repelling them, whether they are conscious of our emotional suffering or in denial about it, lessons are being learned and will be reenacted. Get help for your own sake, but also for the sake of your family.

Not only do we need to be mindful of our own health, we need to recognize when, despite our best efforts to care for our spouse, marriage or children, they are not responding. It is important not to let wishful thinking, misplaced pride, shame, hopelessness or minimizing prevent us from getting professional help early on, before problems become entrenched or escalate.

Remember too, that a child's problem is a family problem. When one of our children has troubling symptoms, we need to recognize that the child doesn't live in a vacuum and so shouldn't be seen as the only family member who could benefit from therapy. Any help the parents receive that strengthens their marriage, own mental health or parenting skills is going to benefit not only the currently symptomatic child but all family members. We need to remember that, when one child has psychological symptoms, there is a good chance other children are also being affected but that their issues are currently dormant.

Therapists who work with adolescents and children often find that parents just want to drop off the child and have him "fixed." In the 13 years that I provided therapy to adolescents in school settings, I can count on one hand the number of parents who contacted me to ask how their child was doing and whether there was some way they could be involved in his treatment. While a young person can benefit greatly from experiencing a nurturing, attuned relationship with a therapist, counseling is usually of greater value when interventions aim to help children build a trusting and secure relationship with their own parents. A family systems and emotion-focused therapy, such as EFT, can guide this process.

Sometimes a spouse refuses to participate in therapy, despite self-defeating behaviors that are damaging to family members as well. This might include a partner with addictions, delusions, abusive behavior or anger problems. It must be noted here that mental and verbal abuse is at least as damaging as physical. Under these unfortunate circumstances, we need to recognize what we can and cannot do. Trying to control others always backfires. The only person we can control is ourself. Far better strategies include:

- Managing our own emotional reactivity so that we are not contributing to a negative cycle.
- Asking our partner to sit with us so we can talk about a problem we are having and then mustering up the courage to share our fears and hurts about the direction we see the family going in.
- Focusing our energies on ample self-care so we can function at our best for our own sake and our children's.
- Seeking the company of those who are healthy and able to respond to our needs and help us maintain perspective, feel supported and explore our options.

With regard to the final strategy, let me be clear that I am *not* talking about a romantic or sexual relationship, which would only cause more harm and complicate the situation further. Nor am I talking about finding someone who will bash our mate and paint us as a martyr. Creating a "shameful one" and "shame-free one" may feel good in the short-run, but it ultimately will not help you to engage in healthy problem-solving or avoid similar predicaments in the future.

When a partner persists in denying his or her need to change and the destructive behavior continues to be detrimental to the rest of the family, the concerned partner may need to make other living arrangements for her own and the children's welfare. While it may be disturbing to the children to see the family separate, it can be far more harmful to continue to subject children to an out-of-control parent. I've known people who wished that their parents had separated rather than subject them to daily misery and torment. Occasionally, when the concerned parent takes such action, it spurs the one who has been in denial into accepting the need to change and seek professional help.

Let me end this chapter by saying that mental health is always about balance. We and our children need to be able to laugh and cry, think and feel, judge and appreciate, do and be. Each of us needs to be able to reflect and imagine, influence and be influenced, relax and be productive. We need stimulation and stillness, serious moments and carefree times. To be fully human we also need to be strong and vulnerable, be accepted and encouraged to grow, give and receive affection and attention, enjoy solitude and connection, respect and challenge authority, be self-disciplined and creative, recognize what is upsetting and what is uplifting, integrate our past, savor our present and dream and set goals for the future.

This may seem like a tall order, but, like all works of art, creating a balanced, full life is not something that can be rushed, forced or chased. We develop organically and mature over time like a fine wine or a photograph. The evolution of each human life has an inherent beauty, which often can't be appreciated with a close-up lens. When we see it from a distance and with a panoramic lens, we are far better able to appreciate how we are, even now. We are far more likely to find balance and the right perspective when we are connected to our inner wisdom—which brings us to our next chapter on Mindfulness, the Higher Self and Being.

CHAPTER NINE

Mindfulness, the Higher Self and Being

WHAT DOES IT TAKE TO FEEL MOST ALIVE; to have the sense that we really are showing up for this trip called Life? What gives us the feeling of operating on all cylinders and thriving rather than feeling cornered by lions, stretched on a rack, hanging off a cliff clutching a loose vine or merely going through the motions? First of all, we need to be fully conscious, awake and in touch with our bodies and senses. That means not drifting in and out of a coma and not being lost for hours in our heads, electronic screens and virtual realities. We need to have adequate affect management skills to allow our emotions to come in the front door, share their messages and move on, having been treated with respect. With those skills, the emotional circulation provides vitality. Without the skills we tread water with our nostrils barely above the water line or develop emotional phlebitis.

What separates humans from animals is our ability to be self-aware. Both animals and humans have consciousness, but only humans can be aware that they are aware. While we have this capacity, it is tremendously underdeveloped and this chapter is about cultivating our distinguishing faculty. When we are merely conscious, we look but don't really see, touch but don't really feel, hear but don't really listen and move without being moved. We get the details but miss the full picture and meaning. Without a well-developed self-awareness, we are at risk of being in a trance in which we live out our past again and again like some *Twilight Zone* episode.

We need to observe and reflect on our life so that we can recognize the patterns in our thoughts, perceptions, beliefs, complaints, urges and habits that keep us in our fatalistic ruts. We need to be able to fully realize when disturbing thoughts, memories and fantasies have invaded the present and not let them hold us hostage. We fear the future because we're still feeling vulnerable and helpless from the past. We fear we are going to be hurt again if we don't control everything. We don't trust ourselves, others or the world enough to feel safe. Our preoccupation with the past is because it has been boarded over alive like Edgar Alan Poe's *Tell-Tale Heart*. It's imperative that we be proactive in resolving the past with a trauma treatment, such as EMDR, so that we can catch up to today, relieved of the ghosts of the past and the burden of carrying yesterday.

Without energy being invested in resisting the unwanted or dueling with fears, we have more energy and attention available for noticing not only the disturbing, but the wonderful. When we have faced and worked through our unresolved memories, the radar screen of our attention broadens tremendously and a new reality presents itself. When we're not fixated on threat and defending ourselves, when we're not exhausted and burned out from chronic stress, we are able to see the daily evidence that we are in the midst of a mind-blowing miracle called Life. We have the chance to live according to the words of the contemporary spiritual teacher Ram Dass, "Be Here Now." Then we will experience breathtaking, heart-rippling moments that counterbalance every trial and tribulation. When we're fully conscious of the universe's artistry and generosity, who needs psychedelics or Prozac?

Functioning at our best means processing emotional experiences as they arise, rather than creating a backlog. It entails keeping ourselves open to experience, even when we've been put through the wringer. Many years ago I attended the funeral of a very young family member. A few days later, I decided to go to Longwood Gardens for the day. Being in the presence of abundant and sublime beauty was tremendously helpful to me, so inspiring and reaffirming of life's fundamental goodness. We never can predict what gifts will be laid before us if we keep our eyes and hearts open.

This reminds me of Mick, a former client of mine, who had a history of mental and physical cruelty at the hands of his older siblings. When he first came to me, he was in a chronic state of anxiety, distrust, anger, contempt and hostility. He was always anticipating being judged and attacked and ready to prove his fearlessness and superiority. Because of his determination to make a better life for himself, our heartfelt connection and with the help of EMDR, Mick was able to resolve his traumas and develop feelings of self-worth, safety and competency.

Because torment was no longer dominating his mental and physical states, Mick's attention was now freed up to see what was before him in the present moment. He recently called and told me that he is amazed at how many serendipitous experiences he has been having. When he opens up to people about his life, he finds out that they have similar interests and they end up sharing their experiences and resources. This same man, who previously had experienced so much violence, first as victim and later as aggressor, is now enjoying meeting people and enthusiastic about learning and developing his spirituality.

Reexperiencing and acknowledging your childhood relational history is most certainly a courageous task: the emotional equivalent of scaling Mount Everest. As you face the challenge, one step at a time, your sense of self expands and strengthens. As you reach each peak along the way, you gain perspective on how far you have traveled and you come to know your inner fortitude and dignity. You also discover the wide world that couldn't be seen while your mind was glued to the threats that dominated your awareness. You wake up from a nightmare and feel relieved to find that reality is far more benign and sweet than you could ever have imagined.

One of my favorite images is a poster from the Sixties that showed an old guru, with long flowing white hair and a loincloth, standing on a surf board. The words underneath the picture read, "We can't stop the waves, but we can learn to surf." Each one of us will face losses, crises and challenges over the course of a lifetime. Some people have most of them in their childhood years. Some have several coincide within a particularly horrific month or year. Some have them spread out with time in between each to fully recover. Our life experiences vary in intensity over time, like the variations of the sea. Sometimes the ocean is like a placid lake. Sometimes it is furious, with waves crashing from every angle. Other times the waves roll in evenly, rhythmically, gracefully and in manageable sizes.

Some people overdo being out in the waves, to the point of chills, wrinkled skin and exhaustion. Some people face the waves, chest out, with an insulted, self-centered attitude of, "Hey, what are these big waves doing here on my day off!" Others turn their backs to the waves and never see anything coming. Then there are those who cling to their beach towels, afraid to even enter the water. Others enjoy the exhilaration of body-surfing the waves, now and then misjudging the timing and getting tossed about, but that doesn't stop them from wanting to go back out. Attitude is everything when it comes to life.

There has been much research that shows that optimists are more effective, successful and happy than pessimists, in every category: relationships, politics, finances, education, employment, sports, health, you name it. The "can do" attitude ensures that the person will rise to the occasion and find whatever means necessary to achieve their goals. They don't give up easily and are resilient. They recognize and capitalize on resources and opportunities. They aren't intimidated by obstacles, but see them as challenges that exercise their intelligence and creativity. People with fewer natural gifts have surpassed those with in-born talent and higher cognitive intelligence. The determining factor was optimism. Pessimists in contrast, don't expect success, so their efforts are half-hearted. Pessimists' lives are a bland and meager fare compared to the banquet that optimists enjoy.

There are four qualifying points that belong here. First, we all have personal and circumstantial limitations and it is important that we recognize these, otherwise we will bang our heads against the wall and the long term result could be falling into a depression. Being able to distinguish legitimate obstacles from perceived obstacles requires an impartial and calm awareness that is able to recognize when we are in over our heads and when the only significant obstacles are fear and self-doubt.

Second, some people are driven to excel in order to meet their parents' expectations and compensate for or avoid feelings of shame, failure and inadequacy. Rather than looking for the sources of those emotions and integrating those experiences into their consciousness, such people bury them with the hope that they will never have to be revealed. Their defenses design a window-dressing for others, that is so convincing, that the person forgets it's just a façade. When people have a hidden part of themselves that retains a shameful identity, it is possible they will eventually engage in shameful acts. At some point they may get caught in illegal, deceitful, disloyal or immoral behaviors that reveal their dark side.

When these people are celebrities, athletes or politicians, everyone is shocked to see how the mighty have fallen. They wonder how someone so bright, with so much going for them, could be so foolish or arrogant. The behaviors could be twisted solutions for avoiding painful emotions, substitutes for comforting human relationships. Or, it could be that the part that misbehaves is sabotaging the person's false persona and trying to give the person a wakeup call to be authentic, experience the disowned emotions and heal the dissociated memories. Symptoms and crises can be seen as our inner wisdom helping us to be honest and whole, to have integrity.

Third, as I said previously, it is imperative that we not edit out or dismiss the negative, particularly when it comes to emotions, experiences and relationships. If we try to skip the step of owning and mourning our losses or dealing with our hurts and unmet needs, and move onto a false optimism, the losses are going to pound on that façade until we shout "Uncle!"

And fourth, I'm thinking right now of a couple in which both partners have inappropriately extreme optimism offsetting deep pessimism, helplessness and despair. The wife's optimism and undying hope is responsible for her putting out huge amounts of energy in the form of talk and complaints aimed at getting her husband to change so that she can feel valued and connected. But simultaneously she has a huge reservoir of emotional certainty that she is unlovable and destined to be alone. At the same time, the husband's optimism and sense of responsibility have him expending huge amounts of mental energy trying to satisfy his wife's needs while on another level he feels immense inadequacy and hopelessness. These opposing internal ego states cause tremendous stress on each individual's physiology as well as mental states. Both husband and wife have a long history of physical ailments.

In his CD and DVD, *The Happiness Prescription*, Deepak Chopra (www.chopra.com) says our life situation is responsible for only 8 to 15% of our happiness quotient. It is not a major determinant. Whether we win a lottery or face a tragedy, one year later our degree of happiness will be the same. Neither changes our set point for happiness. He reports that research on executives in Forbes 500 companies showed that 42% were less happy than the average person. Chopra says that pleasure and immediate gratification are transient; they last a few hours. Fulfillment, on the other hand, is a deeper gratification. What produces a sense of fulfillment are these: personal, meaningful accomplishment; making a difference in the world; creativity; imagination; inspiration; conscious choices and making others happy.

Let me add here that there are those who have the best of everything—the most elite educations, fascinating opportunities, prestigious positions, extravagant parties and vacations, eminent and affluent friends and colleagues and impressive homes and neighborhoods. But if our relationships with ourself and our family members are empty, shallow and judgmental, if our authentic self and needs are dismissed and unknown, if the recognition and love received are conditional on appearance, status and achievement and if our actions are ego-driven, then all that outer glitter is an illusion and misguided substitute for what nourishes the soul.

Just as we are drawn to a marriage partner who is oil to our water, living in contemporary society provides ample challenge to our spiritual development. There are so many temptations and distractions to steer us off course. Our spiritual muscle has plenty of opportunity for work outs, provided we have the awareness and intention to do so. As Peter Russell, author of the excellent book *Waking Up in Time: Finding Inner Peace in Times of Accelerating Change*, states, "Our culture has developed a remarkable mastery of the material world around us; it is time now to develop a similar mastery of the inner world of mind. This is the next great frontier, not outer space, but inner space." (His website, www.peterrussell.com, is a wonderful resource on "The Spirit of Now, Science, Consciousness, Spiritual Wisdom, Global Brain, Meditations and Nature of Reality.")

Developing Mindfulness

The state of mind that is optimal to flourishing is "mindfulness," an intentional, non-judgmental attentiveness and receptivity to the present moment and all its facets. You don't need a prescription and it doesn't cost a cent. Mindfulness practice fosters the ability to see the whole picture rather than an edited, conditioned, distorted, ego-centered or prejudiced one. When we really see things that we normally take for granted, there develops what is called, "beginner's mind," a fresh perception and realization. We also begin to recognize that whatever presents itself to us, whether uplifting or disturbing, is temporary. We experience that we are the awareness that embraces and releases all that comes and goes, like a wedding party reception line.

The process of mindfulness replaces anxious scrutiny and efforts to control with serenity and acceptance. As the churned-up sediment of our internal thoughts, emotions, body sensations and images begins to settle down, we experience greater and greater clarity of vision which helps us discover what, if anything, is the wise action to take. Mindfulness is a state of being that we can cultivate and is most fully present when we experience courage, curiosity, calmness, clarity, confidence and compassion. According to psychiatrist Daniel Siegel and meditation master Jon Kabat-Zinn, the qualities and faculties possessed during mindfulness meditation are the same ones that are developed in a secure attachment relationship. Mindfulness and secure attachment both develop the brain circuits of the mid prefrontal cortex, the part of the brain that is most responsible for emotional and social intelligence.

Calling upon mindfulness, which is an aspect of our Higher Self, makes it possible to heal the past that infiltrates, distorts and taints our present. During EMDR, the abilities to observe mindfully and to access an inherent and wise healing mechanism are the gifts of our Higher Self. Our Higher Self also is present to shower its love on the wounded parts of our personality. I remember a moving therapy session of my own in which my heart connected with the heart of the little girl I once was, sitting alone on her bed. This loving connection was instantaneous and provoked a powerful, compassionate "mother bear" urge to comfort and protect. It seems to me that our first efforts at evoking our Higher Self need to be to heal ourselves. Trying to come through for others is going to be much harder when our personalities are still wrestling with the past. First, we must be whole and at peace with our past.

This reality was underscored in a fascinating article in the *Shambhala Sun* written by Jack Kornfield, the American Buddhist teacher and clinical psychologist. The article was entitled: "Even the Best Meditators Have Old Wounds to Heal." For decades he had traveled to far-off places, studied with esteemed monks, learned ancient methods of spiritual practice and meditated with other students who also devoted large periods of their lives to developing a connection with their Higher Selves. What he found in the East as well as the West, with renowned teachers as well as their conscientious students of meditation, was that their extensive spiritual practices were not sufficient to resolve or overcome their struggles with neurotic symptoms and compulsive behaviors. Even many of the most respected centers of spiritual development were plagued with incidents involving teachers who were financially or sexually exploitative or failed at their duty to others because of addictions. Kornfield found that some people who had already participated in psychotherapy needed spiritual practice to round out their development, while others who started with the spiritual path needed to supplement that practice with mental health services. Why are we so surprised when religious leaders, therapists, high achievers, politicians, celebrities or community leaders succumb to inappropriate behavior? They are just as human as all of us, with their own unattended wounds, misguided defenses and unmet needs.

I have found it interesting that many people's idea of meditation is limited to mastering the mental concentration necessary to tune out stimuli at will. As long as people are in that focused and calm state of mind, nothing gets to them. It's even possible for people to use this kind of meditation as a way to dissociate from painful reality. Some practitioners of meditation connect with a stillness and deep bliss that creates in them a deep knowing that they are one with the universe and its loving wholeness. While this is a truth that is transformative in significant ways, it doesn't necessarily heal their wounded personalities and array of self-defeating defenses. As soon as they resume interacting with the world, they get triggered by all those unconscious beings walking the planet, especially in their family, be it a spiritual family or a nuclear family.

Being able to sustain a Higher Consciousness, the full awareness and recognition as we live our day to day lives that others are an extension of us and we are an extension of them and that there is a beauty and design to the way things are, is a tall order for all but saints. We can, however, begin to behave in accordance with our Higher Selves by doing the work of bringing our personal unconscious to consciousness and peace and security to our childhood selves. Then, our next challenge will be to increase our ability to bring our Higher Self into our place of greatest difficulty—our families. As Ram Dass has said, "Relationships are the yoga of the West." Choosing to commit to and bring consciousness to an important relationship—with ourself, our spouse, our child—is a highly spiritual endeavor.

Eckhart Tolle also sees this as the purpose of intimate relationships, to bring consciousness into the world in each present moment. "How many people does it take to make your life into a spiritual practice? Never mind if your partner will not cooperate. Sanity—consciousness—can only come into this world through you. You do not need to wait for the world to become sane, or for somebody else to become conscious, before you can be enlightened. You may wait forever. Do not accuse each other of being unconscious. The moment you start to argue, you have identified with a mental position and are defending not only that position but also your sense of self. The ego is in charge."

To develop our spiritual natures, we must let go of our egos. What we spent the first chapters of our lives building, we must begin to transcend. Whenever we are able to zoom out from our egocentric perspective to the larger picture, the welfare of the whole, we are in our Higher Self. As I hope you might deduce from this, family, community and international relations require the same capacity if we are ever to create solutions that truly address the competing perspectives and needs of any social challenge. We are a far cry from that day. The human race is still in kindergarten when it comes to accessing the state of mind that knows how to create secure bonds and harmony.

This brings us to the Serenity Prayer of Alcoholics Anonymous, which is relevant to any desire for change: "God grant me the serenity to accept the things I cannot change, the courage to change the things I can, and the wisdom to know the difference." There is so much in the world we cannot change, billions of factors, billions of egos, but if each of us takes responsibility for cultivating our Higher Self, we can have a valuable impact on those around us. Being our best selves in the company of those whose lives we touch is the greatest gift we have the capacity to bestow in this life. Loving others as ourselves is enough work for a lifetime and I can't imagine a more challenging and significant contribution.

Cultivating a higher quality of awareness and more attention to "being" provides a greater sense of harmony, belonging and peace in this life, as it is. On the subjects of change and purpose, we have these insightful quotes from Alan Watts, who has influenced much of the following section and is my favorite philosopher. Many of his books, and even more delightful and charming audio recordings of his talks, can be found at www.alanwatts.com. "What we see as death, empty space or nothingness is only the trough between the crests of this endlessly waving ocean. It is all part of the illusion that there should seem to be something to be gained in the future, and that there is an urgent necessity to go on and on until we get it. Yet just as there is no time but the present, and no one except the all-and-everything, there is never anything to be gained—though the zest of the game is to pretend there is."

Watts also has said, "A living body is not a fixed *thing* but a flowing *event*, like a flame or a whirlpool: the shape alone is stable, for the substance is a stream of energy going in at one end and out at the other. We are particularly and temporarily identifiable wiggles in a stream that enters us in the form of light, heat, air, water, milk, bread, fruit, beer, beef Stroganoff, caviar, and *pâté de foie gras*. It goes out as gas and excrement—and also as semen, babies, talk, politics, commerce, war, poetry, and music. And philosophy."

The Fruits of Mindful Awareness

Developing a higher awareness of the larger picture, and a deep acceptance and appreciation of what is, does not mean fatalism and passivity. It does not mean that we allow ourselves or others to be abused or that we never bother watering the dry plots of land we come across in our lives. It just frees up our energy to invest in what is most essential, including our capacities for creation and love. It means that we take responsibility for making personal decisions that are within our control, which might mean choosing to not associate with those who flail out at others in their pain. It means that we do our part to nourish those around us, as well as ourselves, knowing full well that we are responsible only for the effort, not the outcome. We do what we believe is right and loving in the present moment, without it being dependent upon results in the future. We live mindfully enough so that we have the mental space, energy, awareness and inspiration needed to cultivate the creative seeds that are ours alone to bring to fruition. In so doing, we experience the enthusiasm and passion of creation and we may bring joy, hope, inspiration, understanding, peace and energy to others.

As we experience the full spectrum of what life entails, illness and health, failure and success, pain and glory, drought and bounty, we go with it, knowing to resist is futile and all things will pass. Being able to live this way is equivalent to relaxing our body and mind as we walk into a cold wind and being aroused by its energy, rather than stiffening up against it with a scowl on our faces, insisting it shouldn't be there. It *is* there and has a right to be there, just as much as we do. It is a passing event and is just one of the billions of facets of this phenomenon called Life. The more we are able to say "yes" to, the more serene and free we can feel. The more we see others, events and circumstances as wrong or enemies, the more constricted, isolated, disappointing and threatening our lives will be. The more experiences we can appreciate and recognize as colorful fragments in a colossal, engrossing kaleidoscope, the more we can feel at home and enjoy the show.

People who experience chronic anxiety experience a bodily conviction that getting their expectations met, *now*, is a matter of life or death. They make mountains out of every molehill and feel compelled to act on every urge. People who are rigid can only be happy under very limited circumstances—every i must be dotted, every t must be crossed. Life is walking an eternal tightrope. The psychologist Albert Ellis called this way of living "*must*urbation." Mindfulness practice teaches the overly-anxious person that life goes on without disaster when they sit and observe rather than act on an urge. The more they can tolerate and accept, the greater flexibility and freedom they will experience. Flexible acceptance is not passivity, resignation nor subjugation. Instead, it is greater focus on what you *can* experience, appreciate and do right now, under these particular circumstances. It's broadening your possibilities. It's a mental jujitsu move.

Alan Watts said, "The futility of the strain to make "white" win [i.e. whatever it is you deem "true, right and necessary"] and improve the world; that entire futility, the frustration of it, is what you mean by 'I.'" Again using the metaphor of the ocean, it's like an ocean full of waves with each wave trying to control some of the other waves, not realizing that they are all one entity and it is the nature of that entity to rock and roll against each other. The less we combat, resist and try to control others and situations, the less pain we experience from banging our heads against each other's apparent wall. We begin to experience the "We" rather than "I" versus "You."

It is the nature of the universe to have opposites that go together. Watts also said, "Saints need sinners," because you can't have one without the other; one implies the other. They are two sides of the same coin. Each makes it possible for the other to exist. They arise together like birth and death, night and day, male and female, approach and avoidance, backs and fronts, heads and feet, bees and flowers, chickens and eggs.

The more we can tolerate, accept and appreciate the diversity of personalities, lifestyles, personal preferences, idiosyncrasies and habits, physical appearances, customs, cultures, politics and spiritual beliefs and practices, the better off we all will be. It is the contrasts in the world that make the world so fascinating and colorful, rather than bland like white bread. Think of Lennon and McCartney, Charlie Brown and Lucy, Mother Teresa and lepers, Sonny and Cher, Dennis Wilson and Charles Manson, Scarlett O'Hara and Melanie Wilkes, Bush and Cheney, Abbott and Costello and Jimmy and Billy Carter. A universe without contrasts, conflicts and variation would be one-dimensional, meaningless and lacking vitality. In his talk, "The Game of Yes and No," Watts spoke poetically about the creative spectrum of human personality and our spiritual essence: "Your personality is a phantom even more insubstantial than your body. A personality is a work of art; it's like music, which vanishes as soon as it's played."

Related to this is the realization that we simultaneously possess an individual ego or self with its own particular, limited consciousness and a Collective Mind, Cosmic Consciousness or Higher Self with a higher level of awareness, capacities and wisdom. All of our social conditioning in Western Civilization blinds us to this larger identity, primarily because it doesn't provide the conditions for it to be accessed and experienced. Our society cultivates thinking, doing, achieving, controlling, competing and strengthening our sense of individuality. Our love affair with reason and measurable, material evidence delegates our higher faculties and personal experiences to the category of unscientific and therefore unworthy of attention. For many of us, our spiritual practices and beliefs are more cognitively driven than a deeply felt and experienced inner knowing.

When we think of relationships that we potentially could nurture, we may think of family, friends, co-workers, pets and ourself. We have faint awareness of the most essential relationship of all: our relationship with our wholeness, our largest sense of self and our creative force, which is a seed that is dormant within us and waiting to be watered and cultivated. The vast majority of us have not experienced this level of self-knowledge or have had only a fleeting glimpse of it, perhaps in a moment when we lost our smaller self in the splendor of nature. We live in accordance with a largely unconscious belief system that has us identify ourselves as isolated beings living in a world that is *not us*.

Yet, when we consider the environment that is the bare minimum needed for each of us to exist—energy fields, the sun, the atmosphere, the clouds, the earth, the plants and animals, our parents and all the previous generations, a life force—we realize that the organism called "I" is as large as the universe. We arise together and are inseparable. As Alan Watts has said, "We must see that consciousness is neither an isolated soul nor the mere function of a single nervous system, but of that totality of interrelated stars and galaxies which makes a nervous system possible." He also said, "As the ocean 'waves,' the universe 'peoples.' Every individual is an expression of the whole realm of nature, a unique action of the total universe. This fact is rarely, if ever, experienced by most individuals. Even those who know it to be true in theory do not sense or feel it, but continue to be aware of themselves as isolated 'egos' inside bags of skin."

Many of you may have heard about Jill Bolte Taylor, PhD, the neuroscientist who had a stroke and wrote about her experience in the book, *My Stroke of Insight: A Brain Scientist's Personal Journey*. A YouTube video of her speaking spread like wildfire throughout the world. Taylor was able to experience her higher consciousness when the left hemisphere of her brain hemorrhaged. With only her right hemisphere functioning, she was able to see the world from beginner's mind and was enthralled. Fortunately, we don't have to depend on having a stroke in order to discover our interconnectedness and the rapture of being alive.

In order to access this Higher Self, we need to reduce the power and seductiveness of our left hemisphere with its limited, language-centered and ego-centric perspective, and experience a larger percentage of our present moments from our right hemisphere and our heart. There is a time for our rational brain to be in charge, and there is a time when it only gets in the way. Spiritual guides over the centuries have advised that we first determine our sense of life purpose and values through attending to our heart and Higher Consciousness and then use our rational capacities to implement those intentions.

E. F. Schumacher, author of two excellent books, *Small is Beautiful* and *Guide for the Perplexed*, said, "The most important and universal teaching of all the religions is that clarity of vision can be attained only by him who succeeds in putting the 'thinking function' in its place, so that it maintains silence when ordered to do so and moves into action only when given a specific task." He also observed, "Our ordinary mind always tries to persuade us that we are nothing but acorns and that our greatest happiness will be to become bigger, fatter, shinier acorns; but that is of interest only to pigs. Our faith gives us knowledge of something much better: that we can become oak trees."

When we practice mindfulness meditation or when we take time to just be with the wonder and beauty of nature, we find the space and stillness between all our conditioned, misleading thoughts. As with music, there needs to be space between the notes; otherwise, all we hear is noise. Recently, I have been playing again and again the moving, melodic and captivating music created by my son, Michael Mikulka (www.michaelmikulka.com). He composes classical music in a range of moods: tranquil, wistful, playful, soul-stirring and enthralling. I am realizing how instrumental music is the pure language of emotion as there are no lyrics that might distract from, or fall short of, the feelings being elicited. Listening to such music is another way of clearing the mind of the chatter that relentlessly hounds us.

Listening to moving instrumental music may be especially beneficial to people who are shut off from their emotions. It connects with the body, heart and right hemisphere. I remember once lending one of my favorite recordings, *Piano—French Masters, Greatest Hits* to a neglected, dissociated and under-stimulated client in the hopes of getting her emotions flowing again. But first, there in my office, we danced to the music, each of us expressing ourselves through our individual freestyle movements.

For those whose nervous systems and bodies suffer from too much agitation, panic and overwhelm, coming to a full halt and listening with full attention to serene music such as guitar, piano or orchestra might be a good idea. Those of you who saw the exceptional movie, *The Shawshank Redemption,* will remember how listening to angelic operatic voices (sung in a foreign language) brought the experience of peace, humanity and love to hardened men within prison walls. Other forms of art, such as dance and movement, can also be beneficial to those overwhelmed with emotion or thoughts. Whether engaging in dance classes or being a member of a dance audience, the reprieve from preoccupation with relationships, stresses and inner chatter helps to bring another dimension to being alive.

The natural world is a highly overlooked source of peace, joy and bliss. We don't have to wait for a vacation in Vermont or Yosemite to have our body and heart soothed or thrilled. We don't need Three-D glasses or an IMAX theater to be transported and transfixed by visual wonders. When we clean our mental lenses, beauty is in the eye of the beholder. Every day, Mother Nature creates a stunning new work of art across the canvas of the sky. The image continues to evolve throughout the day. We are also blessed with snowflakes and icicles, clouds and shadows, cleansing rains, wind patterns or diamonds on a lake, raindrops or sunlight on hundreds of evergreen needles, rushing streams, violet and gold sunsets and balmy breezes.

Even if we live in a major city, there is so much to admire if we have the eyes and heart to see. The virtuosity, diversity and juxtaposition of architectural creations are fascinating, as is the array of human faces, fashions and body language. The city parks provide lovely landscaping and humanity at play and rest. If we bring our full attention to a flower, seed pod, tree or animal, surprising details can amaze us and take our breath away. Indoors or outdoors, the play of light on the earth, buildings, walls, rugs or the person sitting across from us can be stunning and magical.

Exploring Central Park one autumn day, I must have passed ten thousand people, all of whom meandered the paths in complete harmony, whether on foot, bike or horse-drawn cab. It was a view of human nature at its best. I did not witness one scene of aggression or offensiveness. People were in good spirits, apparently fully in the moment, their problems and burdens nowhere in sight. In one location, dozens of little birds darted out of bushes and zoomed past the sea of humanity at head level. Again, cooperation reigned. As I stopped periodically to listen to talented street musicians and watch a young boy do astounding juggling acts, golden autumn leaves drifted down from the trees and collections of dried leaves danced across the walk. Cathedral arches of trees gracefully provided an ever-present but silent canopy. Toddlers and young children stopped, hypnotized by the live music and attempted to move their feet in rhythm. One child held her ground in front of an accordion player, feeling the strain of her mother's hand, yet captivated by the gifted hands of the musician and his song. Throughout the day I ambled aimlessly, soaking up the ever-evolving collage, my heart full, wanting nothing more.

Looking out my window today I saw that the blackberry and raspberry bushes that surround the perimeter of a magnolia tree look brown, dry and barren. In five months, they will be a mass of greenery filled with thousands of sweet, juicy and deeply-colored berries. The return of lush life after the apparent deadness of winter is as predictable and reassuring as the sunrise following the dark night. The natural world is full of metaphors for life. For too many of us, these lessons at our fingertips might just as well be covered with a heavy curtain. This reminds me of a Japanese proverb that caught my attention almost 40 years ago, "Do you need proof of God? Does one light a torch to see the sun?"

My best friends know that my favorite activity with them is to "walk, talk and gawk." There are just as many times when I love the solitude of walking and gawking in silence. There is a veritable banquet of beauty that brings us pure delight when we are present to receive the riches. The gifts of nature can feed our souls during the most difficult times of our lives and inspire us when things are going well. Walking or sitting amidst nature provides a wordless, comforting refreshment. Just as with music, dance, poetry and art and eye contact and touch, nature speaks directly to our hearts and Higher Self in ways that left-brain words can't begin to know or express.

The more we develop our connection and relationship with our Higher Self and larger identity, especially at the level of the heart and our inner, intuitive wisdom, the less vulnerable we are to feeling isolated, lonely, insignificant, helpless, afraid and depressed. Research has shown that those without a connection to some purpose or community larger than themselves are more likely to experience depression. Relying on a narcissistic preoccupation with our ego's self-centered interests to sustain a sense of purpose, wholeness and security is a recipe doomed to failure. We are simply not designed to go it alone and to perceive others as simply means to our ends. The psychologist Erik Erikson developed a theory of human development in which the full fruition of adult life is evidenced by "generativity," which is a concern for people beyond self and family, especially a desire to nurture and guide younger people and contribute to society.

While developing a secure attachment with our partner is achievable, desirable, nourishing and an inherent human need, the more we experience ourselves as integral to the whole of a benevolent universe, the less pressure we put on our intimate partner to help us feel secure, lovable and fulfilled. The broader our base of belonging is, the greater our sense of security. In contemporary society, we place too much emphasis on our intimate partner as the source of our happiness and security. Since the vast majority of us arrive in adulthood with a foundation of emotional insecurity, we tend to be two slender reeds leaning upon each other, trying to prop each other up. I believe that our best chance for thriving comes from nurturing several layers of significant relationships: our relationship with our younger selves, inner experience, intimate partner, children, dear friends, others who share a common purpose beyond the ego and nuclear family and the miraculous creation called the universe.

In addition to developing relationships and contributing to the welfare of others, life gives us the opportunity to become creators: to take various ingredients, experiment with different arrangements and find the ones that please us and possibly bring joy, inspiration, peace or relief to others. One of my most fulfilling experiences was developing a repertoire of songs that I loved to sing. Discovering each gem and then expressing it with personal feeling was pure delight for me—and hopefully touched the hearts of at least a few listeners. During a more recent period, I fell in love with fabrics and sewing quilts. Whatever we bring our love and attention to will bloom to its fullest dimensions. When the idea of writing a book first crossed my mind, it was a small kernel that quickly grew to be many kernels. As my attention shone on those kernels like a magnifying glass under the sun, the heat that was generated created an explosion of popcorn in the form of energy, passion, ideas and images that filled my awareness and the pages on my computer.

As my clients become free of their living nightmares and the trance that has ruled their lives is broken, we wonder together what creative endeavors will emerge now that they are no longer in survival mode.

The mindfulness that set them free from their traumas and that they are bringing to their relationships, can now also be used to make contributions, help solve problems, play and possibly spin gold.

Mindfulness Meditation

So, how do we cultivate the connection with our Higher Consciousness, Wise Mind or Higher Self, which is our essence and greatest source of wisdom, peace, love and creativity? While our consumer-oriented, achievement-focused and over-stimulated society certainly is not conducive to its development, there are resources and methods that will support us, provided we free up the time to exercise this mental and spiritual muscle. If there were one skill or practice I would recommend that you integrate into your daily life, it would be mindfulness meditation.

The foundational requirement for mindfulness practice is the discipline to do what we know is in our best interest. Ironically, the less mindfulness we have, the less likely we are to be self-disciplined. With the huge quantity of objects, resources, opportunities and activities available to us, on every conceivable subject and interest, all of them pressing on our attention, you may be tempted to move onto something else as soon as you finish the last page of this book. That is the kind of world we live in today. Most of us are on a hamster wheel, twirling, twirling, always reaching for the next rung and never staying at rest for long. This is the antithesis of the mental and spiritual exercise I have in mind. Mindfulness practice helps us access a sense of timelessness that quiets our brain and entire nervous system. Mindfulness is being, breathing, pausing, observing and allowing space.

Over the past 25 years or so, there has been a tremendous surge of interest in mindfulness meditation. Many clinicians and others who explored spiritual and meditation practices in the Sixties and Seventies began to introduce them to their psychotherapy clients and patients with chronic health problems. Scientists have been carrying out research to determine the impact of meditation on the brain, body and mental health. Some researchers have been studying the brains of Buddhist monks who have been practicing meditation for decades. Since psychologist Daniel Goleman wrote the book, *Emotional Intelligence,* efforts have been made on many fronts to bring "emotional intelligence" into the classroom. Daniel Siegel has suggested that there be a fourth "R": reading, 'riting, 'rithmetic and reflection.

As mentioned earlier, mindfulness meditation and secure attachment relationships both have a positive impact on the social-emotional parts of the brain. According to Siegel, mindfulness has been found to promote growth in the mid prefrontal cortex, the site responsible for the following nine crucial functions:

- Regulating the body through the autonomic nervous system
- Attuned communication, which is the ability to perceive the mental state of another and respond harmoniously
- Emotional balance, activated sufficiently for life to have meaning and vitality, but not so much as to be chaotic
- Response flexibility, the capacity to pause and consider options and consequences
- Insight and self-awareness
- Empathy or the capacity to know how another feels
- Modulating and even unlearning fear
- Intuition, which is the body's wisdom, the deep visceral ways of knowing through the heart, lungs and intestines
- Morality, the ability to see the larger picture and do what is best for the whole, not just the individual

Put in less abstract terms, mindfulness practice has numerous practical benefits. It has been shown to:

- Reduce stress and anxiety
- Recalibrate the nervous system to a sense of safety
- Improve the immune system
- Develop self-awareness
- Increase concentration
- Develop tolerance and management of distressing emotions
- Develop equanimity; a resilience and composure in relation to life as it is

- Foster radical acceptance, the antidote for the judgment that fuels depression and anxiety
- Reduce the experience of emotional and physical pain and treat depression
- Reduce impulsivity, emotional reactivity and compulsive habits, resulting in sounder decisions and improved relationships
- Create space and stillness around the onslaught of objects and thoughts that vie for our attention
- Broaden our perspective and access a deeper knowing than that of our thinking brain
- Increase creativity
- Change our set point for happiness

So many of us "pendulum-swing" between two types of moments: impulsive moments and remorseful moments, or passive moments and resentful moments. In the former, we act mindlessly and later regret it. In the latter, we fail to take appropriate initiative and responsibility and then feel angry and helpless for our lives being the way they are. Practicing mindfulness develops an internal "pause button" that moderates the intense emotions that get in the way of making wise decisions. When we are calm, alert, open-minded and aware, we can see clearly the likely consequences of what we do or fail to do. Mindfulness can be used to "urge surf," a term coined by Alan Marlatt for those seeking to maintain sobriety. Urges, fueled by emotions, inevitably rise and fall. A typical urge will last up to half an hour. When we develop the capacity to sit with and observe the urge have its impact on our thoughts, images, body sensations and emotions, *without taking action*, the urge eventually recedes. The more we practice observing and tolerating compelling emotions, thoughts and urges, the more we build the muscle of self-discipline and true autonomy and freedom. Not only are *others* less able to control you, but impulsive parts of *you* have less power to control your actions.

Mindfulness can be a formal practice in which you designate a period of time to sit, walk or do yoga while bringing full attention to each moment. You can also experience it informally by bringing consciousness into all the activities that comprise your daily life. When you chop vegetables, just chop vegetables. When you eat, just eat. This is the opposite of what most people do. The ability to multitask is considered advantageous and a source of pride to some. Yet it prevents us from fully appreciating any one activity and fosters a sense of time pressure. It hurts and deprives those who are trying to connect with us and it leaves us feeling frazzled and unfulfilled. Alan Watts said, "The reason we want to go on and on is because we live in an impoverished present." Too often, what is lacking is not a rich-enough world, but the quality of our attention. Mindfulness makes each moment and all its dimensions more fully felt. It fosters beginner's mind, the capacity to really see things that all but young children take for granted. It helps us to suspend judgment and brings back a sense of awe and wonder at this miraculous life. As Jack Kornfield has observed, "Those who are awake live in a state of constant amazement."

When we practice formal mindfulness meditation, an image that is commonly used to assist us is a spacious sky. So many things pass through the sky: the sun, clouds, storm systems, snowflakes, birds, insects, planes, smoke and balloons. Whatever enters the sky moves on. Nothing is static. The objects that are in the sky are not the sky. The sky doesn't resist anything entering and doesn't make things appear. Everything has its chance to be noticed and then moves on. When we meditate, we see that the thoughts, images, emotions, urges and body sensations that enter our awareness also come and go. Whatever arises, recedes. This is the nature of all forms; nothing is permanent.

When the mental, emotional and physical events that appear in our awareness are disturbing, we may have the urge to make them disappear. But the more we resist, the more they will pound on the door of our mind to be let back in. When an emotion gets stuck and frozen in us, it defines us, becoming our sense of self. The more we surrender and welcome emotions in, the less energy we waste and the more the emotions flow on through as only passing experiences. The mindfulness dynamic inherent in EMDR has proven to me abundantly that good things come to those who have the courage and willingness to invite all who had previously been rejected to fully speak their minds.

When we experience something desirable, we may wish for it to stay just as it is forever. But it won't. Being fully aware of what is before us in the present moment makes it possible for us to savor and appreciate it while it exists. We also may chase after more of whatever makes us feel good, because we haven't yet cultivated the art of being in stillness and discovered its value. In our society, this is the last thing we consider when we raise and educate our children. Many of us are addicted to objects, thinking, doing and achievement, which is probably a major reason why we are intolerant of boredom and fear death. Let me say at this point that I found Eckhart Tolle's chapter on "space consciousness" and "form consciousness" in *A New Earth* to be very valuable.

The following words of Crowfoot, a Blackfoot Warrior and orator, capture the ethereal and transitory nature of life:

> "What is life?
> It is the flash of a firefly in the night.
> It is the breath of a buffalo in the wintertime.
> It is the little shadow which runs across the grass
> And loses itself in the sunset."

Mindfulness Exercises

Talk Image Touch Feel

I learned a number of valuable mindfulness meditation exercises at a workshop conducted by Shelly Young, MA (www.boulder coloradotherapist.net). She is the author of *Break Out of the Sugar Prison: You Can Overcome Sugar Addiction With The Powerful Basic States Mindfulness System and A Cutting Edge Nutritional Program.* The techniques she teaches come from meditation teacher Shinzen Young (www.basicmindfulness.org). One of the mindfulness meditation exercises that I've introduced to many of my clients is called "Talk Image Touch Feel."

While sitting in an erect and dignified posture, with your eyes closed, bring your attention to your breath, just following its movement without trying to control it in any way. To me, each breath, an inhale and exhale, is like a measure in music. Within each measure there are various notes. As you bring your attention to your *inner* world, begin to notice and label your experience. Any language, talk or words, whether vivid full sentences or soft, mumbled fragments of speech are labeled Talk. If you prefer, you could say Word or Speech if you find those words more helpful. Any images, whether explicit visual memories, fantasies, scenes or abstract designs, are labeled Image, but you might prefer the word Picture. Any physical sensations are labeled Touch, but you could say Body, Feeling, or Sensation. Examples of Touch include noticing your mouth is dry, your feet are warm and tingly, your forehead is itchy, your stomach is in a knot, your face feels flushed or your belly feels relaxed. Any emotion, such as sadness, guilt, anger, fear or happiness, is labeled Feel but you could choose to say Emotion.

At the end of each breath, say one of the four words in a soft, matter-of-fact, calm voice. So whether the image you just witnessed was disturbing or amusing, say the word Image in the same accepting tone. This is one of the ways to develop equanimity. You may very well have a mix of talk, image, touch and feel within each breath and it isn't significant which one you choose to say. It is important, however, to be aware whether you seem to be stuck in one category breath after breath. Some people who suffer from racing thoughts and pressured speech may need to consciously scan their inner experience for images, body sensations and emotions to break up the intensity of the thoughts. Some people whose emotions are more expressed by their bodies than language are preoccupied with their body sensations and need to intentionally scan for thoughts, images and emotions in order to get unstuck.

People often ask, "What do I do if I hear a sound?" If the sound provokes an image, such as a car or bird, then you say "image." If it provokes a thought, like "boy, that car needs a new muffler!" then you say "talk." If the sound annoys you because you had begun to feel peaceful, you say "feel." If the truck is so loud you feel the floor vibrate or your gut tightens, you say "touch."

During the exercise, you may become bored or antsy. You may tell yourself, "That's enough for today." You may remember something you want to write down. You may realize that you never put the wash in the dryer. Instead of following any urges, just notice the urge and label the corresponding thoughts, images, emotions and body sensations. In other words, everything is grist for the mill. This exercise helps us to relinquish our habit of swallowing thoughts, beliefs and images hook, line and sinker and absorbing them as *reality* or our identity. When we allow them instead to flow in and out, we experience a sense of being the whole process rather than a passive victim of external events.

Two images may help you understand and access the state of mind that is mindfulness. First, when you are flooded with disturbing emotions, thoughts, images and body sensations, you may feel as if you are swept away in a deep river current, unable to feel the ground under your feet, helpless with your nose barely above water level. With mindfulness, you are standing on the water bank, sensing and seeing the force of the water very close but feeling firmly on solid ground. Another metaphor that a client and I recently co-created is the following. When we are being drenched with powerful emotional material it is like a stain bleeding into a beautiful fabric. Mindfulness is like *Scotchgard*™, a thin film that protects our true nature from being stained and our mental and behavioral composure from being damaged. The emotion bleeds in and then back out.

For people who are usually battered by fears or self-critical thoughts, doing mindfulness meditation can be very challenging, especially initially. You may have trouble seeing or hearing anything else but this disturbing content. With practice and perseverance, however, you will be able to train your mind and attention to broaden enough to take in what is benign, too. Then, the disturbing content will lose its vise-like grip. As you evolve in your practice, threatening content will be seen for what most of it really is, echoes from the past and imaginal pollution. If you find Talk Image Touch Feel too difficult to do because of the onslaught of distressing material, other mindfulness exercises may be a better fit and I'll tell you about them momentarily.

A new client (the one who came up with the image of *Scotchgard*™ when introduced to "Talk Image Touch Feel"), told me that one morning as she was practicing, she became aware for the first time of all the birds on her property. One bird flew up to her window sill and sang to her for ten minutes. She was so touched by this experience and felt that it was a sign from above that life was going to get better. As she told me about this, both of us had tears in our eyes. What was especially valuable about this experience for this particular client was that her strong emotions tend to compel her to be impulsive, always seeking happiness somewhere else. This puts a lot of strain on her relationship with her husband, who feels abandoned and threatened by her constantly seeking happiness and other relationships outside the home. Through mindfulness meditation, she was able to find peace in the present moment, right in her own heart, right in her own home.

This ability to be open to the present, to discover richness in what may seem like an empty, inconsequential moment, is what author Peter Russell is referring to when he talks about the value of letting go. "We need to recognize how the creative process occurs and work with it rather than against it. When do most of us have our best ideas? In the shower, walking the dog, driving home, in the middle of the night. Seldom while we are at our desks struggling with a problem. But what do most of us do when faced with a problem? Seldom do we pause and say, 'Maybe I should take a shower or take the dog for a walk'; usually we try harder and harder to get to resolve the issue. Yet not trying may be the very thing that would help us most."

When major inventors, Nobel Prize winners or those of genius are asked where they get their ground-breaking ideas, they often answer that it comes during periods of calm, open-minded and alert awareness when they experience moments of inspiration, being and observing, not when they are analyzing or doing. This is one of the reasons that people who take time to reflect and recharge their batteries while out in nature or while enjoying their families tend to be more effective at their work than those who are workaholics, grinding out long hours at their desks.

Typically, people who seek mental health services have experienced chronic and/or severe stress and have nervous systems in great need of repair. Some people are predominantly stuck in the revved-up mode, as if they have their finger in an electrical socket. Others feel shot and drained. I therefore strongly encourage these clients to practice "Talk Image Touch Feel" for a total of one hour a day, whether a half hour twice a day, twenty minutes three times a day or fifteen minutes four times a day. Those in sympathetic over-drive will become more in touch with space and stillness and less agitated. Those in parasympathetic shut down will become more connected with their bodies and emotions and feel more activated.

Sight Sound Touch

Another mindfulness exercise I acquired through Shelly Young's workshop is called "Sight Sound Touch." This is an excellent technique for reducing emotional overwhelm and compulsive urges. Instead of giving full attention to your overwhelming inner experiences, bring your attention to specific things that you can see, hear and touch in your immediate environment. This practice dilutes emotional intensity to a more manageable level. It counterbalances a preoccupation with disturbing thoughts, images and emotions. If you are feeling highly panicked and agitated or at risk of zoning out from overwhelm, naming out loud what you are noticing will be especially helpful. "This table is smooth, hard and brown. The carpet is red, green and gold. I hear traffic outside and people's voices downstairs. This candle smells like vanilla." Just taking in your environment with all your senses fully activated, tends to be very soothing.

Remember, mindfulness always entails non-judgment; you are noticing without analyzing or critiquing. "Sight Sound Touch" is an excellent exercise for bringing calmness into your body and day and for more fully appreciating your environment. Whenever I introduce Talk Image Touch Feel to my clients and they practice it for the first time, at the same time I practice Sight Sound Touch. I focus my attention on the details of the room that I normally don't get to appreciate, while at the same time noticing the gentle ebb and flow of my breath. Unless we intentionally stop and consciously observe and take in what is right before us, we live in the shadow of life.

For those people who are prone to feeling a sense of threat, it may be helpful to say something like the following to yourself as you look around the room: "There is nobody here with a weapon. There is no tiger in the room. No one is threatening my life. I'm not speaking before 1,000 people. These feelings in my body are a traumatic memory fragment. My amygdala is misreading the environment's threat level like an oversensitive smoke alarm. The room is quiet. The breeze is blowing the curtain gently. There is music playing in the next apartment. I'm safe now. I'm an adult now. I can relax now."

Walking Meditation

Another form of mindfulness meditation that elicits peace and calm in some of my most stressed clients is the "Walking Meditation." Again, all of your attention is intentionally brought to the present moment with a non-judgmental open-mindedness. In this exercise, you are still aware of your inner experience, but you substitute internal images for environmental ones. This meditation can be done either indoors or outdoors. You can walk a very short distance going back and forth, or you can cover a lot of territory never retracing your steps. Whenever the weather has been conducive, my clients and I have chosen to do it in the beautiful, spacious backyard of my office. Just keep in mind that anyone who observes you from afar may think you look like a zombie. In fact, you are just the opposite—more alive and open to experience than ever.

Most of my clients rarely savor nature and doing the Walking Meditation opens them up to the fascinating or pleasing sights and sounds they would normally overlook. With this meditation, you're able to lose your self-preoccupied tunnel vision and broaden your perspective of the world before you. Normally, when people walk it's with the purpose of getting somewhere in order to accomplish something. When they walk, jog or run, they are either listening to an MP3 player or lost in their thoughts, memories, plans and fantasies.

In a walking meditation, however, there is no destination, nothing to accomplish and your mind isn't a million miles away. You're simply in the present moment and noticing whatever there is to notice, including the space and stillness in between. Whenever your mind begins to drift, gently bring your attention back to the present. When doing this meditation, hold yourself erect in a dignified posture and move slowly enough to notice every minute movement and body sensation involved in this normally automatic behavior. *As with other mindfulness exercises, you are making the unconscious conscious.* Once you get used to it, walking at a pace that takes about ten minutes to go only about 100 feet is quite calming and grounding. The experience can be surprisingly refreshing and enjoyable.

For those whose minds are greased to slide into disturbing content, this meditation may be more of a challenge, just as in Talk Image Touch Feel. But if you bring your attention to the slightest movements of your body, it will provide a cushioning around the disturbing content, just as awareness of the breath does with Talk Image Touch Feel. In fact, any time we catch ourselves feeling tense and rushed (not just when doing this exercise), we can intentionally slow our every movement down and feel the tension melt away. For example, if we are getting ourselves a cup of coffee, we can breathe deeply as we wait for the cup to fill with water from the faucet. Then we can slowly walk to the microwave and open the door. We continue to observe our breath as we wait for the microwave to finish. Once the water is hot, we can gradually lift the lid of the instant coffee tin and slowly remove a spoonful of coffee. Then we stir slowly, followed by slowly taking a sip and savoring the taste.

Because most of us live in a fast-paced environment, doing anything slowly may at first provoke anxiety. There is the sense, for so many of us, that, "Whatever I'm doing isn't right or enough. I should be doing something else. If I don't hurry and get this done and move onto the next thing, something bad will happen." When we, instead, realize how untrue this is, we can enjoy the peace that comes when we slow ourselves down. Even if we catch ourselves being stressed and uptight ten times a day and take a few minutes each time to slow our actions way down, that's a good start at helping to bring peace to your body and mind.

The Body Scan

The "Body Scan" is a mindfulness practice that involves bringing your full attention and curiosity to your body, starting with the toes and ending with your head. Just as we check in on our young children in their bedroom to see how they are doing, we need to check in with our bodies to see if all is well. You can do this lying down, sitting or standing. It can be done for a few minutes multiple times throughout the day or once a day for forty-five minutes. In the latter case, you linger far longer with each part of the body. As our mind focuses on each part of our body, we may feel that area vibrate with more life energy and warmth, just by our paying close attention. We may find judgmental thoughts and difficult emotions bubbling up such as fear or inadequacy. When this happens, we observe mindfully these events, neither suppressing nor buying into them. The more we release these judgments and attend with a kind curiosity, the more we notice a softening of body tension.

Mindfulness Resources

There are many excellent books, recordings and trainings on mindfulness meditation practices that can go into much greater depth than what I am offering in this chapter. Eckhart Tolle has written a number of books, his best being, *The Power of Now* and *A New Earth*. He also has a large collection of talks in CD and DVD formats.

Jon Kabat-Zinn, PhD and Jack Kornfield, PhD are two of the leaders in mindfulness who have wonderful Mindfulness Meditation recordings, books, classes and retreats to help us develop our practice. Jack Kornfield is founding teacher of the Insight Meditation Society and Spirit Rock Meditation Center. He has written many books, including: *After the Ecstasy, the Laundry; A Path with Heart;* and *The Wise Heart: A Guide to the Universal Teachings of Buddhist Psychology.*

Kabat-Zinn has written a number of classics, including: *Wherever You Go, There You Are* and *Full Catastrophe Living: Using the Wisdom of Your Body and Mind to Face Stress, Pain and Illness.* He started the highly-respected Stress Reduction Clinic and Mindfulness

Based Stress Reduction (MBSR) Program at the University of Massachusetts. The Center for Mindfulness in Medicine, Health Care, and Society, now led by Kabat-Zinn's long-term colleague, Saki Santorelli, EdD,MA, has just celebrated its 30th anniversary. (www.umassmed.edu/cfm/index.aspx)

A Silent Retreat

We don't need to wait to attend an organized retreat at a meditation center in order to experience the benefits of silence and a slower pace. In our own home, we can carve out a period of time—one hour, half a day, one day or three days—to devote ourselves to a deeper connection with the present moment. During this time period we refrain from talking, listening to talk or music, reading, writing and tending to electronic devices of any type. We, likewise, catch ourselves in the past or future and bring our attention to the nuances of the present. Some people may find this to be stressful at first, but over time, serenity arises.

Wise Mind Meditation

It can be very helpful to start each day with the conscious intention to be fully present for each moment and to maintain a balance of being and doing, thinking and feeling. There is a wonderful "Wise Mind Meditation" that I learned in a workshop led by EMDR practitioner and consultant Debra Wesselmann, MS, LIMHP. She is the author of a wonderful book, *The Whole Parent: How to Become a Terrific Parent, Even If You Didn't Have One.* She is also a workshop presenter with special expertise in treating children with attachment trauma and co-founder of the Attachment and Trauma Center of Nebraska (atcnebraska.com and debrawesselmann.com).

I record the Wise Mind Meditation for my clients and recommend they listen to it at the start of each day. Whenever you listen to and participate in an experiential exercise, it is important that you give it your full attention in a place where you will not be interrupted or expected to be responsible for anything. That means no listening while driving! Here is the Wise Mind Meditation:

"As you get comfortable, follow your breath. Follow your breath in and out and with each breath in, you are inhaling peace and calm and with each breath out, you are letting go of tension. In and out, noticing where in your body you feel the most comfortable right now. You can just notice the most comfortable place in your body and just enjoy as that feeling of comfort spreads and moves into other parts of your body. As your legs and feet become heavier and more relaxed, heavy and relaxed. As your arms and hands become heavy and relaxed, let go of tension, heavy and relaxed. As your back and shoulders let go; relaxed and comfortable. Your neck, your head and your face muscles letting go, relaxed, smooth and relaxed. And as I count backward from ten, you can enjoy, sinking down into a deeper place within yourself, calm and peaceful, relaxed. 10, 9, 8, 7, 6, 5, 4, 3, 2, 1.

And as you enjoy this relaxed, calm and peaceful place within yourself, here is where you are more in touch with that wise, serene part of yourself some people call the Wise Mind, some people call the Higher Self or the Guiding Self. The Wise Mind, intuitive and yet rational, an integration of emotions and reason. I would like to invite that Wise Mind within to help you this week and the next, each day, each hour, to stay grounded, centered and calm, always feeling your feet on the ground, feeling yourself in your body, connected to your breath and your inner resources for calm and serenity. I would like to invite that Wise Mind to help you this week to stay in your adult ego state, grown-up, sensible, competent, strong, intelligent.

Your Wise Mind can help you this week to stay mindful and aware of your emotions, the feelings, the sensations in your body, without judgment, just acknowledging, observing, witnessing your own inner experience, your felt sense within. And knowing that feelings cannot hurt us, we do not have to act on our feelings, I would like to invite your Wise Mind to notice and acknowledge your inner experience, to observe the feelings flowing through you, naturally, flowing on through, as you stay calm, grounded, centered in your competent adult self, sensible, rational, able to think about what is needed. Your Wise Mind can help you listen to your inner feelings, to what your body needs to stay calm and grounded. To self-soothe with the senses, whether music, a warm bath, a walk or a moment to yourself, quiet, following your breath.

Your Wise Mind can help you let go of what cannot be changed, turn it over, let go and let God, while changing what you can, thoughtfully, sensibly, rationally, one step at a time, one day at a time. Your Wise Mind can help you acknowledge the positive experiences, emotions and sensations, focus one-mindfully on the little things, the profound things in life; the smell of a rose, the pleasure of a good book, a talk with a friend, a good joke or the pleasure of a pet. Right now at this moment, you can enjoy the experience of calm, comfort or peace, just being in the now, in the present moment, centered and grounded, peaceful and calm . . . And when you are ready, you can slowly move your arms and hands, your legs and feet and open your eyes feeling calm, relaxed, awake and alert."

Sustaining Awareness and Reconnecting with Composure

Whenever we complete a formal mindfulness exercise, we want to transition back to regular life with as much of the calm, alert, aware, open-minded mental state as possible. There are many opportunities throughout our day to keep this mental state alive. Perhaps the simplest way of pausing in the three-ring circus of our daily life is by practicing "Breath Awareness." This exercise involves bringing our attention to our body and noticing with friendly, non-judgmental attention the lilting rhythm of our breath, like a boat rocking gently on the water. We can be mindful of our breath and being in our body while waiting for a red light to change, someone to answer the phone, our computer to turn on, a webpage to appear, our turn in a check-out line, the water to boil, the microwave to turn off, a family member to vacate the bathroom and the people ahead of us in a crowded auditorium to move forward.

We can also have the intention, as we start our day, to recognize more quickly and more often when we are doing something with only partial attention and twirl the dimmer switch to full illumination. When we are watering the garden, are we rushing to get it over with so we can get onto the next activity? Are we rehashing the argument we had with our boss earlier in the week? Or, instead, can we notice the sunlight weaving through the spray, enjoy the birds flitting from branch to branch and feel our body at rest with just our arm gently swinging back and forth? When we are doing the dishes, can we catch our body tensed and hunched over the sink and our mind pressuring us to be finished? With that awareness, we can let go of the tension, straighten up, breathe more deeply and begin to notice how the warm water feels on our skin. We can appreciate the pattern of the spray bouncing off the plate. We can sink deeply into the fullness of the moment.

Recently, my husband and I were cross-country skiing on a frozen lake and when we stopped to take in the panoramic view, I also looked back to see our tracks. I did this a few times and noticed that when I brought my full attention to my movements, my tracks were straight and efficient. When my mind was elsewhere, my tracks were ragged and inconsistent. For me, this was a good metaphor for the difference between living mindfully and mindlessly.

Wisdom from a Buddhist Master

A resource that has been extremely helpful to me and my clients is *The Art of Mindful Living: How to Bring Love, Compassion, and Inner Peace into Your Daily Life*. It is a recording of talks by Vietnamese Buddhist Zen Master, Thich Nhat Hanh. When I first heard it, I was struck by how much Buddhist psychology, which has been around for 2,500 years, coincides with the psychological perspective I have been acquiring over the last 10 years. His gentle, kind and light-hearted presence, clarity of thinking and straightforward guidance cuts through the fog and confusion of modern life to simple truths about effective living. It's the type of resource you can listen to again and again to be re-grounded, reminded and refreshed. I highly recommend it.

And speaking of recommendations, we have arrived at the last chapter of *Peace in the Heart and Home* in which I offer some conclusions and explicit recommendations.

CHAPTER TEN

Final Conclusions and
Recommendations

OUR NATION AND THE WORLD face major challenges that impact our present and future, such as health epidemics, natural disasters, pollution, global warming, hunger, terrorism, war and nuclear threat. And yet, in the Western world in contemporary times there is sufficient economic, political and social stability for most human beings to bring their attention to matters beyond physical survival. In fact, facing the above worldwide challenges requires both large scale and small scale interventions because the larger world is a macrocosm of our family life and a material manifestation of our inner world.

On the large scale organizational level, we have political, legal, intellectual, scientific, volunteer, grass-roots, coalition, international, humanity and social justice endeavors and interventions. Then there is the responsibility of each one of us to clean up our own act, to recognize and purify our own personal and interpersonal toxic waste sites. As most spiritual leaders have long recognized, the ultimate responsibility for bringing peace and security to the world lies within each individual soul. In Gandhi's words, "We must be the change we wish to see in the world." Unrest inside the human heart and family is the portion of human suffering we are in the best position to heal.

How we use the precious days given us determines a lot. In the last several decades, most of us have had the luxury of exploring and enjoying a wealth of opportunities, probably never before known in human existence. Work, family, worship and community have been replaced or augmented by recreation, sports participation and watching, hobbies, exercise and fitness, psychotherapy, Eastern martial and spiritual practices, arts and crafts, culture, adventure, travel, higher education, continuing education, culinary arts, eating out, fashion, shopping, extensive consuming, television, listening to recorded music, electronics, the information explosion, the Internet and electronic communication bites. In our over-scheduled, over-active, over-stimulated lives, time has become unavailable for what is most essential to creating a life worth living and that is: pausing, breathing, being, centering ourselves, reflecting, discovering, really seeing and experiencing the universe before us and within us.

Stopping to clearly see the choices we have been unconsciously making and how they shape our lives can lead to more conscious, wise and creative decisions that enhance our lives and those around us. Every day is full of choices and possibilities if we have the awareness to see them. We can use our time to veg out, dumb-down, lose ourselves and focus on what discourages us. Or we can bring our awareness to aspects of life that inspire and vitalize us, leading us to see things anew, take new paths and invest proactively in efforts to improve our relationships with ourself and significant others.

As I said at the beginning of this book, I'm not offering you a quick-fix for happiness. I haven't said, "Just do this and from then on you can relax and go back on automatic pilot." Instead, what I'm writing is a prescription for showing up and being fully awake for each moment of your life. I believe I've made abundantly clear the consequences of not facing our fears and not being self-aware, conscientious and emotionally competent. Living well involves a lot of sustained work. Don't blame me; I'm just the messenger.

Perhaps you initially reached for this book because you're exhausted from working so hard at trying to feel good and effective. And now I'm giving you more to do? Yes, the path I'm recommending requires being more conscious, courageous, open-minded, compassionate toward yourself and others, moderate in your level of emotional arousal, disciplined about safe-guarding space and time for stillness and willing to take risks, make repairs and perceive anew. It also involves the willingness to delay action while you allow the whole picture to develop in the calm waters of your resolute awareness, so you don't respond to all situations in the same rigid way. But while embarking on this particular journey requires as much mental effort as what you've already been experiencing, it's a very different kind of inner work. It will make a huge difference in the quality of your relationship with yourself, others and life itself.

When your actions are right on the money for meeting your own and your loved ones' most essential needs, you will be far more efficient and effective. You will interact more harmoniously with others and you will have much more mental and physical energy to enjoy your life. Being responsible and healthy doesn't mean being a bore or being solemn and intense. You will experience the full gamut of emotions. When you're receptive to uncomfortable and painful emotions and sensations, you also open up to all the bright colors that exist on the spectrum. In fact, when you invest energy in ways that truly heal, empower and nourish you as well as others, and when you align yourself with and appreciate the world as it is, you have more moments when you are that guru on the surf board, gliding on top of the waves, supported by the exhilarating rush that propels you forward, and loving the view. This is what it feels like to be high on life.

So, here are the key points and recommendations I would like to make crystal clear. I hope you will find many of them worthy of integrating into your life, some right away and others gradually over time. Please take the extensiveness of this list in the most realistic and reassuring light. I don't mean to intimidate you, but to show you how much potential and hope exists. I want you to be fully aware of the range and types of actions and attitudes that will give you the "best bang for your buck" when your intention is to better your life.

Small but Significant Changes to Weave into Your Daily Life

- Allow more moments of noticing and being and far less analyzing, reacting and doing.

- Catch yourself mentally lost in the past or future and bring your attention back, again and again, to what is actually happening right here and now. Really see, listen, touch, taste and breathe in and out all of what is present—both what is desirable and what is not.

- Spend more moments observing with appreciation and wonder the world before you, especially people and all forms of nature, and less time hypnotized by your thoughts or an electronic screen or device. You are in the midst of a miracle; don't miss it.

- Cherish your solitude. Let it be an oasis for reconnecting with the simplicity of your lilting breath and ever-present stillness.

- Throughout the day, take breaks to walk mindfully at a very slow pace. It is very refreshing and calming, even when done for about five minutes.

- Recognize that every life has assets and liabilities, opportunities and limitations. Every gain may have a corresponding loss. Every loss may carry a corresponding benefit. Nothing will ever be aligned perfectly according to our personal expectations. But we can continually develop our ability to live gracefully and wisely with whatever the moment presents. Jack Kornfield's teacher, Achaan Chaa, said, "Praise and blame, gain and loss, pleasure and sorrow come and go like the wind. To be happy, rest like a great tree in the midst of them all."

- Know that experiencing a deep and full self-knowledge, self-efficacy, and aliveness is possible with each moment of our life.

We are provided countless opportunities to live more artfully. As Jack Nicholson said in *As Good As It Gets*, when he realized that his first kiss with Helen Hunt was clumsy, "I *know* I can do better than that."

- Keep yourself open to learning. Allow yourself to change your mind and recognize new perspectives. Once we've figured everything out and nailed it down, life stops. As entrepreneur Ray Kroc said, "When you're green, you're growing." Cultivate an open-minded curiosity. It is one of our most valuable mental states.

- Remember that change and growth are not linear, but tend to move in a spiral: two steps forward and one step back, three steps forward and one step back. Falling back on old habits is a normal aspect of the change process. Often it is through relapse that we learn some new aspect about ourselves that helps us handle future challenges more effectively.

- Check in with yourself frequently throughout the day, to identify what, if anything, you need in that moment to calm and refresh yourself. Review the chapter on Self-Care and make sure to use the potent forms, as well as the more commonly known strategies.

- Help the calming parasympathetic branch of your nervous system kick in by creating a soothing and secure environment. Strategies may include turning off or lowering the volume of television, wearing earplugs, retreating to a quiet, less stimulating environment, playing a musical instrument, singing, talking softly, listening to serene music or looking through a magazine or book with comforting, inspiring and heart-warming pictures or stories.

- Catch your mind relentlessly making judgments. In *Buddha's Little Instruction Book*, Jack Kornfield says, "A day spent judging another is a painful day. A day spent judging yourself is a painful day. You don't have to believe your judgments; they're simply an old habit." Kornfield quotes Master Sengstan as saying, "Do not seek perfection in a changing world. Instead, perfect your love."

- Recognize the value of the love you bestow upon another by being emotionally present, attentive, receptive and responsive. This is far more nourishing than praise. There is no greater gift.

- Ask for and offer hugs more often; they are a natural tranquilizer. They access your internal pharmacy, are free of charge and have no negative side effects.

- Maintain a balance in your relationships and life between being the sun and fertile soil for another's growth and receiving sun and soil from others.

- A wonderful place for you to start anew with your loved ones is to just be more curious, aware, open-minded, patient and emotionally present. From that state of being, any actions you eventually choose are more likely to be effective.

Valuable Resources to Support Your Growth

- Be more attentive to your body sensations and the emotions and needs they are expressing. To better understand the language of emotions an excellent book that builds emotional intelligence is, *The Courage to Feel; A Practical Guide to the Power and Freedom of Emotional Honesty* by Andrew Seubert.

- Learn more about caring for your inner family by reading the book by Richard C. Schwartz, *Introduction to the Internal Family Systems Model*. It is written in a clear and humane manner.

- Visit www.healthjourneys.com to obtain one of Belleruth Naparstek's guided imagery recordings. Be sure whenever listening to any self-care recording to do it in a quiet, private place when you don't have to tend to other responsibilities. That means, no listening while driving.

- Find out more about Imaginal Nurturing by going to April Steele's website: www.april-steele.ca. She has CDs available for purchase that guide one through the imaginal nurturing experience as well as CDs for developing one's adventuring spirit.

- Read Sue Johnson's book, *Hold Me Tight: Seven Conversations for a Lifetime of Love.* Watch the DVD of the same name to witness live examples of what effective conversations look and sound like. Observe yourself more carefully to discover how you contribute to a negative or positive cycle with your partner.

- Read Stephen R. Covey's, *The Seven Habits of Highly Effective Families,* an insightful and practical book.

- For a deeper understanding and appreciation of compassionate parenting, read Jon and Myla Kabat-Zinn's *Everyday Blessings: The Inner Work of Mindful Parenting.*

- For further guidance in cultivating mindfulness, compassion and awareness of the present moment, turn to the wise and inspiring writings and recordings of Pema Chodron, Jon Kabat-Zinn, Jack Kornfield and Eckhart Tolle.

- *The Gift*, poetry of the Sufi mystic Hafiz as translated by Daniel Ladinsky, is mind-blowing, delightful and insightful. His poems, in a playful manner and with contemporary images, speak great truths and help us see that we are diamonds in the rough.

- Alan Watts' perspective and articulation are so fresh, witty, provocative and illuminating. Fortunately, his many lectures were recorded while he was still alive. You might want to visit the website that his son has created, www.alanwatts.com. Some particularly brilliant talks include:
  - Seeing Through the Net
  - Veil of Thoughts
  - Game of Yes and No
  - We as Organism
  - Who Am I: Myth of Myself
  - Limits of Language
  - Man and Nature

Understanding your Emotions and Needs

- Take responsibility for becoming an expert on your childhood and emotional history and how it continues to impact you today. Become curious about your inner family. Notice feelings of vulnerability or distress and recognize that they are young parts of your personality in need of comfort and reassurance. Become familiar too with the younger parts of your personality who feel compelled to defend you. Help them turn over to your Adult Self the responsibility of managing difficult emotions and relationships.

- Reclaim your disowned emotions and memories. Cognitive insight is not a substitute for processing emotions directly through the body. This is challenging work and you will most likely need the support and guidance of a mental health professional to do so. You buried them for a reason; they are intense and painful. You will need to unveil your emotions gradually in a psychologically safe environment and the average friend or family member does not have the skills or experience to provide that. Too many people are unaware of what is in this book and will feel uncomfortable with the depth of your emotion. They may dismiss your concerns, urge you to put them behind you and move on, give you simplistic advice or reassurance, tell you to focus on the positive or quickly switch to some other subject. They may try to boost your spirits and self-worth by brushing a thick layer of gold-gilding over the difficult truths that deserve to see the light of day. This process is too important and sensitive to have mishandled.

- If you're very new to recognizing, admitting and expressing emotions and you fear being judged by others, slowly start out acknowledging to yourself the new realizations you are making by reading this book. Learn what you can about yourself and reassure yourself frequently that almost everyone around you is grappling with similar emotions, insecurities and relationship issues. Once you take the next step of meeting with a therapist, you will probably be relieved to find that sharing with a warm and understanding person can feel very reassuring and comforting.

- If you chronically feel guilt and shame or, on the other hand, feel disrespected, victimized and angry, there is most likely a reservoir of hurts, deprivations and losses for you to discover and grieve. How might others have failed *you* as a child? Who should have been responsible, instead of you or your sibling, when things went wrong in childhood? What unmet emotional needs do *you* have?

- If you chronically feel anger, hatred, distrust, disgust, contempt, rejection or coldness toward others, who might have made *you* feel shameful, undeserving, unlovable and inadequate when you were young?

- If you find yourself annoyed by others' emotionality and feel superior and smug, be aware that dismissing others who are in pain is as harmful and offensive an act as their subjecting you to their blinding emotions. You are putting gas on a fire and both of you are getting burned. Maybe it's time to end "the drama of the pained and the numb."

- If you have always—or never—experienced feelings of unworthiness, inadequacy, helplessness, sadness or despair and your children are having emotional, behavioral or relationship difficulties, it might be that they are absorbing your stuck or disowned emotions. Children are like radios; they will pick up any emotional signals you blare or tune out from your own consciousness.

- If you often feel self-pity and alternate between drowning in it and hating yourself for being such a baby, what you experienced in childhood probably fully justifies your feeling intense sorrow for yourself. The emotion that would get you unstuck is self-compassion. But you can't feel compassion unless you connect with the memories that validate your need for compassion.

- If you are very sensitive to others' suffering—whether people or animals—and devote much energy and heart to rescuing and protecting others, you are probably simultaneously neglecting and depriving yourself. The child inside of you, who has suffered so long without compassion, would be so grateful and relieved if you would turn your caring attention toward him or her.

- If you have chronic or recurrent physical ailments, whether minor or major, follow your physician's advice. But also consider this: trauma, stress, emotions and relationship issues may be significantly contributing to your vulnerability. Mental health services should be an integral part of your treatment.

- If you constantly feel that you're facing more than you can handle, you're external life won't become manageable until you consciously bring order, clarity and calm to your inner experience of chaos.

- If you feel either revved-up all the time or chronically fatigued, your nervous system has been through the wringer and you must make self-care your absolute first priority. The longer you delay, the more vulnerable your body is to developing severe symptoms and chronic conditions. Make use of the various self-care and mindfulness techniques described in this book and "get thee to an EMDR therapist."

Taking Responsibility, Being Proactive

- Beware of solutions to one part of your life that just push emotional issues underground to another part of your life. If a solution to our marital difficulties does not address deep personal, emotional issues, they will reemerge or be played out some other way, either in our physical bodies or other relationships. If we build a secure attachment with our spouse but fail to sufficiently address childhood trauma, we may still be symptomatic. If we develop a formal mindfulness practice but don't address childhood trauma, we may continue to experience emotional hijacks and compulsions. If we do trauma work but don't integrate mindfulness into our daily lives, then we might become emotionally reactive when totally unpredicted events trigger old wounds.

A multipronged approach provides the greatest protection and assures optimal functioning.

- Take 100% responsibility for your own behavior. Identify in what ways you are not evidencing personal integrity. Reduce behaviors that reinforce your partner's sense of you being unavailable, threatening or hurtful. The challenge for each of us is to function at our most mature and wise self, even when our partner is not. If you are prone to putting the blame on others, *be at least as curious about your own contribution to relationship difficulties as you are aware of the other's role.* Take responsibility for cleaning up your own act, but do so with self-compassion and patience. We always have room to grow and life isn't a race.

- Take responsibility for recognizing and acknowledging your own fears, sense of shame and unmet needs so that you don't project them onto others, misperceive others or seek out others to express them for you. Likewise, seek to express the full range of your human capacity: your physical, emotional, mental, social and spiritual dimensions.

- If your partner begins to express any annoyance or defensiveness when you talk about the contents of this book, don't push the issue. Just quietly integrate into your own life what you are learning. Do your part. You are responsible for your effort, not the outcome.

- Whenever your partner, or some other important adult, behaves in an appalling, offensive way, recognize that the person has just been sideswiped and taken over by a protective part of their personality. Don't take it personally and don't join in the futile game. Aim to keep your cool and mindfully observe the whole picture. Think of this as a passing hail storm and only one dimension of your partner's repertoire. Stay in your body, hold onto your non-judgmental awareness and don't react. In the state of mind your partner is in, there is not much you can say that is going to be productive. This is not the time to sell your perspective or reveal how you are being hurt. By not engaging in battle with irrationality, you will conserve your energies for times when your partner's better self is present and receptive. Well after your partner has calmed down and you've had a chance to internally process the event, then approach him or her with information about how you were affected.

- If you've had a pattern of being drawn to high-maintenance people—those who act like it's always about them, express a lot of intense emotion and put excessive demands on you—recognize that you have unmet needs and unresolved emotions of your own.

Until you've recognized and processed your own emotions and learned to express your own needs, you will be drawn to partners who express enough emotion and have enough needs for two people. It's crucial that you bring attention to your inner being to discover what's been overlooked for too long, perhaps guilt, disappointment, helplessness, inadequacy, shame or anger. Stop putting so much energy into placating your high-maintenance partner's every demand or, alternately, avoiding him or her to focus on activities that leave you no time to reflect. Begin to set limits with your partner *and* with the compulsive parts of your personality that won't let you discover your emotional life. Put less burden on yourself to be a rock. Take time to discover who you *really* are.

You need to raise the volume on your inner and outer voices and develop assertiveness, the ability to speak up for yourself in a self-respecting and respectful way. It's important that you become comfortable with having expectations of others and letting them know what you need in order to feel secure in the relationship and that you matter too. High-maintenance people can't read your mind. They have so much with which they are preoccupied, your concerns won't be on their radar screen unless you send steady, strong signals that you need their attention, respect and support. They need to know what would make *you* feel safe enough to come closer. They probably don't know what you feel or need and the time is long overdue for you to identify how *they* can come through for *you*, so that connecting with them will be more appealing.

If you're real new at looking inside and can't imagine what could be worth finding, set aside blocks of time daily to practice mindfulness. When you abstain from your usual focus on the outer world, inner landscape will begin to percolate up for you to observe. Some of what surfaces will probably be unsettling and seeking therapy to help you work it through would be wise. Processing the memories of high-maintenance people in your childhood will help you increase feelings of confidence and worthiness. As a result, you will find yourself relating to your partner more as an adult and less as a helpless child.

- You may, on the other hand, have had a pattern of longing to find someone who will value, understand and validate you and make you feel safe, significant and at peace. Instead, you keep being drawn to people who have difficulty understanding and expressing emotions and being sensitive, available and responsive. You may have felt like you were trying to get blood from a stone. Your attempts to control each partner and the relationship have probably made matters worse. There is a good chance that the intensity of your emotional expression and neediness has been intimidating, smothering, frustrating or aggravating to these people. It would be in your best interest to learn to take responsibility for validating yourself, managing your emotions and practicing imaginal nurturing.

By soothing your inner child you will feel more empowered and less dependent on others to rescue you. By calming your emotions down to a more moderate level and accessing more reason and equanimity, you will feel less panicky and more secure and serene with life as it is. Making a conscious effort to soften your approach with your partner will pay off as you discover that "less is more." It is important for you to recognize that your partner is hyper-sensitive to strong emotions and long-winded relationship speech is very hard to follow. The calmer, more reasonable and more succinct you become, the safer your partner will feel and the more available and responsive your partner will become.

As opposed to your avoidant partner, you need to bring more attention to the world *beyond* your mind, emotions and intimate relationship. Develop hobbies, interests and friendships. Bring more of your attention to the natural world. Go out of your comfort zone and practice mindfulness meditation until you begin to acquire familiarity with the pleasures and benefits of solitude. Be more aware of what life has to offer beyond relationships to counterbalance your preoccupation with human connection. You then give your partner more breathing room for him or her to move *toward* you, instead of *away* due to being pursued, overwhelmed and drained.

Also, you need to process, preferably in therapy, the experiences that you had in childhood that left you feeling so lonely, insignificant and helpless. This includes the relationships with adult caretakers who were distant and insensitive, as well as those who radiated emotional distress. The irony is that, the more you do your own healing work and provide self-care, the more your partner will take initiative to offer you attention and comfort. You move in the direction of giving to each other, not because you are two halves who feel incomplete, but because you experience a sense of generosity and compassion that comes from deep self-knowledge and being whole.

- Know that when you heal your childhood traumas and acquire affect management skills, you are rewiring your social-emotional brain circuitry. This means that you will most likely be drawn to and attractive to people who also have a secure attachment status, whether developed in childhood or earned in adulthood.

Considering Professional Help

- If you've had therapy experiences in the past that were disappointing or provided limited benefits, seriously consider working with an EMDR practitioner. When seeking an EMDR therapist, be sure to choose someone who is certified, which signifies that they are invested in developing expertise and using this approach. EMDR is very powerful and you need someone who understands how to keep the experience safe. EMDRIA (www.emdria.org) is the international organization with a directory that allows you to identify EMDRIA certified therapists by city, state or zip code. The EMDR Institute (www.emdr.com) is also very helpful in providing information about EMDR, including the research that substantiates its effectiveness.

- If you have never been in therapy or have not done the kind of healing work I've described in this book and you now recognize how much has been infiltrating your adult life and relationships, invest in psychotherapy. I recommend that you "shop" until you find a therapist who is warm, genuine, attentive, attuned, responsive and emotionally engaged. It is important that the therapist is comfortable with and skillful at accessing and processing deep emotions and body sensations. You may have to travel further when you have higher expectations, but it will be well worth the investment.

- While EMDR is the approach that I have been mastering and finding very effective, it is not the only method of deep experiential therapy. You might also look into the following approaches:
  o Diana Fosha's Accelerated Experiential-Dynamic Psychotherapy (www.aedpinstitute.com)
  o Pat Ogden's Sensorimotor Psychotherapy (www.sensori motorpsychotherapy.org)
  o Richard Schwartz's Internal Family Systems (www.self leadership.org)
  o Peter Levine's Somatic Experiencing (www.somatic experiencing.com and www.traumahealing.com)

- If you are already attending psychotherapy and benefiting from a therapist who is trustworthy, sensitive and skillful, by all means, continue your work together. If your therapist is not doing trauma work with you, there is significant progress that can still be made including creating stability, experiencing a safe haven and secure base, developing a framework and language for what one has experienced and developing skills such as affect management, self-care, mindfulness and assertiveness. If you reach a point of diminishing returns or if you still remain stuck in disturbing emotions and self-beliefs, you may want to discuss with your therapist the possibility of a referral for EMDR work. In some cases, the EMDR intervention is short-term and the client's original therapist remains the primary therapist. In other cases, the therapist and client may decide together that the client is ready for a new form of treatment and that an EMDR therapist will take over the treatment.

- If you have experienced trauma in adulthood, such as a rape, an accident, hospitalization, loss of a child, loss of livelihood, violence, war or a natural disaster, EMDR could provide tremendous relief. Don't wait for someone else to recommend this to you. Most people, including physicians, either don't know EMDR exists or have misinformation about it.

- In the face of emotional or relationship difficulties, it is always in your best interest to get help sooner than later. The longer you delay, the more harm deepens. When any one member of a family is suffering, the others experience it vicariously. Pain multiplies. It's important to not take struggling and suffering for granted. A competent professional will be able to guide you to a level of functioning you might not have believed was possible. The benefits of good psychotherapy will be significant, not only to you and your family, but also to coming generations.

- If you know you had traumatic experiences in childhood or that your parents' mental health or marriage was far from stable, don't wait for things to go wrong before seeking professional help. Once problems start percolating, the underlying emotions and beliefs have a hypnotic power to entangle you in their familiar spell. They become like slow-moving quicksand that sucks you in without you knowing it. Then new painful experiences get layered on the previous ones and reinforce your negative self-beliefs. Being proactive is wise.

Nurturing Your Intimate Relationship

- If you are in therapy, share with your partner what you are experiencing and learning about yourself. The more your feelings, perceptions, traumatic experiences, difficulties, unmet needs and treatment plan are understood, the more your partner will be able to have compassion and come through for you. The more you acknowledge and verbalize, the less projections, misperceptions and assumptions will damage the relationship. Also, it is important that your relationship with your therapist doesn't replace your connection with your partner. You need to get into the habit of revealing your softer feelings with your spouse, not just with a professional. At the same time, you need to help your partner understand what you need in order to feel safe enough to talk about the things that matter most. Don't begin to share the more delicate subjects until your partner has assured you that he will be emotionally present and sensitive.

- Dare to bring up with your partner whatever emotionally significant issues you confide to your best friend. Again, it is important to do this so that your marriage does not take a back seat. You need to talk directly to the person you are having relationship issues with. A friend can help you clarify your thoughts, feelings and needs, but then you have to bring these issues to your partner so that he or she can understand and respond.

- Be alert for any intense relationship that creates a triangle with your spouse on the outside. This could be your parent, mother-in-law, child, clergyman, co-worker or best friend.

- Remember that most of the time when partners hurt us, they aren't being malicious, they are being mindless. Seek to recognize how *both* you and your spouse have suffered, *both* have been unconscious, *both* have caused harm through use of defenses, *both* need to replace defenses with authentic sharing and *both* deserve understanding and care.

- "Know your audience." You have the power to evoke your partner's worst self or better self. Find out all you can about what upsets your partner and why. As long as the expectations are not at odds with your needs, try to be responsive. If the expectations are unrealistic, inappropriate or trigger your deepest wounds, seek professional help. Couples therapy is preferable, but if your partner is opposed to going, then seek individual therapy.

I say couples therapy is preferable when both partners are willing to participate because addressing relationship problems with half of the couple present often results in the therapist getting a one-sided, distorted view of each partner and the relationship. Those therapists who only see individuals and are not familiar with ego state, systems and attachment theories, may not appreciate that
  - *both* partners' defenses and unresolved emotions shape intimate relationships
  - how the client presents him or herself to the therapist isn't necessarily how the client behaves with their partner
  - the individual client is missing large pieces of their partner's emotional experience
  - the individual client may not recognize his or her own behaviors as threatening
  - with this partial perspective, the therapist may perceive the relationship as untenable
  - working with only one partner increases the chances of one partner outgrowing the other and feeling an even wider divide

- Whether your relationship is just starting to go sour or has been unrewarding for a long time, seek the help of someone trained in Emotionally Focused Therapy for Couples as soon as possible. Don't assume it will get better in time. Don't assume it will do no harm to put it on the back burner while you focus on the children or your career. Don't assume that the relationship can't be

246 Peace in the Heart and Home

improved or saved. Don't assume that your partner is incapable of learning, growing or loving. Don't assume that you made a mistake or that there is someone out there who is going to be a lot easier. Don't tolerate abuse, contempt, ridicule or being totally ignored thinking that it's inevitable for relationships to hurt this badly. EFT therapists have a relationship map to guide you to a secure and rewarding bond. It is in your best interest to find an EFT therapist who is registered or receiving ongoing supervision and/or consultation to ensure receiving the best possible treatment. You can find an EFT therapist at their website: www.iceeft.com.

- Remember the four "R"s of healthy relationships. We need to be able to do all of them.
  - o Request—the ability to ask for comfort, support and reassurance
  - o Receive—the ability to allow your partner to come through for you and take in the gift of caring
  - o Reach—the ability to initiate acts of comfort, support and reassurance
  - o Respond—the ability to come through for your partner in the ways that are most meaningful *to him* or *her*

- Let's add a fifth R: Repair—the crucial element that reestablishes trust and safety. Looking back over 33 years of marriage, there were many times when I thought my husband and I had hit a dead end. Yet we were able to recover trust and caring through reflection, emotional investment and honest dialogue.

- Expand your awareness of the world around you so that the disturbing behavior of your family member doesn't define you and your life. The narrower your universe, the more you feel disappointed and deprived by your family member. Your relationship is significant, *but he or she is not responsible for your emotional state.* Become attuned to other sources of comfort and fulfillment: the beauty and wonder of the sky, the trees, an acorn, the marvel of your hands, the smiling eyes on the faces of strangers, the dignity and vitality of children, the grace of dancers. Invest ample time and full attention to really contemplate these riches. A five second noticing won't register in any meaningful way. Instead, try minutes at a time and soak in these ever-present miracles. There have been countless doors before you and perhaps you've been transfixed on the one that is locked. Don't keep knocking and pulling on the knob. Notice the open doors and go in.

Coming Through for Our Family

- Identify the times and places where marital or family conflicts are most likely to occur—at the dinner table, on weekday mornings, whenever your child procrastinates with homework or after your parents have just visited? These are the times when you most need the qualities of mindfulness. If possible, do a mindfulness technique or listen to the Wise Mind Meditation just beforehand. Or start each day with a brief period in which you state your intention to find your "pause button" and observe mindfully when you feel your emotions begin to surge. In any marriage, attachment wounds inevitably get triggered, over and over again. The best hope for any couple is for both members to actively build their mindfulness muscles through daily practice.

- Starting when your children are very young, get in the habit of putting feelings into words and talking about the thoughts, motivations, beliefs, concerns and emotions behind behaviors. Do this in response to real relationship events, not just as an educational exercise. Keep the dialog brief, five to ten minutes maximum. Don't turn it into an ordeal. Your own and your children's ability to acquire this skill will greatly diminish the need for harmful defenses and contribute to more harmonious family life with you and their own future families. And by the way, there is no reason why your sons can't develop these skills; they're *not* from Mars.

- Be cautious of advice given by well-meaning friends and family, whether about psychological or relationship issues. People who care for you are generally trying their best to help. But they may minimize, exaggerate or misdiagnose your own, or your family member's, psychological symptoms. They may discourage you from doing trauma work if they see you looking sad and afraid. They may misinterpret your child's behavior and steer you wrong. They may sincerely think they are helping you when they tell you to give up on your spouse. It is easy for others to fall into the trap of seeing things from only one angle or from their distorted lens or to wrongly assume the motives of others.

- Whenever a partner or child is verbally attacking, critical, angry or otherwise carried away, be curious. Later, when things have quieted down, try to discover what the underlying softer emotions might be. If at all possible, provide a calm but warm presence and express interest in how they've been hurt and why they're so upset. This response assumes that the person is not physically aggressive. If an adolescent child or adult is physically aggressive, contact a domestic violence program. In addition, both of you will need mental health or family therapy services.

- If your child is prone to physical distress, such as stomach aches or headaches, don't dismiss them or simply respond with medicine. Show curiosity about your child's emotions and relationships. Giving your child the opportunity to discuss fears and troubles may make a big difference. One client of mine remembers feeling pain in his heart for years, starting at age ten, due to chronic stress, lack of support and feelings of confusion and helplessness. Realizing that he suffered severe stress at the tender age of ten brought tears to his eyes.

- If you have a child or adolescent who is having psychological or behavioral difficulties or physical ailments that might be psychosomatic, first schedule a full physical to make sure there is no underlying medical problem. If the issues are not medical, then engage the services of a mental health professional or family therapist who will look at the difficulties from a family systems and emotionally-focused perspective. Be willing to be involved to see how you and your spouse might be inadvertently contributing to your child's problems. The more you discover what *you* can do differently to help your child, the more empowered you become.

- If you tend to be high-strung and anxious and have your child under a microscope, be aware that your fears for your child are themselves capable of provoking symptoms in him or her. The best way to protect your children and enable them to have a happy and successful life is to investigate *your own* life and what harm was done to you, your siblings or your parents that has resulted in your current preoccupation with the safety and happiness of a loved one. The best gifts we can give our children are parents who are genuinely at peace with themselves, each other and life. Let me repeat that. *The best gifts we can give our children are parents who are genuinely at peace with themselves, each other and life.*

- If your children are already grown, remember you are still a resource to them in their adult life, as well as your grandchildren. My client Peter, who was terrorized by his father and peers, had a loving, supportive relationship with his grandfather. He says that without that relationship, he probably would have become violent, been imprisoned or died prematurely, like many of his peers. If your children don't live close enough for regular contact, there are volunteer programs that could use your help. You could be a mentor or a "Big Brother" or "Big Sister." You could develop a relationship with the family next door. You are a potential source of caring connection to all those who cross your path on a daily basis. Never underestimate the power of simple kindness.

A Few Observations about Groups

- Support Groups can be a life-saver for many people, especially in a society in which so many of us are isolated. When we are faced with ordeals and uphill battles, it is very comforting to have a place to go where we will be heard, understood and encouraged. While support groups can be of tremendous benefit, they might, under certain circumstances, interfere with higher functioning. I have two examples in mind.

- When you attend a group for people with special problems or the parents of children with special problems, be careful if this becomes the only place where you feel understood and not blamed or made to feel shameful. When this is the case, members may validate each other as deserving of understanding and support, but continue to sense that there are others "out there" who judge them and would reject them. The sense of safety and self-worth that this solution affords is a shallow one compared to what one experiences when there has been a thorough healing of the root experiences that first created those feelings of shame and rejection. The emotions the person is feeling in the present could be traumatic memory intrusions or a reenactment. "Once again, I can't trust others to see my worth. Once again, I'm being seen as responsible for what's wrong." When instead these memories are healed, the person isn't preoccupied with the sense of either inner or outer judgment.

- The second example is when people attend support groups, such as Alcoholics Anonymous, almost daily for 10, 20 or more years. While I understand the importance of ongoing attendance, my sense is that there may be an excessive dependence on the group. If the person hasn't done any significant psychotherapy that develops affect management and mindfulness skills, heals the memories that have prompted the need to self-medicate and addresses the emotions that current family relationships are triggering, then the person is going to feel that the group is his lifeline and only safety zone. With proper psychological treatment, the person is much more likely to develop a sense of confidence in his or her ability to manage emotions and urges, transform harmful beliefs about self and others and interact with family members in new ways that are more likely to create a secure attachment. Stopping a compulsive habit is a major achievement, but it's only half the battle.

- Any group that fosters a feeling in its members of being special or superior while non-members are perceived as less worthy is providing a conditional sense of self-worth at others' expense. Albert Einstein's words are quite fitting here, "A human being is a part of the whole called by us the 'universe,' a part limited in time and space. He experiences himself, his thoughts and feelings, as something separate from the rest—a kind of optical delusion of consciousness. This delusion is a kind of prison for us, restricting us to our personal desires and to affection for a few persons nearest to us. Our task must be to free ourselves from this prison by widening our circle of compassion to embrace all living creatures and the whole of nature in its beauty." While we have Mr. Einstein present, let's hear another of his insightful quotes, "There are only two ways to live your life. One is as though nothing is a miracle. The other is as though everything is a miracle." And that means "every one" is a miracle.

- For those of you who enjoy listening to books, *Peace in the Heart and Home* is also available as an MP3 audiobook from my website: www.peaceintheheartandhome.com. Some of you may find that hearing my voice provides an added measure of meaning, encouragement and comfort.

- My last recommendation is this: Consider re-reading or re-listening to parts, or all, of this book from time to time. There is so much here to absorb in one reading. Each time you may discover something new that can help you to stay on the path.

As I bring this book to a close, I'd like to share these final words. Optimal health and well-being depend upon our integrity and wholeness. Integrity means that our values, convictions, intentions and behaviors are aligned, not in contradiction with each other. While we may experience strong emotions and urges, we are not ruled by them. How we behave is how our Wisest Self would have us behave. The various parts of our personality are at peace with each other; each can co-exist and flourish without harming or undermining another. Our behaviors truly are in our best interest and in no way interfere with others' autonomy and well-being. Integrity implies wholeness. There are no parts of our experience that we are shunning or living vicariously. There is nothing shoved under the rug to trip us or others up. Our bodies don't have to act out to make us face what we refuse to acknowledge.

Being fully in touch with reality and the moment sometimes brings us into close contact with disturbing emotions and sensations. It can mean feeling fury, anguish, horror, fear, guilt, helplessness, sadness and grief throughout one's mind and body, but with enough presence and resiliency to take whatever good we can from it, and leave the rest behind. It also brings us in touch with experiences that enrich our lives (and broaden our vocabularies): serenity, joy, zeal, zest, sparkle, splendor verve and vitality, as well as the capacity to frolic, savor, inspire, love and thrive. Those who have fully felt the dark emotions, without being overwhelmed, have been blessed with knowing the uplifting. I wish this bounty for you: that you come to know these flourishing states of being, not just as left brain abstractions like "abundance" and "gratitude" that we *try* to believe, but as body-felt experiences.

On another level, wholeness means being at home with life on several two-sided planes. It means knowing and accepting the good and the bad, past and the present, body and mind, earth and ethereal, power and impotence, self and other, creation and dissolution, time and timelessness. It means embracing both our human, personal, evolving self and our perfect, divine, universal self.

Living well is an art form that over the years we have the potential to refine and master with the help of courage, conscious attention, curiosity, enthusiasm and lifelong learning. I believe that what I have shared in this guide provides a down-to-earth framework that can release the creative process within you. Having a new day to start again may be the most wonderful invention with which we've been blessed. Each dawn is a mini-rebirth like in the movie *Groundhog Day* or in childhood games when we called out, "D O! Do Over!" We have all these opportunities to make a fresh start, to make it better, to be more effective, to fly higher and to hone our co-creation with whatever ingredients the new day provides.

Feeling effective, fulfilled and at peace also requires being able to recognize where and when to invest our energies. The last time I experienced depression was the last time I put my heart into trying to change something I was powerless to change. As the Asian martial arts masters and Taoist philosophers have long known, living wisely and successfully involves aligning with the direction in which energy is already flowing. So, when we attempt to change only what is within our control and only our right to reshape, when we recognize and accept what is inevitable and when we take delight in what is perfect just the way it is, we are in flow. We don't need to force anything when there's plenty of opportunity in this life to marvel, play, create, improve, help, share and love.

I hope this book has answered a question some of you might have had: "How can I hope to live the vision of Eckhart Tolle, Jill Bolte Taylor or the Dalai Lama when I haven't had a mind-blowing spiritual breakthrough, a stroke or the cultural background and upbringing of a Tibetan monk and when I live in a modern day family and a contemporary world that is stuck on fast-forward?" For there to be a peaceful connection between ourselves and others, we need to become connected to and bring peace to our hearts.

Our hearts can't be at peace unless we heal our broken hearts. Our hearts remain broken when the child within us still feels full of shame and fear. Our hearts remain broken when we don't know and love ourselves fully and blame others for our deprivation and ongoing pain. Our hearts are broken when we're not at peace with our spouse or children. And our hearts are broken when the pain of these disconnections blinds us to a universe that every day is shining love on us. Each of us has several homes: our heart, our body, our mind, our special loved ones, our community, our planet and the divine universe. Experiencing peace in our homes requires being at home with our emotions, the musical current that brings the world to life.

Throughout my life, whenever it came time to sign greeting cards or come up with an idea for a gift, I would often struggle with what to say, what to give. All my ideas always seemed to fall short of what was in my heart. Well, it now seems that this book is the gift that would have said it best. And so let me sign off with these final hopes. I hope this book conveys my heart-felt wish for you to have as full and rewarding a life as possible. I hope your trip through my mind and heart has been enriching and worthy of your time and attention. I hope my style and choice of words have made the messages I've delivered understandable, non-threatening, memorable and encouraging. I sincerely hope your lives will be better off as a result of the lessons I have learned and shared. I would like you to know that I've thoroughly enjoyed the process of creating this guide for you. Writing it has shown me, once again, that we just never know what is inside of us until we give it a warm welcome and space and time to arise. We are all so full of surprises.

May you and your loved ones, and all of us, thrive.

Bibliography

Bolte Taylor, Jill, PhD. *My Stroke of Insight: A Brain Scientist's Personal Journey*. Penguin Group, 2008.

Canfield, Jack and Hansen, Mark Victor. *Chicken Soup for the Soul*. Health Communications, Inc.,1993.

Chopra, Deepak. *The Happiness Prescription*. Harmony Books, 2009. (Also, in DVD and CD)

Cousins, Norman. *Anatomy of an Illness as Perceived by the Patient: Reflections on Healing and Regeneration*. Norton, 1979.

Covey, Stephen, R. *The Seven Habits of Highly Effective People*. Simon & Schuster, 2004.

Covey, Stephen, R. *The Seven Habits of Highly Effective Families*. St. Martin's Press, 1997.

Cozolino, Louis Ph.D. *The Neuroscience of Psychotherapy, Building and Rebuilding the Human Brain*. W. W. Norton & Company, 2002.

Cozolino, Louis Ph.D. *The Neuroscience of Human Relationships: Attachment and the Developing Social Brain*. W. W. Norton & Company, 2006.

Dusay, John. *How I See You and You See Me*. Harper & Row, 1977.

The Editors of Conari Press. *Random Acts of Kindness.* Conari Press, January 1993.

Goleman, Daniel. *Emotional Intelligence.* Bantam, 1995.

Goleman, Daniel. *Social Intelligence.* Bantam, 2006.

Gottman, John. *The Seven Principles for Making Marriage Work.* Crown Publishing Group, 2000.

Hafiz, *The Gift.* Translated by Daniel Ladinsky. Penguin Group, 1999.

Johnson, Sue. *Hold Me Tight: Seven Conversations for a Lifetime of Love.* Little, Brown and Company, 2008.

Kabat-Zinn, Jon. *Wherever You Go, There You Are.* Hyperion, 2005.

Kabat-Zinn, Jon. *Full Catastrophe Living: Using the Wisdom of Your Body and Mind to Face Stress, Pain, and Illness.* Delacorte Press, 1990.

Kabat-Zinn, Myla and Jon Kabat-Zinn. *Everyday Blessings: The Inner Work of Mindful Parenting.* Hyperion, 1998.

Kornfield, Jack. *The Wise Heart: A Guide to the Universal Teachings of Buddhist Psychology.* Random House, 2008.

Kornfield, Jack. *Buddha's Little Instruction Book.* Random House, 1994.

Levine, Peter. *Waking the Tiger: Healing Trauma: The Innate Capacity to Transform Overwhelming Experiences.* North Atlantic Books, 1997.

Miller, Alice. *The Drama of the Gifted Child: The Search for the True Self.* Basic Books, 2008.

Peck, M. Scott. *The Road Less Traveled: A New Psychology of Love, Traditional Values and Spiritual Growth.* Simon & Schuster, 1978.

Real, Terrence. *I Don't Want to Talk About It: Overcoming the Secret Legacy of Male Depression.* Simon & Schuster, 1997.

Real, Terrence. *How Can I Get Through to You: Reconnecting Men and Women.* Simon & Schuster, 2002.

Russell, Peter. *Waking Up in Time: Finding Inner Peace in Times of Accelerating Change.* Origin Press, 2008.

Scaer, Robert, MD. *The Trauma Spectrum: Hidden Wounds and Human Resiliency*, W. W. Norton, 2005.

Scaer, Robert, MD. *The Body Bears the Burden: Trauma, Dissociation and Disease*, 2nd Edition. The Haworth Press, 2007.

Schumacher, E. F. *Guide for the Perplexed*. Harper Collins Publishers, 1978.

Schwartz, Richard C. *Introduction to the Internal Family Systems Model*. Trailhead Publishing, 2001.

Servan-Schreiber, David. *The Instinct to Heal: Curing Stress, Anxiety, and Depression Without Drugs and Without Talk Therapy*. St. Martin's Press, 2005.

Seubert, Andrew. *The Courage to Feel: A Practical Guide to the Power and Freedom of Emotional Honesty*. Infinity Publishing, 2008.

Shapiro, Francine and Margo Silk Forrest. *EMDR: The Breakthrough "Eye Movement" Therapy for Overcoming Anxiety, Stress and Trauma*. Basic Books, 2004

Shapiro, Francine. *Eye Movement Desensitization and Reprocessing (EMDR): Basic Principles, Protocols and Procedures*, 2nd edition. The Guilford Press, 2001.

Siegel, Bernie S. *Love, Medicine and Miracles: Lessons Learned about Self-Healing from a Surgeon's Experience with Exceptional Patients*. Harper and Row, 1986

Siegel, Daniel. *The Developing Mind: How Relationships and the Brain Interact to Shape Who We Are*. Guilford Press, 2001.

Siegel, Daniel. *Parenting From the Inside Out: How a Deeper Self-Understanding Can Help You Raise Children Who Thrive*. Penguin Group, 2004.

Siegel, Daniel. *The Mindful Brain: Reflection and Attunement in the Cultivation of Well-being*. W. W. Norton, 2007.

Siegel, Daniel. *Mindsight: The New Science of Personal Transformation*. Random House, 2010.

Tolle, Eckhart. *The Power of Now: A Guide to Spiritual Enlightenment.* New World Library, 2004.

Tolle, Eckhart. *A New Earth: Awakening to Your Life's Purpose.* Penguin Group, 2008.

Wesselmann, Debra. *The Whole Parent: How to Become a Terrific Parent, Even If You Didn't Have One.* DeCapo Press, 2003.

Young, Shelly. *Break Out of the Sugar Prison: You Can Overcome Sugar Addiction With The Powerful Basic States Mindfulness System and A Cutting Edge Nutritional Program.* Paul Harris, 2010.

List of Websites

www.acrnet.org   Association for Conflict Resolution

www.aedpinstitute.com   Accelerated Experiential Dynamic
 Psychotherapy Institute, Diana Fosha

www.alanwatts.com   Philosopher, Writer and Speaker

www.atcnebraska.com   Attachment and Trauma Center of Nebraska,
 Debra Wesselmann

www.basicmindfulness.org   Talk Image Touch Feel, Sight Sound
 Touch, Shinzen Young

www.bouldercoloradotherapist.net   Mindfulness Now, Shelly Young

www.chopra.com   The Chopra Center The Path to Wellness
 Begins Here™

www.collaborativepractice.com   International Academy of
 Collaborative Professionals

www.debrawesselmann.com   Wise Mind, EMDR, Attachment
    and Trauma

www.eckharttolle.com   Eckhart Teachings, Are You Ready to be
    Awakened?

www.emdr.com   EMDR Institute

www.emdria.org   EMDR International Association

www.gottman.com   The Gottman Relationship Institute,
www.rrinstitute.com   Relationship Research Institute

www.heartmath.org   Empowering Heart-Based Living

www.healthjourneys.com   Guided imagery, Belleruth Naparstek

www.iceeft.com   International Center for Excellence in Emotionally
    Focused Therapy, Sue Johnson

www.instincttoheal.org   David Servan-Schreiber

www.jackkornfield.org   Mindfulness and Buddhist Psychology

www.michaelmikulka.com   Classical music

www.parallax.org and www.plumvillage.org   Thich Nhat Hanh

www.peterrussell.com   Spirit of Now

www.selfleadership.org   Internal Family Systems, Richard Schwartz

www.sensorimotorpsychotherapy.org   Pat Ogden

www.shambhala.org/teachers/pema/   Pema Chodron

www.smartmarriages.com   The Coalition for Marriage, Family, and
    Couples Education

www.somaticexperiencing.com   Nature's Lessons in Healing
    Trauma, Peter Levine

www.terryreal.com   Relational Life Therapy™

www.traumahealing.com   Somatic Experiencing Foundation for
Human Enrichment, Peter Levine

www.umassmed.edu/cfm/index.aspx   Center for Mindfulness,
Jon Kabat-Zinn, Saki Santorelli

www.womentowomen.com   Changing women's health—naturally™,
Marcelle Pick

List of Defense Strategies

Arrogance	Blame/accusing	Sarcasm
Contempt	Criticizing	Teasing
Devaluing	Challenging	Provoking
Domination	Projection	Status-seeking
Tormenting	Displacement	Overachieving
Intimidation	Entitlement	Overcompensating
Hostility/aggression	Power-seeking	Perfectionism
Threatening	Undermining	Risk-taking
Paranoia	Manipulation	Crisis-seeking
Hypervigilance	Passive-aggression	Over-activity
Revenge	Defiance	Excessive self-sufficiency
Scapegoating	Arguing	
Denial	Oppositional	Repression
Deception/lying	Acting out	Suppression

Isolation of affect	Placating	Nagging/ complaining
Minimizing	Compliance	Possessiveness
Defending	People-pleasing	Jealousy
Rationalization	Idealizing	Intrusiveness
Dismissive	Approval-seeking	Self-blame
Indifference	Subjugation	Self-criticism
Intellectualization	Self-sacrifice	Introjection
Conflict-avoidance	Martyrdom	Conversion
Procrastination	Silence	Mental confusion
Worrying	Stonewalling	Suicidal thoughts
Analyzing	Reaction formation	Mania
Obsession	Forced cheer	Delusion
Avoidance	Sugar-coating	Magical thinking
Seclusion, withdrawal	Excessive sociability	Fantasy
Emotional insulation	Overly-dramatic	Regression
Pessimism	Excessive humor	Dissociation
	Whining	

APPENDIX C

List of Self-Care and Self-Soothing Resources

APPENDIX D

List of Questions for Reflection or Journaling

HERE ARE SOME QUESTIONS to stimulate reflection. Take plenty of time to explore each one. You may find it helpful to keep a journal of your realizations and review what you've written from time to time.

* How did my parents deal with their emotions?

* How did my parents deal with *my* emotions?

* How do I typically handle emotions? Do I tend to disconnect from emotions or be overwhelmed by emotions?

* Do I alternate between both strategies?

* What do I do to avoid feeling emotions and what do I do to counter-balance them? (Refer to the examples of defenses in Addendum A.)

* What are my most common defenses and which emotions are they trying to prevent me from feeling?

* What experiences in childhood and adolescence provoked those same feelings?

* What do I do when my partner provokes strong emotions in me?

* What are my softer, more vulnerable emotions hidden under the annoyance, anger or frustration I am expressing?

* In what ways are my key relationships imbalanced with polar opposite behaviors or emotional states? (For example, I'm cynical and guarded, while he's overly trusting and generous.)

* What emotions or behaviors do I need to reclaim to be more authentic and whole?

* Do I recognize that I have the need to be heard, understood, comforted and responded to or do I mostly focus on tasks, interests and work and taking care of others who are emotional or needy?

* How much do I depend on others to change my mood or to validate me? Almost never? Almost always?

* What childhood experiences have I dismissed, minimized, tried to not think about or sugar-coated that truly were painful at the time?

* What experiences have been haunting me that I can't let go of?

* What vulnerabilities or sensitivities repeatedly get triggered in me by people in my life?

* What traits do I see in a family member or others that push my buttons?

* What deep negative beliefs about myself and others did I learn from painful experiences? How does having such beliefs impact my life?

* What beliefs about myself, others or life do I cling to or expect to have validated or confirmed?
(Examples: I can't trust people to tell me the truth, people are going to screw me, I'm not going to be taken seriously, I'm going to be rejected, others always have the advantage, it's easier to do things myself, I have to take care of everybody and no one will ever be there for me.)

* What emotion or behavior do I now exhibit with any of my family members that was not allowed at all or enough when I was growing up? Might I be going overboard? How might this behavior be impacting my current family members?

* How might my interaction with each of my children reflect unmet needs, unresolved fears or unresolved hurts from my childhood?

* How might I be using my relationship with my child to meet my current emotional needs? Is it easier to seek connection from my child than my spouse?

* How accessible, responsive and engaged were my parents with each other? In which ways am I recreating that kind of relationship with my partner?

* Am I over-attuning to one family member and neglecting another?

* Am I doing my part to express my concerns and needs in an appropriate way?

* Am I really listening when others express a concern or need?

* Am I initiating efforts to repair breaks in relationship harmony?

* Am I taking time to listen in on how I'm doing and provide proper self-care?

* Am I deriving satisfaction from my handling difficult situations in a mindful way, even when others don't give me credit or reciprocate?

  * Am I appreciating what is already fine or even great, just the way it is?

Draw your own egogram. (See Chapter Three.) Assess the size of each ego state and estimate a percentage from 0 to 100%. Ask yourself, to what extent:

  * Am I carrying a lot of disturbing emotions? (hurt child)

  * Am I too anxious or shutdown to feel carefree? (carefree)

  * Am I able to make sound adult decisions and act appropriately in my most important relationships or do emotions flood in too often resulting in fight, flight or freeze? (adult)

  * Do I judge myself harshly and put a lot of pressure on myself? (critical parent)

  * Am I able to relate to myself in a compassionate, supportive way? (nurturing parent)

Three months later, draw another egogram to graphically see your progress.

Index

Accelerated Experiential Dynamic
Psychotherapy, 242
acting out, 52, 107, 173
ADD/ADHD, defense mechanisms
and, 34–5
addiction, 17, 52–3, 56, 129, 138,
155, 166, 190, 200
adrenal fatigue, 106
adult ego state, 41, 44, 46, 62, 66,
69–70, 81, 86, 89, 99
affairs, extramarital, 156–7
affect regulation, 7–10, 12–14,
212–14, 241. *See also* self-care/
self-soothing skills.
aggression
defense mechanism, 18, 34–5,
42, 52, 65, 74, 128, 143,
183, 248
male, 35–6
Ainsworth, Mary, 16
alcohol abuse, 155,

amygdala
emotions and, 25, 40, 46, 60
hyperarousal and, 29
role of, 10–12
analyzing, 39
anger, suffering expressed as, 183
anxiety
early home life and, 176
emotional history and, 11,
176
generalized anxiety disorder
and, 27
heart coherence and, 121–2
hyperarousal and, 30
inherited, 171
managing, 46, 204.
mindfulness and, 204, 212
physical illness and, 105
symptoms of unresolved,
46–9
anxiety attacks, 106

About the Author

Dennis Becker

CHARLETTE MIKULKA IS A Licensed Clinical Social Worker. She earned her Bachelor of Arts in Social Work from Fairleigh Dickinson University in 1974 and her Masters in Social Work from Rutgers Graduate School of Social Work in 1976. Charlette's initial work experience included Child Protective Services and Family Life Education. Following that, she worked in schools providing psychotherapy to adolescents. Since 2003 she has had a psychotherapy private practice. Charlette is a member of the Academy of Certified Social Workers (ACSW), the National Association of Social Workers (NASW), the EMDR International Association (EMDRIA), the International Centre for Excellence in Emotionally Focused Therapy (ICEEFT) and the International Society for the Study of Trauma and Dissociation (ISSTD). Charlette is an EMDRIA certified therapist and participates in ongoing training in EFT for Couples.

In 2011, Charlette and her husband, Joe, will have been together for 40 years. They have two sons, Michael, 25 and Christopher, 19. In addition to enjoying her family, her profession and learning, Charlette loves spending time with her friends, appreciating and photographing nature and architecture, walking, biking, quilting, singing, cooking and visiting her favorite places: New York City; the New Jersey Shore; New Hope, Pennsylvania and Vermont.

Charlette can be reached at:

charlette@peaceintheheartandhome.com

www.peaceintheheartandhome.com

Give the Gift that
Keeps on Giving

Order additional copies of *Peace in the Heart and Home*

Available through:

Website: www.peaceintheheartandhome.com

Telephone: 800-247-6553 (BookMasters, Inc.)

or your local bookstore

what % of 25 is 5 ?

what number of 25

$\frac{\text{Pertage}}{100}$ $\frac{\text{Part}}{\text{whole}}$ .5 $\left(4\frac{3}{2}\right)$

$\left(4\frac{2}{3}.\right)$

$\frac{x}{100}$ $\frac{\cancel{25}}{\cancel{25}}$

4-

$+\frac{25}{25}$ $\frac{500}{25}$ $\frac{25}{}$ $\frac{1}{4}$

$\frac{500}{25}$ $\frac{25}{500}$

$\frac{500}{100}$

20

$\times 5\frac{1}{20}$

$\left(\frac{3}{2}\right)^n$ $D \cdot \frac{2}{3}$ $\cancel{3}/4$ $\frac{2}{}$

Prope.
impro
mix fr / mixnu

whole → $\frac{1}{2}.$

arda proper
& 8 → $\frac{3}{2}.$

$4/2$ → is mad·
4